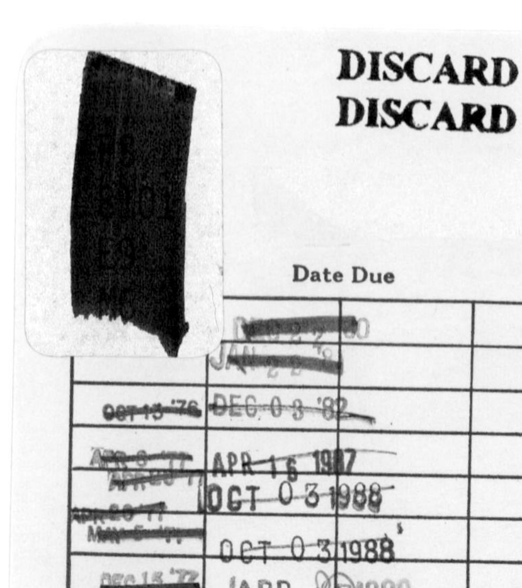

PATTERNS of ISOLATION

Note on the Author

Dr. John G. Moss was born on February 7th, 1940, in Waterloo County, Ontario in the village of Blair. He graduated from the University of Western Ontario with B.A. and M.A. degrees, received an M.Phil. from the University of Waterloo in 1970, and a Ph.D. in Canadian Literature from the University of New Brunswick in 1973. He has worked at over a score of different jobs, ranging from taxi-driver and bush guide to archivist and educational consultant. He presently lives in Montreal with his wife and two children where he is a Professor of Canadian Literature at Sir George Williams University. With his family he spends a good part of each year on their island near Bellrock, Ontario, where they are rebuilding an early nineteenth century log farmhouse by hand. The author is co-founder and Managing Editor of the very successful *Journal of Canadian Fiction*, and contributes literary criticism to a variety of Canadian, American, and British periodicals.

PATTERNS of ISOLATION

in English Canadian Fiction

JOHN MOSS

McClelland and Stewart Limited

0-7710-6568-X

The Canadian Publishers
McClelland and Stewart Limited
25 Hollinger Road, Toronto

PRINTED AND BOUND IN CANADA

Contents

I am indebted to Dr. Fred Cogswell and Dr. Robert Gibbs for providing the authentic interest in Canadian literature that has made this study possible. I would like to express my appreciation to the University of New Brunswick and the Canada Council for their support. Also I would like to thank the women in my life who have borne with me through the various struggles, of which this is the culmination.

Introduction

The patterns of isolation in English Canadian fiction provide one of a number of its distinguishing characteristics. Whether they define concepts of exile, express what I would call the geophysical imagination, or arise from the ironic conflicts of individual consciousness, they equally reflect the progress of the Canadian imagination towards a positive identity. An examination of other patterns might reveal as much about the processes of our emergence into national being. It seems to me that none, however, better displays the indigenous character of the Canadian community.

The preceding paragraph is almost verbatim the same as the concluding paragraph of this book. The intervening pages are, in a sense, no more than an elaboration of the premises they contain. The purpose has not been to assume or to prove that Canadian fiction is unique from the rest of literature written in English. In fact, that it is continuous with world literature is implicit throughout. However, in Canadian, as in other national literatures, there are thematic and dramatic tendencies, tonalities, qualities, concepts, imagery, and incidents more common to that literature than to any other. These I have lumped together under the generic term, patterns. In Canadian literature, and in Canadian fiction in particular, certain patterns have a closer affinity than others; the various patterns of isolation, more than most. For this reason, I have endeavoured to explore the realm of English Canadian fiction from its inception to the present, with isolation in mind as both the common bond linking many of our most notable works and a point of departure for the separate study of a number of the most significant.

A great deal of Canadian fiction does not conform to the patterns perceived in this study. That does not make any of it less Canadian, or of less literary merit. Nor does it make those works not included more cosmopolitan or of greater merit. The objectives of art, no matter how indefinable, would seem to me to be universal. But the experience it embodies or conveys or exploits is indigenous to a particular time and place. When the originating context is Canadian, or part of the Canadian experience–once again, ultimately indefinable–then it falls to us to explore its indigenous characteristics. That, rather than simply defining national identity or national literature, is my operative rationale.

Many Canadian novels exhibit a profound fascination with the implications of exile. This might be expected in a country whose population, with the exception of its native peoples, has come from abroad within the last few generations. The patterns that exile generates in our fiction apparently tend towards one or another of four distinct phases which conform to the historical evolution of Canada into its present state. These, as I see them, are contained by garrison, frontier, colonial, and immigrant experience. None precludes the simultaneous presence of the others.

A variety of works belong to these separate phases and they are discussed, but the novels I have examined as principal examples of each seemed almost to offer themselves for the purpose. *The History of Emily Montague* (1769) is an unparalleled work of garrison fiction, the more effective because the palisades are as much in the minds of the characters as around them. *Wacousta* (1832) exploits the frontiers of historical, literary, and psychological possibility as well as those of the New World wilderness, while *The Imperialist* (1904), with definitive clarity, explores the colonial experience. *The Sacrifice* (1956) sounds the depths of immigrant confrontation with opposing orders of reality. These novels portray exile from quite different perspectives. I have tried to explain the central vision of each, only after first examining them in relation to the criteria of their particular phase and to Canadian literary patterns of exile in general.

Regionalism is an ambivalent term in Canadian literary circles. More often than not it is used in a pejorative sense. However, it seems to me that the patterns of isolation engendered by the proximity, the immediacy, of the physical world on the creative imagination provide a moral dimension in our regional fiction that elevates a number of works to the first rank of excellence. These include Maritime novels, *The Channel Shore* (1954) and *The Nymph and the Lamp* (1950), the Prairie classic by Sinclair Ross, *As For Me and My House* (1941), and two novels set primarily in the British Columbia Interior, *The Double Hook* (1959) and *Swamp Angel* (1954). In each of these novels, there is an uncanny correspondence between the various characters and their environments that their authors appear quite consciously to exploit. None does so more effectively than Ross, and I have treated his novel separately. The others are paired, not according to their regional affinities but for their contextual similarities. These three studies follow a general discussion of the geophysical imagination which provides an explanation of some of the premises on which they are based.

In the third and final section I have considered a number of our best and best-known novelists and some of their separate works. The common factor in my discussions is the ironic nature of their concepts of individual consciousness. In exploring the patterns of individual isolation in Canadian fiction, it is inevitable that Frederick Philip Grove should demand separate treatment. His lone protagonists loom large in the literate Canadian imagination and I have endeavoured to provide an overview of the major portion of his writings while remaining aware of their ironic conception. Hugh Garner's *Cabbagetown* (1950) is a work of original merit that has been badly used by critics although it continues to enjoy popularity with the general reading public. I have attempted to resolve this seeming contradiction through a brief examination of its ironic structure. Morley Callaghan and Hugh MacLennan have been considered for their similarities and their more striking differences, with a view to showing the common assumptions they share in regard to the personal solitudes occupied by individuals in a Canadian context. Finally, three novels that stand out from the midst of contemporary Canadian fiction for their sheer accomplishment are examined: *The Mountain and the Valley* (1952), *Son of a Smaller Hero* (1955), and *The Stone Angel* (1964). My purpose with these three has been to show how Buckler, Richler, and Laurence have in their separate ways effectively used the Canadian milieu in order to portray the conflict for their protagonists between interior and external realities, self-concepts, and the experience of others.

Each of my three major divisions is concluded with a brief section suggesting alternative patterns of isolation to the ones considered. These, I hope, serve to unite the principal concepts presented in the preceding material, while offering possibilities of different approaches from those I have taken. "The Mentality of Exile" ends with a segment on the recurrent presence of Indian and half-breed lovers in Canadian fiction and the patterns of exile they engender or convey and "The Geophysical Imagination," with a discussion of the seemingly ubiquitous bastard in our regional fiction. Finally, the concept of the fool-saint concludes the section on "Irony and the Individual Consciousness" and the book as well.

In a study such as this, it has been necessary to range freely throughout Canadian fiction. I have had to limit myself primarily to the consideration of novels, although short fiction is not entirely ignored. In an attempt to provide an overview of our literature as well as insight into a significant number of separate works, I chose to remain within that area of the genre which has the longer and, on the whole, more illustrious tradition. I have varied my distance from the texts according to the extent of familiarity with them which I felt I could reasonably expect from my readers. My treatment of *The Channel Shore,* for example, includes a brief plot summary. *The Stone Angel*, I have assumed, would be known well enough to make such a summary unnecessary. It also appears to me that English and French Canadian fiction participate in distinctly separable traditions which only occasionally converge. While this premise does not affect the study itself, it is the basis for my decision to deal with only one side of a dual entity. When I refer to Canadian literature throughout, unless otherwise indicated, I mean that part of it written in English. When I refer to the Canadian sensibility or imagination, I am referring to the English Canadian sensibility or imagination. This is essentially a quantitative delimitation and in no way is meant to be a qualitative judgment.

If I have proven anything, ultimately, it is that a coherent body of Canadian fiction does, in fact, exist and does reward serious investigation. Patterns of isolation such as I have perceived are only one of its distinguishing characteristics. They are, however, one which seems to provide an excellent entry point into the unique visions of a great number of separate works.

On the whole, it has been a very enjoyable pursuit.

J.G.M.

PART I
The Mentality of Exile

The old immigrant gods must fade to inconsequence at the frontier if a new civilization is to mature. If they don't, they bring in relatives and even new acquaintances and keep their subjects colonial forever, always with a sense that this place may not be home or perhaps, at any rate, not one worthwhile defending[1]

–Scann

The *mythos* of such a nation as Canada whose original population came from abroad, usually under duress of either force or circumstance, has taken its present shape through countless stories of exile, stories in which the dualism of isolation remains explicit. Isolation is a transitive concept. One is isolated *from* something and conscious of the state of separation, although not necessarily of its dual antecedents. Except in the most limited of its literal senses, isolation does not describe a state of mind or a locale, but the effect of both. If there is no awareness that a difference exists between the way things are and the way things might otherwise be, if there is not a response to alternative realities, then the effect of conflicting experience is not isolation but disorientation or *angst.* When the alternatives are known and their separation is readily apparent, determined by real or imagined distance, their effect is the particular form of isolation so characteristic of the social dynamics in Canadian fiction, the experience of exile.

As exile is basically a physical and social dislocation, the patterns of its presence in the Canadian novel are primarily sociological. This is not to say that explicitly or by implication they are not also of moral or psychological or some other order of significance. Certainly, the Jewish diaspora, ancient and modern, is found as often in Canadian novels as elsewhere. Inevitably, the patterns of exile suggest the eternal human condition of mortality. In any case, they originate in the experience of two societies being held simultaneously, in conflict, within a single consciousness. One will be actual and the other maintained with the distortions of memory. Which is the more real, which the more alien, depends on a number of variables.

To the immigrant, for whom Canada represents a choice, whether between destruction and survival or merely between the despair of a known future and the promises offered by an uncertain one, the new land is both alien and, often for a generation or more, quite unreal compared to that of the irretrievable past. For the native-born colonial, Canada is undeniably real but seemingly alien, while in the frontier consciousness, although real, it is by the nature of its assimilated presence, not alien. From the garrison ramparts, Canada is neither, however, for it is not of significant consequence upon the cloistered life except as an external context.

In variations such as these, a schema can be perceived into which many of the patterns of exile in Canadian fiction may be arranged–as a critical convenience, but, more importantly, in response to affinities determined by four distinctively different double visions of society, of reality. These visions correspond to a series of metamorphic stages in the country's historical development; a process which, as T.S. Eliot often observed about civilization in general, should not be confused with historical improvement. Each stage anticipates the ones to follow. Each includes the experience of those that preceded. None is mutually exclusive. Yet the nature of isolation from one to the other varies greatly. The garrison is a closed community whose values, customs, manners have been transported virtually intact from some other environment and are little influenced by their new surroundings. It is the stage of occupation. The emotions and relationships sustained by lack of assimilation or reconciliation can be quite foreign to the experience of either world.

The frontier, in contrast, is a context of undifferentiated perimeters, where the experience of one reality comes into direct conflict with that of another, a more immediate and amorphous reality. The frontier provides an alternative to conventional society. It is a place of flight and of discovery, a condition of individual being, in the struggle to endure. As a stage in the historical development of a country, it characterizes that period when the physical world has yet to be mapped out in the consciousness of man, and the need to do so has become necessary.

When the territory is known, its strangeness subdued, then a period of colonial exile sets in. Colonists are seldom colonial. They are usually too prepossessed with the problems of survival to reject local experience for the alien alternative of their immediate past. The colonial mentality comes of being born in exile, of accepting foreign experience as more valid, more relevant, than one's own. It is the condition of an established society having been transported, in fragments, to a newly settled or newly civilized location, and rebuilt according to the specifications of an idealized past.

The fourth stage, that of the established order of a self-determining, self-defining nation, is the context of immigrant exile. The nation exists by virtue of historical and geographic imperatives that have been accepted by its populace as binding. It is a political, cultural, and social entity. To the outsider seeking entry, it is an arena of conflicting orders, of alien conditions, of established chaos. The reclusive self-containment of the garrison, in our history, gave way to frontier aggressiveness which was the only alternative to being crushed by the harshness of the land and its seasons, its immensity and indifference, or being seduced to impotence by its grandeur and abundance. As frontiers became boundaries, a colonial community took shape, sponsored by a distant power, catering to domestic insecurity. The world changed, and a nation-state came into being to which immigrants swarmed, often because they had little choice to do otherwise.

Each stage in the metamorphosis has engendered a corresponding literature of exile. These are no more exclusively separable from one another in our fiction, however, than are the historical phases in our collective memory. Rather, they are all present in any particular work in a hierarchical pattern, according to its particular demands. The garrison experience portrayed in the earliest novel of Canada, *The History of Emily Montague,* suggests more of the pleasant exile pictured by J. M. Barrie in *The Admirable Crichton* than it does the Dostoievskian depths of Adele Wiseman's contemporary novel of human isolation, *The Sacrifice.* Yet the latter is in many ways a garrison tragedy, enacted in a modern urban ghetto. Much of its dynamic tension derives from the implicit remnants of frontier and colonial restraint that characterize Miss Wiseman's anonymous Winnipeg, the place of her protagonist's exile. The passive innocence of *The History of Emily Montague* is given a romantic turn towards demonic complexity in the frontier drama of Major John Richardson's *Wacousta.* Richardson's title-character is an unrequited Englishman who, after a brief attempt at being French Canadian, has become a loin-clothed Indian lord. He is the archetypal frontiersman, characteristically at vicious odds with the opposing values of the garrison. In the madness that makes his exile as much mental as geographic, he embodies the most disturbing aspects of colonial experience, while the mythic implications of the merged identities, the violence, ambivalence, and anguish that are Wacousta's lot, resoundingly bespeak the beginnings of a nation. The national experience prefigured in *The History of Emily Montague* first becomes the colonial experience of a people born in exile, by 1867, when Canada emerged as a political entity and a cultural conundrum. What was taken as nationalism, at the time, was an expression of the Imperial imperative. At the turn of the present century, Sara Jeannette Duncan captured this paradox between the lines of *The Imperialist* if not quite within the story itself. Miss Duncan's Elgin is socially a garrison and politically a frontier. Its self-contempt, of course, is colonial; but, much like present-day Brantford, Ontario, the town on which it is based, Elgin in the Gay Nineties is also a microcosm of its surrounding nation.

While these four types of exile in Canadian fiction spring from a fixed historical sequence, they are in no way restricted to their appropriate historical era which, after all, varies from place to place in Canada by a hundred years or more–the West being newly garrisoned while the Maritimes were already bemoaning, with some justification, the consequences of national sovereignty. On the one hand, a work like Robert Kroetsch's existential reversal of the quest for identity, *But We Are Exiles,* is a frontier novel written in the 1960's, not only because it is set in the barren Mackenzie River district but also because of the sense and structure of fugitive excitement which it shares with such earlier frontier novels as Richardson's *Wacousta.* On the other hand, a work like John Galt's *Bogle Corbet,* written in the 1830's, is dominated by the spirit of emergent national sovereignty, by the frustrations and aspirations of an immigrant populace in a new land; in these respects it is equally characteristic of many novels written more than a century later.

When Northrop Frye and others who have commandeered his facile epithet–I am thinking in particular of D. G. Jones in *Butterfly on Rock*–when such critics refer to the "garrison mentality" that permeates the Canadian experience, their observation is accurate, in my opinion, but imcomplete as a basis for literary analysis. Similarly, Wilfred Eggleston's *The Frontier and Canadian Letters,* while being an informative study of social and literary history, falls short of providing comprehensive insight. Eggleston, like Frye, tends to interpret the whole of Canadian literature according to the social criteria of only one of the metamorphic stages through which it has passed, accumulating a multifaceted personality along the way. It is the common characteristics of these stages, however, and not their individual differences that can offer the best possibilities for critical insight, and it seems to me these, in the novel at least, are clustered around the endemic concept of exile.

Note

1. Robert Harlow, *Scann* (Victoria: Sono Nis, 1972), p. 134.

1.
Garrison Exile

Garrison palisades in the past have served as more than fortifications against attack by the dissident populace of an occupied land or to hold an encroaching wilderness at bay. They also kept the garrison effectively confined to close quarters. Those on the outside remained outsiders, foreigners in their own country. The surrounding environment retained the characteristic ambivalence and fascination of the unknown. The garrison was a closed community, devoted as much to resisting assimilation as to maintaining an external authority.

Life in the garrison is a form of exile, not only from the homeland far away, but from the world at its gates. Both literally and figuratively, garrison exile provides a vision of reality that tends towards the romantic rather than the realistic, towards the self-indulgence of disengaged impressionism and the self-satisfaction of over-indulgence. From atop the garrison ramparts, whether actual or of the mind, the view is perceived through the filter of previous experience which seems at once more graphic and qualitatively superior. Separation from home may not be by preference but separation from the enclosing milieu, in which the garrison is like a whistle in the dark, is a matter of choice and of satisfaction. Thus, in effect, the response to one form of exile is the choice of another by which the first may be endured and, possibly, enjoyed.

Novels of garrison exile in Canada are the produce of foreign minds. Without degenerating into a discussion of what is and what is not a Canadian novel–such a discussion inevitably misses the point, overlooking the extent of a work's participation in national traditions in the search for its naturalization credentials–there are a number of works by non-Canadians that are clearly a part of Canadian literature. Their authors have been transient residents in this country, and even temporary citizens, and have experienced it without the commitment of the immigrant, or the intimacy and involvement demanded by frontier or colonial life. Often, as in the cases of Malcolm Lowry and Frances Brooke, to name two of the most significant writers of this sub-genre, other of their works have nothing whatsoever to do with the Canadian experience. Lowry's first two novels, *Ultramarine* and *Under the Volcano* are from the hand of an increasingly tormented, peripatetic Englishman. *Hear Us O Lord from Heaven Thy Dwelling Place, Dark Is the Grave Wherein My Friend Is Laid,* and *October Ferry to Gabriola* are brilliantly intense flashes of genius amidst the delirium of a man who seemed to have become Canadian by default and was determined to make the most of it. Mrs. Brooke's *The History of Emily Montague* integrates a thoroughly alien vision of occupied New France during the interregnum between 1759 and 1776 with the form and sentiments of a domestic eighteenth century British romance. Her Englishness, in fact, makes the novel definitively Canadian. Despite the insistent and awesome presence of the landscape and the vitality of its description, despite the ubiquity of indigenous French and Indian peoples, her characters' behaviour and her judgments upon it are imperviously English. This double vision of the New World milieu makes her novel a prototypic portrait of garrison exile.

Mrs. Brooke employs a highly sophisticated, exquisitely controlled counterpointing of what might be called the debits and credits of isolation in a primitive, in some respects primeval, environment. Exile that derives from an author's garrison experience is not always so subtly presented. It may be expressed in an aura of desperate urgency, as in Lowry's works, or it may broil upon a novel's surface. It broils most vigorously, perhaps, in Wyndham Lewis's morbid satire, *Self Condemned.*

Lewis closes the first chapter of his novel with a vivid picture of his protagonist's cynical determinism in response to the destruction, during the London blitz, of houses built by the archetypal British "Jack":

> Some houses built by Jack attracted incendiaries, some did not. But it did not matter whether they did or whether they did not. All in the end had wild cats in their cellars, for civilization never continued long enough to keep the wild cats out–if you call it civilization, René Harding would shout.[1]

Here, Lewis creates an indelible impression of René Harding, but what is equally difficult to erase from the mind is the God-like posture the author assumes in patronizing the whole of human history. This stance lends itself well to satire, particularly that self-indulgent satire which in its cynicism verges on the nihilistic.

Appropriately, the attitudes and antecedents of his character's Canadian exile are founded in an English holocaust. The ensuing bitterness that makes predictable every moment in the novel's story of an outcast British gentleman-professor, stranded in a mythical Toronto called Momaco, transforms incipient bathos into inexorable tragedy. Lewis spent some miserable years of his own in Toronto. To the extent that his novel is satire, it is redeemed from meanness by the uncompromising honesty of the author's fictionalized response to the Queen City during World War II, not by the accuracy of his account. To the extent that it is poorly disguised autobiography, it is morbidly petulant.

Harding's wife, Hester, departs their state of exile in the only way possible, given the rigid context Lewis has placed them in. In her suicide note, she attempts to explain:

> What can I say, René darling, except to ask your forgiveness. I loathe this country so much, where I can see you burying yourself. I cannot leave you–physically–go away from you back to England. I can only go out of the world. Good-bye, my darling. Ess.[2]

Not unexpectedly, nobility and the cruelest self-indulgence are simultaneously present in the form of her escape and her explanation of it. Sometimes, though, even this ambivalence is lacking in Lewis's vision–reminiscent of Swift's Brobdingnagian estimation of mankind as "the most pernicious Race of little odious Vermin that Nature ever suffered to crawl upon the Surface of the Earth."[3] He describes Harding's final escape from Momaco and its University to an Ivy League post:

> . . .in a few months he was installed in a small, warm, wooden dwelling not far from the campus of this much more pretentious seat of learning, five hundred miles further south; and the Faculty had no idea that it was a glacial shell of a man who had come to live among them, mainly because they were themselves unfilled with anything more than a little academic stuffing.[4]

With appropriate irony, the final chapter, of which these are the closing lines, is entitled "The Cemetery of Shells." While also being a general indictment of mankind, Lewis's run-on sentence accurately describes the state of Harding's psycho-spiritual collapse, a state continually prefigured by his response to the conditions of his Canadian sojourn, by the sharpness of the author's satiric prod. I do not mean to suggest that Lewis, himself, felt that the only recourse in life in Canada was, or is, death, nor that he was so misanthropic as to believe his fellow men, universally, to be full of dead matter–stuffing, or whatever. What I do suggest is that his novel is a satire patterned with ominous philosophic shadows suggesting nothing so much as Gogol's morbidly engaging romance, *Dead Souls,* in a garrison context that is as uniquely Canadian as Hell is Christian.

There is nothing alien about the Canadian setting of *Self Condemned* or the author's use of it. In fact, as when he casually notes, for instance, that "In Momaco (unlike Toronto) taxis are allowed to ply for hire"[5], a pedestrian familiarity is assumed which, on the whole, makes the Hardings' despair that much more oppressive than if the place of their exile were exotic or other-worldly. Yet Lewis uses Canada to express a garrison response to personal isolation amidst a social, cultural, and moral wilderness that is as moribund as the torn and bloodied corpse of his wife that Harding is confronted with upon the police-morgue slab. René himself is one of the living dead, buried, as his wife lamented, in this country. When he "landed in Canada, he landed as a dead man, or as good as dead."[6] As he perceives them, the people around him in these nether regions are hollow men, stuffed, dead. This is his view from garrison ramparts which are the product of his spiritual and emotional poverty and of his author's flagrant intellectual bias. It is an extreme that is demanded by the particular bitterness of his satire, or, perhaps, the cause of it. In any case, alone of Wyndham Lewis's novels, *Self Condemned* is a contributing participant in the Canadian experience it so vehemently distorts and condemns. In this respect, its title has an ironic dimension which its author undoubtedly did not intend.

For the embittered Wyndham Lewis, the garrison is a morbid state of mind temporarily occupied by an English gentleman on the way from birthright to oblivion. The parallel, in this respect, between René Harding and his author is too obvious not to acknowledge. In *The History of Emily Montague,* it is not the story but the milieu in which it takes place that is born directly out of the author's personal experience. From the few years Frances Brooke spent in Quebec–exactly how many appears to be debatable, but certainly no less than five–she has drawn a delightful picture of British society in occupied New France. The romantic relationships between her two pairs of lovers on this side of the Atlantic, and the complexities of these affairs, are the products of their exiled context, but the motivations of her characters are determined almost exclusively by their English backgrounds. In her conscious manipulation of this paradox, Mrs. Brooke anticipates a recurrent pattern, in Canadian fiction, of conflicting social orders met in direct confrontation. For this alone *The History of Emily Montague* is an integral part of the Canadian literary tradition–giving the lie to an *a priori* definition of the Canadian novel. That it may also be an English novel, as *The History of Julia Mandeville,* also by Frances Brooke, most certainly is, does not diminish its Canadian status at all.

An interesting variation on the use of the *ancien régime* as a place and time of exile is to be found in Willa Cather's 1931 novel, *Shadows on the Rock.* Unlike Mrs. Brooke, in whose work isolation is virtually inseparable from environment, Miss Cather seems to have found in the historical and exotic qualities of Old Quebec an appropriate objective correlative for her private vision of exile. A sense of exile underlies all of Cather's novels, possibly born of her girlhood dislocation from civilized Virginia to the wilderness of Nebraska, in 1883. While Frances Brooke's characters respond to the New World in a manner quite in keeping with their identities as English ladies and gentlemen abroad, Cather's Québécois are aesthetic translations of her peculiarly American, continentalist vision of alienation and acceptance. The apothecary, Euclide Auclair, for example, finally acknowledges that he is to remain forever away from France, but as one who is absolved from the past, not reconciled to it. Although continuity with the past is broken, he is not entirely free of it. In the shadows on the rock of the old city, he is haunted by that to which he is no longer responsible. The child, Cécile, sees the shadows embodying the legends of the new land, of the wilderness around their petty garrison. But to Euclide, they are the ghosts of a former life, an earlier incarnation of himself at home in France. This is a projection of an American experience of exile into an alien context that bears it well, but only because it has been mythologized beyond any recognizable semblance of the way it was, or is. Cather's *ancien régime* is an admirable theatre for the re-enactment of an almost archetypal, but alien drama.

In most respects, *Shadows on the Rock* cannot be said to depict garrison exile, not arise out of it, and I make no claim for it as a part of the Canadian literary tradition. It would be rather presumptuous to do so only on the basis of the Canadian "materials" made use of by the author–comparable to suggesting that Saul Bellow's *Henderson the Rain King* is an African novel, or that Graham Greene's *The Quiet American* can be clearly identified with the traditions of Vietnamese literature. Yet there are similarities between Miss Cather's work and the Canadian novels of such aliens as Brian Moore and Malcolm Lowry, imposed perhaps by the common foreignness of their visions of Canadian experience. All three portray the Canadian physical and social environment with graphic, even intimate, attention to detail, to specifics; and yet, in each case, it is romanticized, manipulated, but never confronted as an integral fact of their novels' fictional reality, only as the background context. However, Lowry and Moore both write from personal knowledge about Canada as the context of isolation. Unlike Cather, their visions are from within and not from beyond its reaches. Their novels, particularly Lowry's, sustain a sense of garrison exile that is not to be found in *Shadows on the Rock.*

Lowry's works contain a visceral sense of dislocation often bordering on vertigo and at other times suggesting disembodied rapture. In *Under the Volcano,* the oppressive confusion of Geoffrey Fermin's latter days are inseparable from the self-indulgent, self-consuming vision of the author that is implicit in the hallucinogenic intensity of the entire novel. That is, the entire reality of the novel is representative of a deteriorated spirit and the protagonist merely provides a fragmented focus on that condition. The author is ever present in Geoffrey's spiritual torment and yet, with the schizoid objectivity of a brilliant artist, reminiscent of Van Gogh's self-portrait done in the asylum, he is also the indifferent executor of Geoffrey's fate, consigning him to an oblivion necessitated by the momentum of his creative vision.

Hear Us O Lord From Heaven Thy Dwelling Place represents a deeper turning inward, on Lowry's part, than he achieved in his first two novels. In an opening sequence called "Through the Panama"–I hesitate to call it either chapter or novella–Sigbørn Wilderness, unlike Geoffrey Fermin, is not a mere creation of the author but rather a personification of the author's whole concept of himself, and Primrose is not a wife-figure but a fictional wife of flesh and blood. But Sigbørn is also Martin Trumbaugh, the fictionalized character of *his* creation and Primrose is his wife as well. "Through the Panama" portrays a coming together of the author with his creative and his suffering selves.[7] By the final section, "The Forest Path to the Spring," Lowry has thoroughly subdued all three beings within himself to a joyous harmony. Artistic objectivity gives way to a supreme subjectivity wherein the reader cannot perceive the difference "between the dancer and the dance." This section, addressed not to Primrose but to Margerie, the author's wife, is narrated in the author's own voice, which is the very sound of creation. Lowry, the man, has become inseparable from his art.

It is not surprising, then, that "The Forest Path to the Spring" was to have been the final scene in a long sequence (parts have been published posthumously) that Lowry intended to appear under the title "The Voyage That Never Ends." The Lord in His dwelling place from Whom Lowry has been exiled, toiling as a mortal in hope and despair, assumes a transcendent imminence through which life and art are integrated in the forest setting by the seacoast of British Columbia. Lowry's garrison is a spiritual one. Entirely at ease with the rhythms and the details of their rustic home, Lowry discovers the meaning of spring as a completion of the seasonal cycle, as the life-giving source of water, as personal rebirth. But a forest path led to his revelation. He is not a part of the natural setting: he has walked through it time and again, "Tyrannized by the past," only gradually discovering that it is his "duty to transcend it in the present.[8] The landscape itself, his setting in time and space that he seems almost to caress with his quiet eloquence, is not something he participates in. It is observed. In its patterns, which he comes to adore but never venerate, he discovers a higher reality. Describing the spring water, he explains:

> In the deeper reaches of the forest, the somber damp caves, where the dead branches hang bowed down with moss, and death camass and the destroying angel grow, it was haggard and chill and tragic, unsure measurer of its path. Feeling its way underground it must have had its darker moments. But here, in springtime, on its last lap to the sea, it was as at its source a happy joyous little stream.[9]

Natural imagery provides the perfect metaphor for what he has discovered of life from his cloistered perspective within the natural world.

Brian Moore I would place on the periphery of the present discussion. His novel, *The Luck of Ginger Coffey,* belongs more properly with the Canadian novels of national exile that play out the themes of confrontation between the landed immigrant and established order. His other novels, fiction and non-fiction alike, only participate in a Canadian tradition by the most conscious of designs–providing material for his works but never their informing principles. This is the case even in, especially in, his imaginative documentary, constructed after the manner of Truman Capote's *In Cold Blood,* in which he manipulates some of the events and personalities central to the political confusion in Quebec during the autumn of 1971 into an exploitive dramatization entitled *The Revolution Script.* Moore is an Irishman, first and foremost, in fiction as, it appears, in life. He has been a Canadian, is presently an American, and has exploited both experiences with considerable brilliance and aplomb from the indigenously Irish point of view of an artist unable, by his own creative genius, to go home.

Unlike Lowry, Moore is not a spiritual exile, He is an ethnic exile who displays none of the commitment to place or action or idea nor implicit resentment to his severed state that might normally be associated with a perennial immigrant. Instead, there is in his fiction an overwhelming sense of dissociation which his characters are seldom adequately able to resolve. They are nearly without values, their lives without meaning–which is not to say that his novels are without values or meaning. In *The Lonely Passion of Judith Hearne,* for example, Judith is not at middle age an alcoholic spinster, vulnerable, disillusioned, unfulfilled, by chance or bad luck or poor timing. She is alone and afraid and the walls of her prison are the flaws and the strengths of her own personality. Her incapacitating humility before an ignorant God derives from the confusion of pride and compassion that she has helplessly cultivated within herself as a means, in her mind, of survival. Ultimately, boozed in the best hotel in Belfast, she defies the personality she has constructed for herself and the God of her creation. Her salvation is in the anaesthesia of acceptance, which is a reconciliation with Hell. The eloquent simplicity of her story and the complexity of its themes together articulate a conception of life's significance and its order that is paradoxically signified by Judith's lack of either, in her own life. Her utter isolation is a form of social, spiritual and psychological exile, from which the only escape is the acceptance that there is no escape. Moore seems to be subscribing here to a sort of benign existential determinism.

In the manipulation of his reader's consciousness to a somewhat similar end, Moore leads the title character in *I Am Mary Dunne* through a long day's search for her identity, only to discover that she has none. In the twenty years since leaving Nova Scotia, she has continually pared it away until there is nothing left–or else added to it until she is unrecognizable even to herself. The anxious retrospective review of the sequence of accumulation or attrition, as the case may be, by which Mary has reached her present-tense vacuous state is motivated by guilt and remorse. Ultimately, Moore founds her salvation in the discovery she is led to make that she has no identity beyond her present self. For Mary Dunne, there is mild relief and the promise of another day in which her quest will have become a contributing part of her residual past. For the reader, her exile from reality is ended as she seems to prove that reality itself is a form of exile.

Moore's contemporary interpretations of universal themes are compatible with those of modern Canadian fiction, but except for *The Luck of Ginger Coffey* they suggest nothing that is more characteristic of Canada than of any other place. The particularities of his vision are drawn from a cosmopolitan experience which has as its frame of reference the same disembodied Ireland of the soul that James Joyce explored with somewhat more attention to its antecedents, and Brendan Behan, to its personal legacy. That is not to say that a good number of Canadian novels are not also the products of an alien vision–the point of the present discussion is to show that some definitely are. But in novels of garrison exile the Canadian materials of the foreign writer transmute that vision into something that has particular relevance to the Canadian experience. This is not generally the case with Moore, whose fiction suggests an imperviousness to the conditions and sensibilities of his characters' environment.

Quite the opposite, in this respect, is Frances Brooke's epistolary novel, *The History of Emily Montague*, in which there is a responsiveness to the broader world that fiction in English did not again achieve until Joseph Conrad brought the whole arena of international commerce and high adventure into the scope of his imagination. In the happiest of coincidences, Mrs. Brooke's novel combines eighteenth century British social and literary conventions with intimations of the sublimity and degeneration that characterized Quebec during the brief period between 1759 and 1776 when it was an integral, if occupied, part of British North America. Admittedly, her husband was a garrison chaplain during her stay on this side of the Atlantic in the mid-1760's. But apart from the military presence of a petulant occupation, the garrison consisted mostly in a lack of social and moral commitment on the part of the neophyte English community. Their host's intercourse with France has been dramatically terminated, of course, and the virulent republic to the south did not yet exist. Here was an enclave within the wilderness in which to test the principles of enlightenment against those of nature. In so doing, Mrs. Brooke created a *tour de force* out of what might otherwise have been a rather ordinary story of love as a set of social complications to be resolved by good manners and right reason.

The natural surroundings of their enclave are overwhelming to the newly arrived British. Colonel Rivers describes his initial response to the landscape in a letter to his sister:

> The country is a very fine one: you see here not only the *beautiful* which it has in common with Europe, but the *great sublime* to an amazing degree. . .I felt a kind of religious veneration, on seeing rocks which almost touch'd the clouds, cover'd with tall groves of pines that seemed coeval with the world itself.[10]

Arabella Fermor, as prodigious an epistolarean as Rivers, writes eloquently, also to Lucy, about the falls at Montmorency in the winter:

> As you gradually approach the bay, you are struck with an awe, which increases every moment, as you come nearer, from the grandeur of a scene, which is one of the noblest works of nature: the beauty, the proportion, the solemnity, the wild magnificence of which, surpassing every possible effect of art, impress one strongly with the idea of its Divine Almighty Architect.[11]

Arabella is generally as fickle in her opinions as Rivers is droll in his. Yet the observations of both are consistently acute and adroitly phrased as both approach the landscape with an almost devotional sincerity. Their experience of it is immediate. The sublime in nature is a reality to them and not an abstraction to be found at Versailles or in an English garden. In matters of natural phenomena, England invariably suffers by comparison. Her sun is not so cheering, her evenings are not so pleasant, and the changing of her seasons is not so stimulating. Even her waterways are lesser channels, according to the comparison of them with the St. Lawrence made by Arabella's father in one of his numerous reports to the Earl of ________: "I found *the great river*. . .assert its superiority over those petty streams which we honour with the names of rivers in England. Sublimity is the characteristic of this western world. . . ."[12]

This is the world, then, in which are set the fragments of society which Mrs. Brooke portrays. It is a larger context than anything of man's creation. It is not a backdrop nor, as in Brian Moore's novels, fifth business, but the stage itself. On this stage a group of static ethnic fragments have been forced together by the arbitrary whim of history. The Indians, on the one hand, are variously extolled for the nobility of their ways and condemned for their demented savagery. On the whole, they are admired for their capacity to endure. The French Canadian peasantry, on the other hand, are described as being "hospitable, courteous, civil," despite their also being the odious parasites of a bounteous land, whose "Bigotry, stupidity, and laziness, united, have not been able to keep [them] poor."[13] The response of the British minority to Indians and to peasantry derives as much from the world of nature as from the intellectual currents of Europe. The noble savage of Rousseau and the happy rustic are illusions which the density and the plenitude of their Canadian setting help to foster. The illusions are recognized as such by Mrs. Brooke, for the attitudes towards them of her proper English characters runs the gamut from idealization to insult, depending upon the particular narrator's particular state of mind at the time of writing about them in one letter or another.

Only "society," in the restrictive, class-conscious sense of the word, is apparently independent of the land. It was transported whole from the motherland in English minds–values, customs, culture, manners, all intact. The French Canadian elite, it seems to have freely admitted to its midst. Yet society made distinctions. With puckish subtlety, Arabella deflates their masculinity:

> . . .the French ladies are handsome, but as to the beaux, they appear to me not all dangerous, and one might safely walk in a wood by moonlight with the most agreeable Frenchman here. I am surpriz'd the Canadian ladies take such pains to seduce our men from us; but I think it a little hard we have no temptation to make reprisals.[14]

In another of his reports to the Earl of ———————, William Fermor declares of the French Canadians that "their religion, to which they are extremely bigoted," is the reason for

> the superior increase of the British American settlements compared to those of France: a religion which encourages idleness, and makes a virtue of celibacy, is particularly unfavourable to colonization.[15]

Mrs. Brooks exploits the distinctions between French and English, at the expense of the former, by providing both Emily and Arabella with local competition in their respective efforts to win Rivers and Captain Fitzgerald. In the latter case, Madame La Brosse is merely a passing coquette. But Madame Des Roches is a more formidable obstacle between Emily and Rivers. She is, in Emily's words,

> the noblest and most amiable of women, and I have been in regard to her the most capricious and unjust; my hatred of her was unworthy my character; I blush to own the meanness of my sentiments, whilst I admire the generosity of hers.[16]

Not only that; she is a woman of experience and property. But, of course, she loses out to Emily, despite the latter's simpering nobility that occasionally makes one wonder at the justice of it. Madame Des Roches is French and, as Colonel Rivers notes, "There is not perhaps on earth a race of females who talk so much, or feel so little, of love as the French."[17] In a world of values such as these, it is fitting that Rivers have an English wife.

Both principle affairs of the heart in the story take place in Canada. Yet the sentiments and the social values, the manners and customs of courtship and love are entirely alien. They are as typically English as those of John Temple and Lucy Rivers, back in England. The courtship rituals in Canada are not so rooted in the social market-place, perhaps, but otherwise they are indistinguishable from their counterparts at home. With little passion and a great deal of emotion the various participants write to one another of their loves. They are conventional lovers. When Rivers, for example, seems to have no chance in the competition for Emily's affection with Sir George Clayton, he graciously desires nothing more of life than to be her friend–an entirely normal response within his social and historical context, albeit his description of his rival is, spiritedly, somewhat untoward: "he resembles the form my imagination paints of Prometheus's man of clay, before he stole the celestial fire to animate him."[18] Emily, in similar fashion, rather insipidly wishes Rivers all the best, on believing he has been lost to Madame Des Roches. The emotions and opinions of all six lovers are invariably conventional, excessive. There is nothing in the expression they give to them to indicate that two of them dwell in central London and the other four amidst the wilderness on the outskirts of civilization.

Their sentiments are independent of the land. But their relationships are not. In this dichotomy lie the novel's most engaging complications. The affairs conducted in Canada turn on the effects upon them of their impelling environment. On determining to pursue Emily for his wife, Rivers declares in a letter to his sister that some parts of Madame Des Roche's estate are necessary for his purpose. Referring to Emily, he explains:

> . . .I will not suffer my tenderness for her to make her unhappy, or to lower her station in life: if I can by my present plan, secure her what will in this country be a degree of affluence, I will endeavour to change her friendship for me into a tenderer and more lively affection; if she loves, I know my own heart, that Canada will no longer be a place of exile; if I have flattered myself, and she has only a friendship to me, I will return immediately to England, and retire with you and my mother to our little estate in the country.[19]

But, of course, Canada remains a place of exile for Rivers and Emily, for whom consummation is concomitant with a return to England. Nevertheless, it is significant that not only does the land offer the incentive to Rivers of righting an awkward economic imbalance, but also the means of doing so. The person and property of Madame Des Roches provide the romantic complication which, by its threatening near-miscegenation, assures a providential outcome to the primary relationship. Before true love prevails, however, Emily turns Rivers down in an ironically logical, if somewhat perverse, response to his aspirations:

> I would therefore marry him tomorrow were it possible without ruining him, without dooming him to a perpetual exile and obstructing those views of honest ambition at home, which becomes his birth, his connexions, his talents, his time of life; and with which, as his friend, it is my duty to inspire him.[20]

Thus Emily will marry Colonel Rivers only if they return to England and he will marry Emily only if they remain in Canada. Filial devotion, fortunately, finally calls him home to the presence of his heart-sick mother. Emily goes with him and there the restoration of lost relatives and estates rewards their mutual selflessness.The relationship of Arabella and Fitzgerald is more subtly the product of their British behaviour in confrontation with the Canadian environment. For Emily and Rivers, both of whom are steadfast sorts, Canada is a pawn in the game of garrison romance. But for Fitzgerald, who is an incorrigible flirt, and Arabella, one of the most charmingly audacious coquettes in literature, Canada is the board on which the game is played. Much of the vitality which is the source of their mutual attraction for one another is in their response to the sublime stolidity surrounding them. Arabella, for instance, alternates between the assertion, in a letter to Lucy, that

> . . .the elegant arts are unknown here; the rigour of the climate suspends the very powers of the understanding: what then must become of those of imagination,[21]

and the contrary view, also to Lucy and only two months later, that

> . . .the British [belles] set the winter of Canada at defiance; and the season of which you seem to entertain such terrible ideas, is that of the utmost chearfulness and festivity.[22]

Finally, four months later, she tells Lucy, now Mrs. John Temple, that

> I had rather live at Quebec, that it for all in all, than any town in England, except London; the manner of living here is uncommonly agreeable; the scenes about us are lovely, and the mode of amusements makes us taste those scenes in full perfection.[23]

True to herself, in her fashion, Arabella is consistently lively in her diverse estimations of the society in which she finds herself and, as I have suggested, never loses her sense of awe at the natural surroundings. The vitality of her romantic affections is prefigured, stimulated and sustained in her response to society within a Canadian context. She is both fickle and curiously faithful. Similarly, Fitzgerald, though he is much less in the novel's foreground, displays a charming inconstancy.

Ironically, it is this very characteristic of inconstancy that saves them, in the light of their surroundings, from being *only* gallant and coquette. The relationship that develops between them is the extension of their mutual capacity for self-indulgence which has enabled them to survive their exile, socially and personally, with aplomb and good humour. In the Canada of Mrs. Brooke, society is not a homogeneous process as it is with such robust fluency in Fielding's England, or as it is, so sanctimoniously, in Samual Richardson's. Nor does she focus consciousness on one dynamic segment in a continuous flow, as in the novels of Jane Austen. Society, in the midst of which the courtship of Arabella and her Captain transpires, consists instead of static microcosms of worlds far off in space–the distant homelands of the privileged French Canadians and their British overlords–or in time–the better days once known by the Indians and the Canadian peasantry at the garrison gates. Rather than submit insipidly to the rigidity of a self-conscious interregnum society as Emily does, Arabella manipulates it for her own amusement. Nor is she intimidated by her setting for, although her appreciation of it is acute and reverent, she berates it to her friends at will. Such a mercurial personality as hers would dissipate their romance in the vanity fair of England, but in the confined and arbitrary mode of life in Canada it makes their marriage not just possible but inevitable.

Just as the courtship rituals in *The History of Emily Montague* attain consequence because of their Canadian setting, so the entire novel is redeemed from the mediocrity of its story line by the highly sophisticated use that Mrs. Brooke makes of a garrison dichotomy in the Canadian experience. The measure of society is drawn against the measure of the natural phenomena in which it lives: the victors and the vanquished, the indigenous and the alien, are counterpoised; home and exile correlated; urbane and rustic, civilized and savage, juxtaposed; and, of course, the differences between male and female are extensively exploited. Reality, so thoroughly divided, itself becomes the subject of her fiction. This is not because her Canada is universal but because her treatment of it is. That, perhaps, is why the last part of the novel, set in England, while continuing the story-lines to completion, dissipates into the conventionally predictable. Her England is merely regional. The dimensions of reality displayed in the Canadian parts, however, have been deftly drawn apart for observation.

The superficial structure of her novel, through which her social perspicacity is conveyed, is not remarkably inventive. It is not, however, "little more than a convenient thread upon which to hang natural description, social comment, and moral preachment" as Desmond Pacey states in an essay entitled "The First Canadian Novel."[24] It is a finely contrived arrangement of relationships and characters in counterpoint. Subsidiary roles played offstage, such as those by Madame Des Roches and Sir George Clayton, are effective in revealing the characters of those writing about them as well as forwarding the action, and broadly contribute to thematic development. The subplots are neatly deployed to recapitulate in miniature the thematic implications of the main plot and to anticipate its further development. The tale of the Kamaraskas hermit is an ironic cameo showing the tragic consequence of using Canada to facilitate a marriage of love that in England would not be opportune–the exact situation of Emily and Rivers. Similarly, the latter part of their affair is suggested by the Fanny Williams digression about Sophia and Sir Charles Verville that tells of love and responsibility, misplaced identities, and fortunes retrieved.

Of prime importance to an epistolary novel such as this is Mrs. Brooke's ability to unfold the structural fabric of interwoven correspondence so naturally, with neither the self-consciousness of Richardson's *Clarissa* nor the artifice of Fanny Burney's *Evalina.* The action of her story is not in the behaviour of her characters but in their anticipation of behaviour and responses to it. Letters are the perfect medium for the reflections, analyses, and gossip of which such action is composed. The distance imposed upon her correspondents, even when they write from neighbouring rooms, prevents their letters from ever appearing to be the products of literary convention rather than of diverse needs to communicate as defined within their texts.

Where Mrs. Brooke most gives evidence of genius, however, is in the structural arrangement of her perceptions of an ambiguous reality. Not at all unlike Herman Melville's achievement in *Moby Dick,* written almost a century later, she exploits the possibilities in fiction of documentary detail. Neither Mrs. Brooke nor Melville were naturalistic novelists in that their factual accounts are, at least to a considerable extent, separable from the narrative flow of their novels, But Frances Brooke, like Melville, has interspersed her story with numerous expository essays. Melville's are on whales, the sea, and whaling. Mrs. Brooke's are on the people and the landscape of Canada and on the conditions of its British occupation as seen, primarily, through the eyes of William Fermor, Arabella's father, in his reports to the Earl of ____________. Mrs. Brooke covers a broader spectrum than Melville does, but with less intensity. Nevertheless, her essays are vivid, articulate, and highly informative.

The documentary accounts in *Moby Dick* provide a solid middle ground between a rather esoterically conceived adventure yarn and the profound complexity of its moral implications. Straightforward accounts of blubber being stripped and oil processed are made to bridge the gap between the ambiguities of fictional particularity and of universal reality. In *The History of Emily Montague* the documentary function is somewhat similar but more complex. It lends authenticity and weight to a cluster of rather frivolous affairs of the heart. It provides the ironic context in which society and manners come to represent the experience and conditions of humankind. Most significantly, the documentary details arouse an awareness of the duality of man's existence that may not have been consciously intended but which is unavoidable, nonetheless, and an important part of the novel's achievement.

This duality is not the Manichaeistic moral split portrayed by Melville. More typical of its age, it is the classic confrontation of rational man with an irrational world, of intellect with the sublime. On one hand, Mrs. Brooke documents the new world as a vast indifferent wilderness by which parallel societies are both encompassed and defined. On the other, she informs it with the intellectuality of the old world. Her characters debate the role of women, the structures of society, the nature of mankind, the meaning of life, all with casual authority. They refer to Montesquieu and Rousseau without affectation. They are, in short, quite civilized. But their context is not. This ambivalence is continually reinforced by the ironic mindlessness of her most clever maxims and in the grace by which her characters' exile is endured. Such a duality is a fundamental characteristic of garrison life, for a garrison is enclosed by walls, each of which has two sides. In Mrs. Brooke's version, the walls are figurative, making it sometimes difficult to tell which side is inside and which out. Thus, her ambivalent vision is ambiguous as well, prismatically dimensioned rather than bi-focal.

Ambiguity is a resonant characteristic of the novels by other writers of garrison exile. As in *The History of Emily Montague,* it is generated by an apparent lack of conviction on the part of the author as to whether the point of view is from within the garrison or outside it, even when it is as successfully exploited as it is by Mrs. Brooke. In Moore's novels and in Lowry's, the result is a tonality consistent with their themes of rootlessness and isolation. In *Self Condemned,* it lends to Wyndham Lewis's voice an air of hysteria which is also an air of authenticity. The garrison is, after all, a state of mind whether it is sustained by force of arms or circumstance or habit. Its walls are difficult to perceive even while their effect is clearly evident.

Notes

1. Wyndham Lewis, *Self Condemned* (London: Methuen, 1954), p.14.
2. *Ibid.,* p. 392.
3. Jonathan Swift, *Gulliver's Travels* (New York: Modern Library, 1958), p.101.
4. Lewis., *op.cit.,* p.407.
5. *Ibid.,* p. 369.
6. *Ibid.,* p.659.
7. This arrangement suggests nothing so much as a prosaic analogy of Blake's representation in the Major Prophecies of the fragmented creator as the Poet, Inspiration, and Selfhood in the struggling forms of Los, Enitharmon, and the Spectre of Urthona, respectively.
8. Malcolm Lowry, *Hear Us O Lord From Heaven Thy Dwelling Place* (New York: Lippincott, 1961) p.279.
9. *Ibid.,* p.283.
10. Frances Brooke, *The History of Emily Montague* (Toronto: New Canadian Library, 1969) p.19. (London: Dodsley, 1769, 4v.)
11. *Ibid.,* p.123.
12. *Ibid.,* p.186.

13. *Ibid.*, p.33.
14. *Ibid.*, p.37.
15. *Ibid.*, p.167.
16. *Ibid.*, p.173.
17. *Ibid.*, p.24.
18. *Ibid.*, p.44
19. *Ibid.*, p.127.
20. *Ibid.*, p.169.
21. *Ibid.*, p.90.
22. *Ibid.*, p.122.
23. *Ibid.*, pp.220-21.
24. Desmond Pacey, *Essays in Canadian Criticism 1938-1968* (Toronto: Ryerson, 1969), p.35.

2.
Frontier Exile

The garrison is an enclosure; the frontier, an expansive milieu. The garrison implies the confrontation of two realities–two social or moral or philosophic visions–one of which is coherent and comprehensible and the other, apparently chaotic and indeterminate in scope. The frontier is a context, relatively uncomplicated, in which duality consists of a single vision of reality confronted by itself as in the concave reflection of an encompassing mirror. The redundancy and distortion of the ensuing image is a characteristic typical of frontier literature. In the Leatherstocking Tales of James Fenimore Cooper, for instance, variations of the same theme are played over and over: as Natty Bumpo grows, matures, ages and dies, as he is transformed from proud and predatory youth to wasted anachronism, he continues to straddle the distance between civilization and the natural world, and that is always his story. There is a similar consistency in the frontier fiction of Major John Richardson. In *Wacousta* and later, in *The Canadian Brothers (Matilda Montgomery),* and even in two of the potboilers he tossed off in New York during the last three years of his life, Richardson repeatedly exhibited a fascination for the types of violent conflict indigenous to North America. His considerable talent was devoted primarily to the elaboration, to the making complex, of simple themes born out of violence. This, of course, is in the romantic tradition, its object the opposite to realism which attempts to clarify the complexities of human experience, albeit sometimes (most notably in *Finnigan's Wake*) the reality perceived is so complex that its clarification approaches incomprehensibility.

Richardson and Cooper are romantic novelists. Reginald Morton, otherwise known as Wacousta, and Natty Bumpo are both romantic protagonists. Both of them are outsiders, fugitives amidst the wilderness from the menace of civilization. But Natty is the personification of an American dream. He is the individualist seeker of egalitarian truth, in the tradition of Daniel Boone and Davy Crockett and Ralph Nader, and with their same killer instinct. Wacousta is the ominous and violent embodiment of a much different vision, a vision of the frontier as a place of exile in which one with violence might redeem the past. Natty Bumpo is an ignorant intermediary between Jean-Jacques Rousseau and Henry David Thoreau. He is rational man self-immersed in the natural world but pursued, to his death, by civilization. Richardson's Wacousta is pursued by himself. Unlike Cooper's ambivalent garden wildnerness, Richardson's frontier is a reduction of context to primeval chaos in which the ambivalent purpose of Wacousta's exile is achieved.

Garrison exile tends to be communal–it is part of a shared experience in an urban setting or, as in the case of Lowry, an urbane mind. Frontier exile is solitary, the experience of an individual in the wilderness. The garrison is a form of prison, its occupants in a form of stasis, and it is often from this very state that the frontier exile is a fugitive. His flight, usually, is a quest for either a private alternative or personal redemption. The fugitive, solitude and wilderness, romance and moral drama, the search for meaning, these characterize the frontier effect in Canadian literature of exile.

Such contemporary novels as Robert Kroetsch's *But We Are Exiles* and Fred Bodsworth's *The Atonement of Ashley Morden* are clearly within this tradition. A case might be made that something in the primeval malevolence bred by Caleb Gare's lust for the soil and the spontaneous piety of his daughter Judith's naked embrace of the earth place Martha Ostenso's *Wild Geese* there also. Ostenso's novel is similar, in this respect, to Mazo de la Roche's *Possession* which likewise describes rather bizarre activities beyond the margins of acceptability as it is implicitly defined. Miss de la Roche's lone protagonist, Derek Vale, quite consciously has placed himself apart from the morality of his Nova Scotia heritage and the values of the rural Southern Ontario society in which he lives. When he buries Buck, his half-breed infant son, he denies him the final possibility of escaping the utter isolation of his brief existence:

> Nor would Derek have Mr. Ramsey sent for to read the burial service. The conception of Buckskin had been secret; their life together that winter had been secret; now in death, let him strike

> his tent in secret and join his dark forebears without benefit of clergy.[1]

In this denial, Derek seals his own fate to be forever an outsider–a fate confirmed by the return to him of Buckskin's Indian Mother, Fawnie. *Possession* and *Wild Geese* are two of many novels which, to varying degrees, exhibit characteristics of frontier exile. The prototype, as I have indicated, is Richardson's *Wacousta.*

There is a recurrent strain of heterosexuality in Canadian frontier fiction. Without being seduced by Leslie Fiedler's statements about the pervasiveness of inter-racial homosexuality in American fiction, it is nevertheless quite evident that relations between the sexes are limited to perfunctory intercourse, at best, in many American novels, particularly those of Cooper, Twain and, in the same frontier tradition, Zane Grey. In contrast, Canadian works of the frontier lean heavily on the heterosexual impulse. The five just mentioned are all tales, at least superficially, of love, lust, and infidelity between the sexes. And interestingly enough, there appears to be a correlation between the degree or depth of exile and the perversity of sexuality displayed.

In Ostenso's *Wild Geese,* sexuality is both link and barrier amongst her characters. Working as a teacher in northern Manitoba, Lind Archer is billeted with the Gares:

> The teacher was lonely, and even more conscious of the stark loneliness of Amelia, of Judith, of Ellen and Martin, each within himself. Work did not destroy the loneliness; work was only a fog in which they moved so that they might not see the loneliness of each other.[2]

Lind is ignorant of Caleb's power over his family. She is not aware that he is blackmailing his wife Amelia into a continuing submission nor that he threatens to reveal her past indiscretion to its bastard offspring, the seemingly well-bred Mark Jordan. Lind and Mark are both outsiders. A combustion of isolation without alienation allows them to recognize the peculiar quality of their frontier environment as well as fall in love with each other. They speak of "the strange unity between the nature of man and earth here in the north, and of the spareness of both physical and spiritual life."[3] Mark explains:

> We are, after all, only the mirror of our environment. Life here

> at Oeland, even, may seem a negation but it's only a reflection from so few exterior natural objects that it has the semblance of negation. These people are thrown inward upon themselves, their passions stored up, they are intensfied figures of life with no outward expression–no releasing gesture.[4]

They do not understand, however, the extent to which the land and Caleb, together, have the power to reduce those within reach of their malignant union to abject servility. They are not innocent witnesses.

The land is Caleb's only love and it is an exacting mistress which finally swallows him into the depths of its muskeg while the flax their union yielded is consumed by fire in the surrounding background. Clearly nature finds his lust unnatural and destroys him. But it is this lust, combined with the perversity of his marital relations, that determines Caleb Gare's demonic behaviour, as well as being the product of it, and characterizes his small and ugly world. Escape from this sexually derived oppression inevitably must come through sexuality. Ellen, the eldest daughter, has not the strength of character to run off with Malcolm, her half-breed lover. But Jude, the great, strong, beautiful, rebellious antithesis of her father Caleb, makes love to the earth, and to Sven Sandbo. She conceives as much from one as from the other: from the first, a will to prevail; from Sven, a more conventional pregnancy. She tries to kill her father and is virtually imprisoned by him; but she runs away, escapes, and Caleb's world collapses. With his death each of them, locked within himself, is let out. Perhaps their whole dramatic story is no more than a gothic metaphor for the complexities that underlie the more pedestrian affair between Lind and Mark. As these two lovers prepare to leave for civilization, their innocence unblemished, the world of the Gares recedes like the memory of a dream but its disturbing effect lingers:

> Lind felt humble as she heard the wild geese go over. There was an infinite cold passion in their flight, like the passion of the universe, a personal mystery never to be solved. She knew in her heart that Mark Jordan was like them–that he stood inevitably alone. But because of the human need in him, he had come to her. It warmed her to dwell on the thought.[5]

Lilka Frahm, in Bodsworth's *The Atonement of Ashley Morden,* combines the visceral earthiness of Jude Gare and the spirituality of

Rima, the ethereal forest nymph in W.H. Hudson's *Green Mansions.* Unlike Jude, Lilka is sexually naive and, unlike Rima, she is very human, but like both of them she has lived utterly apart from society and her relations with the masculine world have been correspondingly unnatural. In contrast to Margo, whom Ashley Morden had loved through their growing up together, Lilka is morally incorruptible. Significantly, when Margo is seduced by Ron Dorkett during World War II, she dies in the blitzed ruins of their London rendezvous. Twenty years later, when Dorkett attempts to make love to Lilka in the midst of the Canadian wilderness, it is he who dies. For Bodsworth, relations between the sexes are emblematic of his larger vision, and used to serve its larger purpose. As in *The Last of the Curlews,* he is here concerned with survival, only this time it is the survival of mankind.

His thesis is that the implements of man's aggression are not evolutionary but invented. Man has not the instinct of the wolf, for example, either to conquer or submit but not to kill except for sustenance. Human beings are like the pair of rabbits or the doves in a cage who kill each other. Because they are built for flight and not for battle, they have not instinctive behavioural restraints. Man's indiscriminate aggressiveness is graphically suggested by Dorkett's psychopathic lechery. Man's capacity to endure through flight, even to prevail, is represented by Werner Frahm's outpost hospital, Kawogamee House, to which he retreated after Auschwitz. On the road to the concentration camp, Frahm had witnessed the multiple-rape and murder of his wife–the link between sex and death is once again shown–and he responds by cloistering his daughter Lilka away from society, particularly white masculine society, in the wilderness. Such an action anticipates eventual sterility, however, and not survival. But in the love that grows between Lilka, the naive child of nature, and Ashley Morden, the battered fugitive from a self-destructive, self-consuming civilization, Bodsworth offers the possibility of man's endurance. Their choice of frontier exile represents a positive moral disarmament, social disengagement, and the return to nature and to natural law. This is a movement in quite the opposite direction to that of Ostenso's novel.

In *Wacousta* and *But We are Exiles,* novels at the opposite ends of the temporal spectrum of frontier fiction, the central love relationships exhibit a vicariousness, a rediffusion of identities. As Kroetsch's novel opens, the *Nahanni Jane* is dragging off Norman Wells for Mike Hornyak's corpse. Peter Guy has precipitated Hornyak's death by letting him take an unshielded electric light into a storage tank, which thereupon explodes. Hornyak is ignited, but with characteristic dispatch he manages to reach the cooling river waters. He chooses death by drowning, a master of his destiny to the end. Even when, six years earlier, the two of them had made their zany voyage across the Canadian prairies, Hornyak had been in pursuit of water. After they picked up Kettle Fraser, Peter's girl friend, and, by nightfall, Mike's mistress and incipient wife, they went to the hot springs at Lake Louise. (The Kettle and the Fraser are both rivers in British Columbia.) In a medley of suggestive allusions, Kroetsch describes the scene:

> 'This is it!' Mike shouted. He slammed on the brakes, 'We've found it! Quick! Get out.' And he left the Rolls in the middle of the road, horns honking. 'Run!'
>
> They took off their shoes, They sat with their feet in the hundred-degree water in the sunlight on the mountainside. The smell of pine and spruce over the smell of sulphur. Kettle with her dress up past her knees and Peter grinning and Hornyak kneeling in the spring, trying to get closer.
>
> And when they started to sing, to laugh, a wrinkled old man who couldn't die came out from behind a rock wall: 'Take your feet out of that damned water.' Which made them stop singing. . .
>
> 'You're supposed to pay. Up there,' the guard called.
>
> 'You can't pay,' Mike yelled back. 'Not to be reborn.'[6]

Although early in their story, this section is related near the novel's end. Consequently, the allusions to salvation and damnation, to life, death, mortality, natural order, and the ultimate futility of man's purpose, are not lost. Within their context of retrospective hallucination, they represent the completion in Peter's mind of a metamorphosis that began with Hornyak's death by water amidst the sulphurous stench of burning flesh–a death followed almost immediately by resumed intimacies between Peter and the widowed Kettle. In the evening of the hot springs episode, Peter had peered into Kettle's room and seen, reflected in the mirror

> . . . the image of two raging bodies, a tumble of dark hair. And he was caught. He fled and fled and was caught there, trapped, doomed in that long mahogany frame. He fled and went on searching and could not see himself.[7]

It is as if Peter had deposited his own identity in their mirrored coupling. He fled northwards, away from all external expectations of himself, from family and a promising future, to become a pilot on the Mackenzie, "a white river bum with a river in his head to keep everything else out."[8] During the time of Peter's learning, and of his forgetting, Hornyak was forcing a way through the world, making money, gaining power, and taking his wife along with him. His death began the process of Peter's confrontation with the self that he had left in the mirror, that he had fled six years before. The affair with Kettle continues it, not so much as a catalyst but as a lubricant.

Peter comes to realize that "nothing would be enough to kill the isolation. Nothing. Nothing to kill the nothing."[9] And Kettle is likewise in a spiritual vacuum–the legacy of her life with Hornyak. When they had met at the university where she had been sent by her father, "the wilderness she had been exiled from was a forbidden land, yet a world to which she dreamed of returning, for it had become dream and excitement and utopia to her."[10] But at their coming together again, it is a wasted land, caught in the vicious onset of the early winter snows, a land they wish desperately to leave. To do so, however, would be to escape from their own identities as they are frozen in the past. When Kettle pleads with Peter, "Break the mirror for me. Break it, break it please, smash it, Peter. Listen to me, smash it," he can only look out "beneath the trees at the distant water."[11] Kroetsch portrays their mutual agony in a brilliant blend of metaphor and memory fragments. Peter has gone too far towards becoming the other image in the reflection that has impelled him through the last six years, too far towards becoming his mirror opposite, Mike Hornyak. He cannot also be the antithesis of what he has become. In final surrender to the metamorphosis, he tips Hornyak's appropriately defaced corpse from the canoe where it lies, into the water and wrapped against the cold in a tarpaulin takes its place.

In Kroetsch's vision of reality confronted by itself, the possessed and the possessor, the pursued and the pursuer, ultimately are one. It is the disturbing vision of an existential romance in which, through the violence of sexuality and death, the past is redeemed–and discovered to be a void. Identity is obliterated by awareness, the future by the present. Exile sought at the periphery of consciousness is a desperate temporary measure with which to withstand oblivion, and doomed to fail.

Wacousta is the exemplary novel of frontier exile. The complexity of its character-relationships far outstrips that in *But We Are Exiles,* although Kroetsch's metaphysics are somewhat more subtle than Richardson's and, certainly, they are less histrionic. But then, there is not another novel in the whole of Canadian literature that can match *Wacousta* for the resounding enthusiasm with which it exploits a seemingly universal inclination for depravity, perversity, and bad taste. In comparison, the Leatherstocking Tales are as anaemic as a nun beside a painted lady. And as entertaining.

Richardson is nothing if not thorough in his exploitation of the grotesque, the morbid, the sordid. For instance, in the death of Frank Halloway, after wringing every possible emotion out of the last meeting between the wrongfully condemned Halloway and his beloved Ellen, pathetically disguised as the drummer boy for his funeral procession, and then offering the possibility of reprieve through the fugitive who runs towards the execution scene, Richardson's hand moves swiftly:

> "Oh, stop–for God's sake, stop! Another moment and he will be here, and I–"
>
> He said no more–a dozen bullets penetrated his body–one passed directly through his heart. He leaped several feet in the air, and then fell heavily, a lifeless, bleeding corpse, across the coffin.[12]

Halloway is dead, but not departed. A tomahawk aimed at the fleeing man, thrown by Wacousta, misses its mark but cleaves "with a deadly and crashing sound into the brain of the weltering corpse."[13] Next, the widowed Ellen appears and falls across the body of her husband, "imprinting her warm kisses on his bloody lips":

> Suddenly she started from the earth; her face, her hands, and her garments so saturated with the blood of her husband that a feeling of horror crept throughout the veins of all who beheld her. She stood upon the coffin and across the corpse, raised her eyes

> and hands imploringly to heaven, and then, in accents wilder even than her words, uttered an imprecation that sounded like the prophetic warning of some unholy spirit.[14]

She screams her prophecy of destruction–the subtitle of the book is "The Prophecy"–for all the family of Colonel De Haldimar, whose withheld clemency has condemned Halloway to his death. She is then carried off by the triumphant Wacousta to become, demented, his wife. But Halloway's part is still not done. That same evening, Captain Frederick De Haldimar and Lieutenant Everard Valletort, in rustic disguise on their way from Detroit to Michilimakinac to warn of Pontiac's treachery, approach the place of execution and discover Onondato, Wacousta's "wolf-dog lapping up from the earth in which they were encrusted, the blood and brains of the unfortunate Frank Halloway."[15]

Richardson's imagination may be somewhat garish, but it is by no means undisciplined. The sequence I have just described is not atypical in the extent to which even the most extravagant image is integrated with the whole. The exotic repast of Wacousta's wolf-dog is an excellent case in point. Onondato is, like Lupe in *The Atonement of Ashley Morden,* an extension of its master's condition in the world. But, whereas Lilka's wolf is the embodiment of natural law, Wacousta's is the spectre of his most unnatural appetite. Like so much else in this novel, the form of his derangement echoes elements of Jacobean tragedy and ghoulish folk-lore. His loss of Clara Beverley to Colonel De Haldimar, twenty-four years before the present action, has reduced him to the level of a creature possessed, driven by a lust for evil and vengeance. The Indians, who accept him as their better, are described as "whooping hell fiends."[16] Amongst them, he is likened "to the spirit of darkness presiding over his terrible legions."[17] The flag he flies from the captured schooner is black, the emblem of death. But he is more than demonic. He is lycanthropic, a beast, howling inarticulately from cover to cover of his context, the embodiment of natural chaos. So often is he described as emitting bloodcurdling yells that when he finally does speak in articulate and cultured English, the extent of his depravity is heightened by the contrast. Ellen, too has been reduced to animal dementia. She and Wacousta couple. But Wacousta turns out to be Sir Reginald Morton and Ellen, hearing this, exclaims that Halloway was also, really, Reginald Morton: "Yes, Ellen Clayton, you have been the wife of two Reginald Mortons."[18] In the light of this revelation, the image of Wacousta's spectral self devouring Halloway's remains becomes less arbitrary–a grotesque metaphor for actuality. As Richardson exclaims in the second paragraph following this explanation of the merged identities of Ellen's husbands, "ours is a tale of sad reality.. . .Within the bounds of probability have we, therefore, confined ourselves."[19] Ironic? Yes, but accurate according to the novel's implicit purpose which is to offer provocative entertainment through moral complexity in the midst of chaos.

Identity is not a stable commodity within Wacousta's sphere of influence. His own has many facets: first as Reginald Morton, then Scots renegade, then as a French officer with Montcalm on the Plains of Abraham, and finally, at the farthest reaches of his exile, Indian Chief second only to Pontiac amongst the Ottawas. This movement in Richardson's cosmology represents degeneration from order to the embodiment of natural chaos. In the course of achieving his purpose, however, on both a dramatic and a metaphysical level, Wacousta also remains the English gentleman, abused by life and abusing it in turn. He eventually becomes one with his nephew, Halloway, who ironically was devoted to the De Haldimars, particularly to Frederick who alone of the family survives their accursed lot. Wacousta takes Clara De Haldimar as a surrogate for her mother, whom he had lost to Clara's father. His confusion is pathetic, yet also pathological:

> . . .he imprinted a burning kiss upon her lips. "Even thus was I once wont to linger on the lips of your mother; but hers ever pouted to be pressed by mine, and not with tears but with sunniest smiles did she court them." He paused, bent his head over the face of the shuddering girl, and gazing fixedly for a few minutes on her countenance, while he pressed her struggling form more closely to his own, exultingly pursued, as if to himself: "Even as her mother was, so is she. Ye powers of Hell! who would have ever thought a time would come when both my vengeance and my love would be gratified to the utmost?"[20]

In taking her, he is taking Clara Beverley, her mother, and simultaneously avenging himself upon Colonel De Haldimar, her father.

Wacousta's love had begun in a Scottish Eden where Clara Beverley was hidden away from mankind by her misanthropic father, much as

Lilka Frahm had been hidden by her father in Northern Ontario–in a manner quite the opposite to Gordon Fraser's banishment of Kettle into society, in *But We Are Exiles.* When at last the antithesis of love is within his grasp, it is in a different Eden, a garden of chaos, of dark shadows and savagery:

> . . .the hour of retribution is at hand, and revenge, the exclusive passion of the gods, shall at length be mine. In no other country in the world–under no other circumstances than the present–could I have secured it.[21]

The course of his exile has led him to the frontier–of civilization, of morality, of individual identity, and of sanity.

Richardson's manipulation of identity leads to even more bizarre, and more subtle, effects than these. Clara and Charles are said to bear striking likenesses to their mother. Ironically, they die at Wacousta's hand while Frederick, their brother who closely resembled Colonel De Haldimar, survives them all. I would suggest the reason, conscious or unconscious on the author's part but sustained by the text, is that Frederick and his first cousin, Madeline De Haldimar, to whom he is betrothed, represent a new order. His younger siblings embody the decadence of the old. In such a weltering chaos as Richardson perceives the world to be, the nobility of Frederick and the attractive magnetism of Madeline offer a stability of sorts, imbuing their world with an order based on natural virtue and beauty. It is by these characteristics that it survives "the doom that had fallen, without exception on every fortress on the line of frontier in which they lay."[22]

Their enduring Wacousta's vengeance is ironic. But the sacrificing of Clara and Charles to it bears the imprint of a double irony. The two youngest De Haldimars, whose identities are merged with the former Clara Beverley through their physical resemblance to her, suffer the consequence of Wacousta's hatred for their father. More ironic than this, they are the victims of their author's contempt. They are, therefore, expendable where expedient–to fulfil the prophecy. Frederick is described as "brave, generous, manly, amiable, and highly talented–the pride of the garrison, and the idol of his family."[23] In contrast, Charles is said to possess "retiring, mild, winning manners, and gentle affections, added to extreme and almost feminine beauty of countenance."[24] His nature is "affectionate and bland"[25] while Frederick is said to have "had none of the natural weakness and timidity of character which belonged to the gentle and more sensitive Charles."[26] Clara, in every respect, is said to be his counterpart. When she is finally, reluctantly, introduced by the author, she is portrayed merely as "an elegant, slight form" while in the paragraphs to follow Madeline is compared favourably to the Medicean Venus and the Madonna of Raphael.[27] The low regard in which Charles and Clara are held is not, however, merely the result of arbitrary prejudice. It is consistent, perhaps unconsciously so, with their dramatic function.

Before examining that function the relationship of Captain Frederick De Haldimar and his affianced first cousin, Madeline De Haldimar might first be worth considering for the light it will eventually cast upon the far more intriguing, indeed Websterian, relationship of the other two. Union between first cousins lies somewhere just on the short side of incest. Certainly the nature of the bond between Frederick and Madeline makes such a suggestion inescapable. Furthermore, their relationship attains the quality of pagan myth through the ministrations of the ubiquitous savage girl, Oucanasta. In her selfless and apparently unmotivated devotion to Captain De Haldimar, the Indian girl leads him through the night to the camp of the fiends of Hell, and assists in his return to the world of the truly living. She later rescues Madeline from the massacre at Michilimakinac, delivering her, likewise, from death in terms that leave no doubt that that is exactly what she has done. Madeline herself first reappears as a "pale and spectral" apparition amidst the foliage:

> In the centre of the wan forehead was a dark incrustation as of blood covering the superfices of a newly closed wound. The pallid mouth was partially unclosed, so as to display a row of white and apparently lipless teeth, and the features were otherwise set and drawn, as those of one who is no longer of earth.[28]

In one sense, Oucanasta is a dusky Beatrice who leads the lovers through the purgatorial fires of their love's refinement. In another, she is the benevolent impulse that is ever present in the natural chaos which surrounds them.

It is interesting that the young chief who is her brother is her counterpart in sentiment only. There is nothing of redemption or the supernatural in his mien as in hers, nor in his function. When he frees

Frederick from Wacousta's bondage, it is only luck that Wacousta trips, allowing Frederick to escape. When he frees Sir Everard and Clara, they achieve safety only to have their mutually beloved Charles, who is esctatic at their return, restrained by the maniacal Ellen Holloway and cut down by Wacousta. Finally, when the young warrior executes Wacousta on the bridge, Clara plunges from the dying man's upraised arms to her death in the ravine. In all, the young Ottawa chief rather ineptly forces the plot towards its conclusion. As the unfortunate embodiment of natural principle, he is consistent with Richardson's apparent concept of the fundamental centrality of accident and disorder in the experience of man.

The intimations of a love triangle which includes the Indian girl are even more subtle than those of an incestuous union. Only the rather graceless Captain Erskine has the poor taste to mention it at all; jokingly, upon the approach of someone unrecognized in the shadows:

> "Another Oucanasta for De Haldimar, no doubt," observed Captain Erskine, after a moment's pause. "These Grenadiers carry everything before them as well in love as in war." The error of the good-natured officer was, however, obvious to all but himself.[29]

Some things are simply not talked about, the possible miscegenous liaison of a fellow officer and gentleman being one of them.

In contrast to the quiet perversity of Frederick's loves, the same themes in the relationships of his younger brother and sister and their friend, Sir Everard Valletort, are amplified extravagantly. The healthy undertones of sexuality of the other three are, in this effete triangle, replaced by bonds of filial devotion which are a crude disguise for incipient incest, homosexuality, and impotence. I am not trying to suggest that this was Richardson's intent–to devise a Sartrian *ménage à trois.* And it is not the literal truth of their contextual relations. But it does provide a blunt accounting of their function in the novel that cannot otherwise be thematically or dramatically justified. It also helps to coalesce the reasons for the author's attitude of distaste towards all three of them.

A series of brief quotations will highlight the source of my perhaps bizarre contention. Between Sir Everard and Charles De Haldimar,

> not a shade of disunion had at any period intervened to interrupt

> the almost brotherly attachment subsisting between them, and each felt the disposition of the other was the one most assimilated to his own.[30]

They make an unlikely Castor and Pollux, considering that one of them is "bland" and given to crying while the other plays the part of an "ephemeral" fop. In any case,

> Clara De Haldimar was the constant theme of her younger brother's praise. Her image was ever uppermost in his thoughts, her name ever hovering on his lips; and when alone with his friend Valletort it was his delight to dwell on the worth and accomplishments of his amiable and beloved sister.[31]

He does so to the extent that

> while listening to his eloquent praises, Sir Everard learnt to feel an interest in a being whom all declared to be the counterpart of her brother, as well in personal attraction as in singleness of nature.[32]

Inevitably, the baronet is besmitten by Clara, although they have never met, and declares himself to Charles:

> "I have absolutely, I will not say fallen in love with (that would be going to far), but conceived so strong an interest in her, that my most ardent desire would be to find favour in her eyes. What say you, my friend? Are you inclined to forward my suit; and, if so, is there any chance for me, think you, with yourself?"[33]

When eventually, under the duress of violent circumstance, Sir Everard encounters "that cherished sister of his friend, on whose ideal form his excited imagination had so often latterly loved to linger,"[34] he discovers

> the suppression, if not utter extinction, of all passion attached to the sentiment with which he had been inspired. A new feeling had quickened in his breast; and it was with emotions more assimilated to friendship than to love that he now regarded the beautiful but sorrow-stricken sister of his bosom friend.[35]

Forced to witness Wacousta's lusty supplications to the terrified Clara, for whom, it was earlier explained, there are some things "worse even than death,"[36] he shuts his eyes. But when she runs to his embrace

> a thrill of inexplicable joy ran through each awakened fibre of his frame. . .delight mingled with agony in his sensation of the wild throb of her bosom against his own; and even while his soul fainted within him as he reflected on the fate that awaited her, he felt as if he could himself now die more happily.[37]

He is at this time, of course, securely tied to a tree and unable to intervene.

The pattern of their relationships, then, if not the superficial reality, is essentially perverse. It is clear that the obsessive devotion of Charles to his sister promises to be vicariously requited through Sir Everard. With equal clarity, it may be seen that the baronet is actually enamoured not of Clara but of an uncompromising version of Charles. Clara, in effect, becomes an emblem of the attachment that has grown between the two men–to the extent that when Everard and Clara finally meet, she is rather pathetically reduced to being only the object of his friendship, from being his imaginary beloved. His ardour diminishes to impotence because his response to her is as to a surrogate for Charles, a forbidden fruit, and because affection for Charles has been sustained at the level of brotherly fondness, his sexual love for Clara would be incestuous. Nevertheless–and significantly–when Clara embraces him while he is in bondage, when as Wacousta's captive the situation is beyond his control, his ecstasy at their proximity is orgasmic.

When it appears that Sir Everard has shot Captain Frederick De Haldimar, albeit in error, a familiar impasse emerges. How, worries Charles, "could Clara De Haldimar become the wife of him whose hands were, however innocently, stained with the life-blood of her brother!"[38] There is a considerable variation, however, between this and more conventional versions of the same dilemma. In *The Golden Dog,* Le Gardeur de Repentigny kills Bourgeois Philibert, the father of his sister Amélie's beloved Pierre, thus causing Amélie in horror and shame to flee to a convent where she dies. In *The Seats of the Mighty,* potential difficulties are deftly resolved by having someone else intervene for Robert Moray and slay Juste, the brother of his secretly wedded Alixe Duvarney, as it were, by proxy. But in *Wacousta* the dilemma of loving and killing next-of-kin gains an alarming new dimension, for Clara is almost incidental–the strain is between Charles and Everard:

> Frederick De Haldimar a corpse, and slain by the hand of Sir Everard Valletort! What but disunion could follow this melancholy catastrophe? and how could Charles De Haldimar, even if his bland nature should survive the shock, ever bear to look again upon the man who had, however innocently or unintentionally, deprived him of a brother whom he adored?[39]

When it is discovered that the heinous crime did not, in fact, occur, Charles and Sir Everard are reunited:

> Never had Charles De Haldimar appeared as eminently handsome; and yet his beauty resembled that of a frail and delicate woman. . .[accounting]. . .for the readiness with which Sir Everard suffered his imagination to draw on the brother for those attributes he ascribed to the sister.[40]

Perhaps the French surnames given to these particular English characters are a small indication of Richardson's gothic achievement.

What sets *Wacousta* apart as something more than a lurid, subliminally obscene, melodrama of revenge are precisely those characteristics which make it the prototype, as previously defined, of one stream in the flow of Canadian fiction. Exile, in this novel, is a state of mind; the frontier, a state of consciousness. The character relationships, the intricacies of the plot mosaic, the superficial but quite accurate details, these are all subservient to a larger purpose, which is to convey the nature of man's condition in the universe and his perception of it.

Such a purpose undoubtedly grew as much out of the frontier materials with which he was working as out of any conscious intent on Richardson's part. His Canadian setting has neither the social complexity nor the sublime, indifferent beauty and order that Frances Brooke perceived in the Canada of her experience. It is, rather, the landscape of a troubled dream; dark, forbidding, filled with murderous savages and murderous intent, a chaotic malevolence streaked with intimations of virtue and stained with the bloodshed of human depravity. It is the outer perimeter of reality, a morass of limitless depth, and man at its centre is in utter isolation, turned in upon himself–his actions and emotions, the self-fulfilling prophecies of his own demise.

Notes

1. Mazo de la Roche, *Possession* (Toronto: Macmillan, 1923), p.284.
2. Martha Ostenso, *Wild Geese* (Toronto: New Canadian Library, 1971), p.33. (Toronto: McClelland and Stewart, 1925.)
3. *Ibid.*, p.77.
4. *Ibid.*, p.78.
5. *Ibid.*, p.239.
6. Robert Kroetsch, *But We Are Exiles* (Toronto: Macmillan, 1965), p.144.
7. *Ibid.*, p.145.
8. *Ibid.*, p.103.
9. *Ibid.*, p.64.
10. *Ibid.*, p.32.
11. *Ibid.*, p.124.
12. Major John Richardson, *Wacousta* (Toronto: New Canadian Library, 1967), p.85. (London: Cadell, 1832. 3v.) The popular edition has been used in this study, and wherever possible elsewhere, in the belief that availability is an important consideration for the literary critic to keep in mind. My commentary is, I believe, fully corroborated by the original 1832 edition held in Special Collections, Douglas Library, Queen's University, Kingston, Ontario.
13. *Ibid.*, p.87.
14. *Ibid.*, p.87.
15. *Ibid.*, p.105.
16. *Ibid.*, p.230.
17. *Ibid.*, p.134.
18. *Ibid.*, p.224.
19. *Ibid.*, p.224.
20. *Ibid.*, p.234.
21. *Ibid.*, p.270.
22. *Ibid.*, p.298.
23. *Ibid.*, p.28.
24. *Ibid.*, p.58.
25. *Ibid.*, p.58.
26. *Ibid.*, p.151.
27. *Ibid.*, p.165.
28. *Ibid.*, p.197.
29. *Ibid.*, p.214.
30. *Ibid.*, p.59.
31. *Ibid.*, p.60.
32. *Ibid.*, p.60.
33. *Ibid.*, p.66.
34. *Ibid.*, p.245.
35. *Ibid.*, p.245.
36. *Ibid.*, p.178.

37. *Ibid.*, p.247.
38. *Ibid.*, p.62.
39. *Ibid.*, p.28.
40. *Ibid.*, p.66.

3.
Colonial Exile

Superficially, there would seem to be little in common between *Wacousta* and the measured tones of apparent rationality and good taste that characterize Sara Jeannette Duncan's *The Imperialist.* Yet each in its own way expresses themes of exile that are indigenous to its Canadian setting. Richardson's frontier romance undoubtedly conveys more, in a sociological sense, about the literary sensibilities of the 1830's when it was written, than about the conditions of life during the period of the Indian massacres at Detroit and Michilimakinac, some seventy years earlier. But authenticity has never been the criterion of art. *Wacousta* achieves a graphic, almost surrealistic, representation of terrorized humanity driven by motives dark or noble, or by destiny or chance, to the outer bounds of rational experience. In sharp contrast, the themes of colonial exile portrayed with serene diffidence by Miss Duncan in her realistic novel, *The Imperialist,* are undoubtedly reinforced by their historical veracity and relevance. The Imperial question was very much in the forefront of the public mind when her book appeared in 1904. While clearly showing her personal bias, Miss Duncan does not dissipate her political drama by muzzling the anti-British opposition. Her treatment is balanced and thorough. She displays, in fact, one of the most acute political minds that Canadian literature has yet allowed to flourish in its midst.

Documentary and literary significance in a novel may be quite independent of each other. The former is determined by factual considerations, and the latter by the universal implications of facts as they are refined by art. Miss Duncan's primary achievement, quite consistent with the objectives of realism, has been to integrate the two in a most engaging balance of authenticity and aesthetic diversion. *The Imperialist* lucidly portrays the ambiguous and at times ambivalent conditions of life under a colonial dispensation that disorients and demeans even while it ennobles and provides stability. Such a world is Elgin, Canada, in the last few years of the Victorian era–more colonial in attitude than fact, where all experience is incomplete, because it is not happening in England. This world sustains an insidious form of exile, pleasantly and even triumphantly endured; continuously promising a future that it cannot deliver. This is the world *The Imperialist* defines with clarity and charm.

Obviously, Richardson and Duncan perceive quite different orders of reality in their Canadian experience. In many ways, however, *The Imperialist* is more the polar opposite of *The History of Emily Montague* for, while being a world apart, like opposing polar regions they have much in common. Garrison and colonial exile are perceptual inversions of one another. The garrison is a restrictive enclave in an alien context and the colony, an alien or dissociated enclave, however large, restricted by the force of an external presence. The vision of the former tends to diminish the world around it while the later is, itself, by the world diminished. Exile in the garrison as well as the colony or neo-colony is a relatively passive state of dissociated being, characterized by tonality and theme rather than being primarily manifest in plot and characterization as in corresponding novels of the frontier and the nation-state. In keeping with this, *The Imperialist* and *The History of Emily Montague* are rational and reflective, although Duncan has created an analytic representation of reality and Mrs. Brooke, a synthetic one. Mrs. Brooke's concern is manners, social relationships, the appearance of things. She populates a world of limited creation with characters of limited dimension and places them in situations of limited significance. Like Jane Austen, she does it exceedingly well. Sara Duncan, however, is concerned with the underlying social factors that cause appearances to be what they are. She, rather more like George Eliot, portrays a broader spectrum of reality and with deeper insight, although often with less clarity.

By comparison to either of these, *Wacousta* and Adele Wiseman's *The Sacrifice,* an exemplar of immigrant exile in the nation-state, are works of both emotional and actional violence. However, they are not polar but diametric opposites on a horizontal plane. Where lies east and where lies west, which is the established order and which the opposing chaos being confronted, depends entirely upon how the author manipulates the reader's viewpoint. Richardson and Wiseman both exploit the ironic possibilities of this mobility to their respective limits of dramatic complication and dramatic intensity. In *Wacousta,* the frontier that ultimately matters is as elusive, ominous, and insubstantial as are the interwoven shadows of its literal antecedents. Whether it is a frontier within civilized man or all around him, is effectively indeterminant. Exile, there, is necessarily a furtive and perverse condition, resisting static definition. In *The Sacrifice,* the Winnipeg surrounding the Jewish community or ghetto is insubstantial, abstract, unknown. By manipulating its felt presence in the ghetto and in Abraham's experience, Wiseman builds and sustains a tension between a nation's established presence and the exile of the immigrant within it and within himself. The result is an overpowering sweep of emotion which, with Dostoevskian intensity, assaults the reader's consciousness. This is a far cry from the refined sentiments and accomplished dialectics of *The Imperialist,* only one quadrant away from it on the metaphoric compass face of exile in Canadian fiction.

The colonial effect in fiction is in the superimposition of responses to an alien or alternative reality upon indigenous experience. The alien alternative, in this duality, is distant in space and, usually, in time. Exile from it is in the sense of irretrievable loss imposed by the separation. In *The Imperialist,* Sara Jeannette Duncan has given such colonial exile a fine and thorough treatment, but it is present elsewhere in Canadian fiction in a variety of forms.

As well as being thematically the mainstay of Mordecai Richler's *A Choice of Enemies,* colonial exile is also elusively apparent in the author's gratuitous–that is, textually unjustified–contempt for his native land. In a marvelous bit of fatuous introspection, his protagonist, Norman Price, evaluates the Canadian dream:

> Whenever Norman thought of his country he did not, as Americans were supposed to do, recall with a whack of joy the wildest rivers and fastest trains, fields of corn, skyscrapers, and the rest of it. There were all these things in his country. There were magical names in abundance. A town called Trois-Rivières; a mountain pass named Kicking Horse; Saskatchewan–a province. But there was no equivalent of the American dream to boast or knock. The Canadian dream, if there was such a puff, was how do I get out?
>
> I got out early, Norman thought.[1]

It is appropriate that Norman's mind should display this bent, but it is entirely unnecessary and, in fact, tends to undermine the more universal elements of his morally disenfranchised state. Richler has been on an interminable expatriot hegira of his own, with an occasional lapse, and he has exploited the Canadian identity crisis often and effectively–without realizing that it is the crisis, not the identity or dream, that is the "puff," as he calls it, and that his exploitation of it is ironically colonial.

The colonial effect is residual, like a racial memory. It does not derive from the original conditions of colonization, which are more likely to be those of the garrison or frontier, but from the perpetuation by ensuing generations of their forebears' ancillary function as colonists. In fiction, the colonial effect is sustained by the author's response to being born in exile which translates into the self-conscious tonalities of a dissident like Richler, an apologist like Hugh MacLennan, or a mildly embarrassed Robertson Davies.

The embarrassment of Robertson Davies at having been born a Canadian is something he seems to have overcome in the recently published *Fifth Business.* This cosmopolitan novel is set unprepossessingly in Canada and elsewhere, drawing much of its design and texture from the anomalies of life in Southern Ontario. It is, perhaps, a different type of fiction altogether from his earlier novels and this may explain the change. The Salterton trilogy, such as it is, consists of clever *tableaux,* arrangements of surface reality to convey the contours of a facile wit rather than, as in *Fifth Business,* psychic depths. In *A Mixture of Frailties,* for instance, the beneficiary of Mrs. Bridgetower's posthumous machinations is Monica Gall who, being the daughter of a factory cleaner, displays all the characteristics assigned to the working class by effete aristocrats. As described by one such snob, she is a soprano in "the Heart and Hope Gospel Quartet, who broadcast on behalf of the Thirteenth Apostle Tabernacle five mornings of the week, from nine-thirty to nine-forty-five.. . .You should hear them in *Eden Must Have Been Like Granny's Garden* or *Ten Baby Fingers and Ten Baby Toes, That Was My Mother's Rosary.*"[2] Such sniggering by an author tends to set the reader's teeth on edge.

The structure of *A Mixture of Frailities* suggests an unintentional Jamesian parody–or, if intentional, distastefully achieved. Monica receives the endowment to study abroad, while Solly and Veronica Bridgetower remain in Salterton trying to conceive and bear a live male heir in order to recover their rightful estate. The trustees fret. The consternation at discovering that more money must be spent on Monny's foreign education than they had hoped sets them all afussing:

> That night Miss Puss was very severe with her old housekeeper, who had left a light burning needlessly, and Solly went to bed drunk, to Veronica's great distress. Though the difficulties of their marriage had been many since they came under the Dead Hand of Mrs. Bridgetower, this was something new.[3]

Meanwhile, the Canadian girl abroad progresses. The Bridgetowers finally have a son, but he is stillborn: "his navel-cord tight around his neck, strangling as he moved toward the light."[4] Because of this tragedy, a gruesome turn of events in such a frothy novel, Monny continues to receive her remittance from Canada. With part of it, she finances her lover's opera, *The Golden Ass,* and tacitly assists in his suicide. After returning to Canada to bury her mother, she accepts Sir Benedict Domdaniel's offer of himself on her return to London. There is no seal on a poor girl's achievement like a titled husband. Her naiveté and the trustees' worldliness–the Jamesian confrontation of innocence and experience reduced by a heavy hand–offer an ongoing clash of relatively frivolous significance which is, however, perpetuated and resolved by three gruesomely unpleasant deaths.

It is a clever work, nonetheless, and invites facile interpretations. Possibly it is a socio-political allegory of the triumph of innocence and brass over colonial sterility and old-world decadence, or perhaps it is an ironic commentary on cultural and social pretentiousness. Perhaps it is a parody of a conventional colonial romance in which barriers of religion, education, and caste disintegrate along with the barriers of distance and national origins. If the first of these possibilities is true, however, the novel is morally inconsistent; if the second, it is structurally inconsistent; and if the third, it is in excessively bad taste.

Only occasionally in this novel does Davies anticipate his achievement in *Fifth Business* and find the perfect tone to correspond with the subject matter at hand. When he does, the effect is delightful. For example, the wit and the warmth in the following passage are in perfect harmony with the revelation of character and of setting which is being made:

> A superstitious belief persists in Canada that nothing of importance can be done in the summer. The sun, which exacts the uttermost from Nature, seems to have a numbing effect upon the works of man. Thus Matthew Snelgrove, while assuring Solly that he was going ahead at full speed in settling Mrs. Bridgetower's estate, went to his office later in the morning, and came home earlier in the afternoon, and was quite unavailable at night. During the whole of August he went with his wife to visit her girlhood home in Nova Scotia, where he gave himself up to disapproving contemplation of the sadly unruly behavior of the sea. Miss Puss Pottinger, according to her custom, went to Preston Springs for two weeks in June, to drink the waters and then, greatly refreshed. . .[5]

Such rambling prose delights with the same irreverent pleasing wit that characterizes the table-talk and correspondence of Davies' most enduring alter-ego, Samuel Marchbanks. But between the same book-covers with such as this, fetal strangulation, the suicide of Monny's lover and her mother's agonizing death, and the haunting voices of her subconsciousness seem, at best, uncomfortably placed. This schizophrenic effect does, in any case, suggest the anomaly of Davies' response to Canada in its larger world context–an anomaly he finally overcomes when he allows the larger world to subserve his primary setting rather than, as in the Salterton novels, the other way around. The embarrassment of his colonial background overcome, he is no longer in exile, no longer insecure and patronizing and aesthetically obsequious. His talent has blossomed into a rare genius. *Fifth Business* is one of the most accomplished and mature novels to have been published in recent years and, while the protagonist, Dunstable Ramsay, is in a form of exile in his lifelong search for the meaning of sainthood and of himself, there is nothing whatsoever that is colonial about his quest.

In the novels of Hugh MacLennan, exile is more often present in peripheral episodes than as a central theme, while a particular sort of colonial attitude is pervasive. The two manifestations merge in one or another of his recurrent explanations of why things are as they are: MacLennan is an apologist for reality. For instance, the boyhood tragedies of Alan Ainslie, Jerome Martell, and John Knox Cameron seem devised as justifications for plot developments–not in terms of motive but in terms of order, of consistency. Cameron, whose parents were consumed by fire, was brought up by a pair of Calvinist aunts who moulded his character to the shape of their beliefs. This is a minor incident in *The Precipice,* related as a secondhand anecdote, yet it provides a personalized basis for the Cameron girls' three quite different responses to small-town Ontario Presbyterianism. In *The Watch That Ends the Night,* the story of Jerome's origins is gratuitous, if luridly arresting. As a youngster, having witnessed his mother's murder in the backwoods of New Brunswick by a lumbercamp engineer, aroused to violence by her scorn for his impotence, Jerome is taken in by the Reverend Martell, a kindly Calvinist minister. His early experience does not account for a continuity of behaviour, as might have been expected, but it is consistent with his being different, a man apart–it is a mythical rather than realistic accounting of the man. Alan MacNeil, in *Each Man's Son,* is adopted by a Calvinist as well–the dynamically assertive Dr. David Ainslie, whose own origins are mixed in emotional violence and pathos. There is no alternative for Alan, in the catastrophic resolution imposed by MacLennan upon his story, but to live with Ainslie. Ironically, it is Margaret, the barren mother-wife, to whom the boy is drawn. Unlike the other two examples of such tragedy, the murder of Alan's mother, Molly, by Archie, his father, is the dramatic and thematic culmination of his story. Competing for possession of the boy's identity from one direction has been Ainslie, the Highlander, the embodiment of strength in individuality, and from another, Louis Camire, the effete corrupt French socialist, a representative of the masses, and from yet another, Alan's punch-drunk father, Archie, in whom the Highland instinct has been corrupted. With him in the midst of these opposing forces is the longsuffering Molly who is, however, more their casual source than she is surcease from their pressure. With Archie's death at hand, following his abrupt removal of Molly and Camire from the scene, Alan has no option left to him but what Ainslie provides. Thus, MacLennan resolves the conundrum as if it were the Gordian knot, by destructive might. After the fact, the themes resolve reflexively, retroactively. The deaths are not inevitable–dramatically, morally, or thematically. Only superficially do they arise out of the preceding action; but they are consistent with it. And they do not remedy the problems raised, but merely remove their sources.

Of course, plot resolution through catastrophe is not unique in

MacLennan's novels to *Each Man's Son.* War in *The Watch that Ends the Night* and *The Precipice* is a convenience. And the holocaust in Halifax harbour during World War I sorts out most of the problems in *Barometer Rising.* Colonel Wain's lurid demise is quite convenient in that he is removed as an obstacle to his daughter Penny's love, and his reputation is besmirched in retribution for ruining the reputation of Penny's first cousin and lover, Neil MacRae. But the deaths of Jim and Mary Fraser are particularly timely, for little Jean is thereby restored to her rightful parents, Penny and Neil. This is perhaps the most cynical variation of MacLennan's favoured pattern of parental demolition.

The violent separation from parents seems less an analogue than an effect of MacLennan's response to the historical Canadian experience. The child, in each case, is removed from a morally unstructured but genetically continuous world and set within an established order, under the dispensation of an external authority, and the old world suffers extinction. The child cannot turn back upon his past for solace or for definition. Nor can he draw comfort from the alien experience of his adoptive parents. He has been set free of the past but, unlike Huck Finn, he does not take its residue in hand and mould himself in the image of his choice–fulfilling the American dream of individualism and self-determination. He cannot, for the past has been obliterated and the present offers, imposes, a clear and viable alternative, a mould into which to grow without the promise of an infinitely receding horizon but without its uncertainty as well.

The recurrent pattern in MacLennan's vision of change, transfer, and imposition of identity may be seen as conforming to the historical process by which a collection of colonies became a Canadian nation. It accounts for the endlessly self-deprecatory search within his fiction for identity, by one representative being or another, on behalf of a mature self-sustaining sovereign body and for the consequent moral ambiguity which characterizes such a quest. In this respect, John Knox Cameron is a sketchily perceived, ghostly progenitor of small-town Ontario; Alan occupies the peripheral boundary of an elusive Canadian myth and later, as an older man in *Return of the Sphinx,* the uncomprehending ground, itself, upon which a larger, less universal, myth is enacted; and Jerome Martell is both epic hero and, himself, the epic.

In his novels, MacLennan does not provide behavioural parallels for historical events. His response to the colonial heritage of birth-in-exile is more sophisticated than that, and more ambiguous. His novels pursue a sort of retrospective self-inquiry wherein the character representing the author, whether at the narrative edge like Captain Yardly and Angus Murray or as central as George Stewart and the elder Alan Ainslie, has his own perceptions re-enacted, consolidated, verified during his novel's course. Being centres of consciousness rather than voices of the author, they disguise MacLennan's polemics. They contribute to the sustaining illusion that MacLennan's moral and political vision is a complementary extension of the behavioural dynamics of his fiction when, as I have tried to show, the actual situation is quite the reverse. Individual behaviour is subordinate to the conflicting moral and political bias imposed by the author. This may be the necessary illusion of art which speaks consciously to its society. It is an illusion which Thomas Hardy capitalized on most effectively in *Tess of the D'Urbervilles* and, to a lesser extent, in *Jude the Obscure.* It is an illusion which depends for its success upon an entirely unambiguous conception of its social–that is, the fusion of moral and political–intent. There is no doubt in Hardy's mind, apparently, or in the minds of his readers, about exactly where he stands on matters of private sexuality and the public heart. MacLennan's novels offer no such unequivocal insights into social behaviour. While his explicit polemical intent may be clear and well-defined, its contextual achievement is not. Rather, it is refracted and diffused amongst such arbitrary narrative explanations and justifications as the shattered parent syndrome. Other examples abound, but one of the most notable is the recurrent use of facial disfiguration and reconstruction–rather an overburdened symbolic device. Both Bruce Fraser in *The Precipice* and Alan Ainslie, in *Return of the Sphinx,* bear this affliction of their author's heavy hand.

The justification of experience in terms of precedent is typically a colonial response in fiction as in life. Similarly, the explanation of experience by literal example rather than by intimations or explications of causality is a reflection of the colonial sense of dissociation. It is a form of exile subtly endured, subtly displayed. The informing principle of MacLennan's fiction is born of this apologist attitude, thus accounting for the apparent conflict between plot dynamics and theme in many of his novels. This conflict gives them a disturbing internal consistency in spite of their rather alarming plot gyrations.

Consider the cases of a boy with two or more fathers, a woman with different husbands at the same time, dead soldier-lovers returned to the living. Young Alan, for example, is portrayed as a boy bewildered by his own perceptions of the world. His confusion is given concrete representation in the three father figures, Ainslie, Camire, and Archie. He is not the product of their conflicting presence in his experience. They, in effect, are the products of the confusion within him. In *The Watch that Ends the Night,* Catherine Stewart's devotion to George and her mesmeric obsession with Jerome do not so much arouse an emotional ambivalence within her as they personify it. Jerome's return from apparent death in the Spanish Civil War and Neil MacRae's from death and disgrace in World War I are supplied by the author as the dream fulfilments of Catherine and Penelope Wain. Each dream carries a corresponding overtone of nightmare resurrection, as the *status quo* of reality becomes illusion and illusion becomes haunting reality.

More specifically, colonial exile in MacLennan's novels is in the ambiguity of origins, the ambivalence of relationships, and the precedence of definition over awareness of individual and collective identity. Only in *Two Solitudes,* where Athanase Tallard suffers virtual banishment, and in Lucy Cameron's pathetic removal to the United States in *The Precipice,* does exile occupy the forefront of his novels' action. Tallard and Lucy both reject an existence that has atrophied under the imposition of external forces whose values they find alien to the communal good. Interestingly enough, for what it says about their author's colonial determinism, the response of both is doomed to failure. Tallard's life loses all meaning when he cuts himself off from the traditions, history, and places that were his lifeblood and heritage. Lucy, in escaping Grenville, Ontario, merely exchanges the burden of her Presbyterian small-town-Ontario heritage for Steve Lassiter's Princetonian refinement of a similar hell within a smaller, family unit in the midst of a larger, American setting. The colonial conditions to which their separate revolutions are a response are quite differently conceived. For Athanase Tallard, the Roman Catholic Church and Anglo-Canadian Capitalism are the horns of the dilemma on which he is tragically impaled. In *The Precipice,* it is the moral impotence of vestigial Presbyterianism and the sterility of the small-town big-business social conscience that determine the miasmal atmosphere within which the novel's characters attempt to free themselves through sexual, devotional, and marital alliances.

On a more conscious fictional plane, the socio-political conditions of colonial exile characterize community life in *The Imperialist* and expatriate experience in *A Choice of Enemies.* In an essay entitled "Our Latent Loyalty," published in *The Week,* Volume IV, in 1887, Sara Jeannette Duncan proclaimed colonial fealty:

> We owe more to Britain than we are ever likely to pay; gratitude may be detected in it. We love our Queen: for the space of a long lifetime she has been to us the embodiment of all the tender virtues of a woman, all the noble graces of a queen. Thousands of her subjects in Canada were born in her kingdom; and nothing is more contagious than the loyalty they colonized with.[6]

This vision, transformed by art to a subtle mesh of communal and global relationships and value conflicts, informs *The Imperialist* with an air of fantasmal isolation from the reaches of a mundane reality, like that of Prospero's isle. Yet, it makes her novel's separate reality all the more poignant and meaningful. Paradoxically, as in a mirror image of Miss Duncan's world, Richler's Canadian expatriates in post-war London occupy a world that is ephemeral and, likewise, separate from their surroundings:

> At that moment Norman realized something that should have been obvious before: he realized that all his friends in London were aliens like himself.
>
> Proud they were. They had come to conquer. Instead they were picked off one by one by the cold, drink, and indifference. They abjured taking part in the communal life. They mocked the local customs from the school tie to queueing, and were for the most part free of them by dint of their square, classless accents. Unlike their forebears, they were punk imperialists. They didn't marry and settle down among the natives. They had brought their own women and electric shavers with them.. . .For even those who had lived in London for years only knew the true life of the city as a rumour.[7]

Richler continues in this vein for several paragraphs and concludes with an observation which would have appalled Sara Duncan, if she had understood it–"the British didn't care a damn for Canada. . . somewhere out there between lost India and them lay the loyal Dominion of Canada, where Lord Beaverbrook came from."[8] Miss Duncan might have had difficulty comprehending Richler's vitriol, particularly his bitterly ironic conception of colonial exile at its very source. For Richler's expatriate Canadians in their nation's homeland, the antecedents of traditional values have suffered a complete reversal:

> The Canadians had come to conquer. They were the prodigal offspring of a stern father. Coming home again, however, they had not counted on the old man having grown feeble while they prospered overseas. They were surprised that the island was great only in terms of memory or sentiment. The choice of coming to England, where the streets were paved with poets, rather than to the United States bespoke a certain spiritual superiority, so they were appalled to discover that this country was infinitely more materialistic than their own, where possessions were functional, naturally yours, and not the prize of single-minded labour. They were surprised to discover that they had arrived too late.[9]

Norman, in thinking this, of course, misses the point, which Richler does not, and that is, not that they arrived too late or that expectations were not met, but that they had come for the wrong reasons and remained in expatriate bondage because they could not comprehend their error. They chose exile for a system of values, for a way of perceiving experience, that their colonial and provincial past had assured them was better than their own, because it was the progenitor of their own system, their own vision. Inevitably, they are doomed to bear the frustrations of a self-imposed second-rate existence, so long as their exile endures.

In *The Imperialist,* the situation is reversed. Exile is a state of mind and colonialism, the physical fact. The community of Elgin, Ontario, is politically as feckless as Norman's cluster of London expatriates and, in its own way, morally no less stultified, no less decadent. It is as determinedly subservient to alien conditions and alien preferences, only these are exerted residually, from a distance, and not from the immediate surroundings as in *A Choice of Enemies.* Elgin is unabashedly part of a colony set at a great distance from the mother country–to the mutual benefit and relief of each, although the child's strongly ambivalent feelings in regard to its parent are reflected back primarily as benign indifference.

When Lorne Murchison, the intemperate colonial proselyte of imperialist doctrine, visits London, he, like Norman Price half a century later, recognizes the imperilled condition of the homeland:

> "Industrial energy is deserting this country; you have no large movement, no counter-advance, to make against the increasing forces that are driving this way from over there–nothing to oppose to assault. England is in a state of siege, and doesn't seem to know it. She's so great–Hesketh, it's pathetic!–she offers undefended shore to attack, and a stupid confidence, a kindly blindness, above all to Americans, whom she patronizes to the gate."
>
> "I believe we do patronize them," said Hesketh. "It's rotten bad form."[10]

Unlike Norman, Lorne returns to Canada and with his Imperialism that much more resolute for having seen an actual need for it in England, a need that he had only surmised to exist while in Canada. Not all colonial politicians–neither neophytes like Lorne nor the old guard–were of the same mind, however, even in his own political party:

> "The popular idea seems to be," said Mr. Farquharson judicially, "that you would not hesitate to put Canada to some material loss, or at least to postpone her development in various important directions, for the sake of the imperial connection."
>
> "Wasn't that," Lorne asked him, "what, six months ago, you were all prepared to do?"
>
> "Oh, no," said Bingham, with the air of repudiating for everybody concerned. "Not for a cent. We were willing at one time to work it for what it was worth, but it never was worth that, and if you'd had a little more experience, Murchison, you'd have realized it."[11]

Lorne steadfastly honours the cause and, moments later, is asked to renounce his claim to the Liberal nomination in South Fox; which he does. He has directly confronted the ambivalent status to which the community clings for survival. His intransigence forces an awareness of this ambivalence, transforming it into an uncomfortable dichotomy of opposing camps–Imperialist and Annexationist.

As an agent of imperial consciousness, Lorne is nearly, but not quite, rejected by the electorate, following which–through the neat literary expedient of having the election challenged and a by-election called–his own party eases him into a premature political retirement while he is still in his late twenties and, in name at least, a winner. The tenor of life in Elgin depends on the relativist illusion of practical compromise, an illusion which does not bear scrutiny without revealing the profound sense of isolation, of rejection, upon which it is based. It is not Lorne's colonial obeisance that brings him down, but the assumptions upon which his ideology is built that there is not so wide a gap between the colony and its Imperial antecedent that it cannot be closed by preferential economic policies. He does not see that to close the gap would be to move continents. He does not realize that much of what is valued in the British "connection" is the reversal of time. The others are happy merely to impede its progress. They enthusiastically celebrate Victoria's birthday, for instance, with more vigour than in England because she is the past personified. This past the Canadians dearly covet, while simultaneously acquiring American merchandise and American habits as fast as their purses and attenuated sensibilities will allow. Canada, caught between the giant appetites of history and commerce, consumes herself in disaffected compromise, and yet endures with sullen pride.

The Imperialist is not a treatise on economic politics. It is a highly imaginative novel. Sara Jeannette Duncan has deftly balanced a middle-sized Ontario town against the vast reaches of a powerful and indifferent world. She does so by making Elgin come alive, a coherent separate being of many parts. The town's populace, the novel's characters, are its various traits in dynamic interaction. The world around it is the context within which it struggles towards that maturity through which isolation becomes independence. Yet the context is the force of the British and American presence and, as such, it retards maturity and fosters parochial isolation. The conflict between this alien presence and the indigenous characteristics of the community provides the framework for the entire fiction, at every level from amorous fantasy through social realism to political prophecy.

Such an approach invites bathos but, always, Miss Duncan maintains a sense of decorum and of proportion–the more so when her protagonists are bereft of theirs, as is so often the case. She writes in a fine style, tempering her characters' rhetoric with her own wit, balancing their foibles against the insight and keen humour in their presentation. For example, when Dora declares her disconsolate state upon Lorne's departure for England, "She did indeed seem moved, about the mouth, to discontent. There was some little injury in the way she swung her foot."[12] Dora, as the object of Lorne's mindless devotion, receives the author's cruelest blows. His sister Advena, for her pride and independence, receives the most sensitive and sympathetic treatment: when she thinks of the impossibility of consummating her love for Hugh Finlay, for example, she gazes "humbly through tears at her own face in the glass, loving it on his behalf."[13] Even Duncan's cynicism shows a respect for proprietary balance: Dr. Drummond's Christmas Day sermon attacks "the saints' days and ceremonies of the Church of England" while "the special Easter service. . .was apt to be marked by an unsparing denunciation of the pageants and practices of the Church of Rome."[14] Dr. Drummond, of course, is Presbyterian. Similarly, Canadian patronizing of the British–"You haven't been very long in the country, Mr. Hesketh, or we shouldn't hear you saying that"–[15] is followed immediately by British condescension towards things Canadian. Speaking of the coming election, Hesketh announces that "I'll be on hand for the fight. I've had some experience. I used to canvass now and then from Oxford; it was always a tremendous lark."[16] And of course, the speakers of these bits of puffery are more ridiculed by their words than those to whom they speak.

Affairs of the heart provide the narrative superstructure of *The Imperialist.* The plot moves upon the configurations of courtship, while themes are crystallized in the varying expressions of love. Miss Duncan does nothing so ponderous, as is suggested by Claude Bissell in his introduction to the *New Canadian Library* edition, as to arrange heterosexual relationships in her fiction as analogical equivalents of the larger political scene. But then, Bissell can hardly be accused of writing perceptive commentary. His declaration, in regard to Miss Duncan's birth in Brantford, 1861, that "Here, surely, was one reared in provincial bondage–growing up in a small Ontario town and exposed only to the faintly exhilarating winds of the provincial capital,"[17] is contemptuously provincial itself, and bespeaks a damning ignorance about the naive complexity of the small town colonial world that *The Imperialist* reveals with such clarity. Presumably one must also patronize Faulkner for having emerged from Jefferson, Mississippi, circa 1900, or Kipling, from far off India in the abysmally distant 1860's. In any case, Miss Duncan has not written a romantic parable for the explication of a political scheme, but fictional realism. Her deployment of romantic incident and sentiment, and her presentation of politics on the riding level as well as at the level of Empire, reflect common universal traits of human experience from different perspectives. By counterbalancing plot elements of the former with rhetorical explications of the latter–almost every political theory relevant to Elgin, Canada, the Empire, is given its full oratorical due–she has devised an ironic resonance through which these universals are made poignantly specific.

To counteract the potential pomposity or didacticism of her method, the principal relationships contain within their scope an element of self-parody. Advena Murchison and the Reverend Hugh Finlay, both martyrs of forbearance, prove their love to be the higher sort by refusing its requital, in the name of honour. Hugh has previously, by proxy, betrothed himself to Miss Christie Cameron of Scotland, five years his senior. And, as he explains, "I cannot ask her to reconsider her lot because I have found a happier adjustment for mine."[18] Rather than break the bondage of his word, the young lovers maintain their distance, savouring their tragedy even while suffering it. In the light of Miss Cameron's apparent indifference about her prospective marital arrangement, their martyrdom takes on an air of absurdity which even Advena finally laughs at, but does not attempt to alter. Ultimately, the precipitous action of Dr. Drummond in proposing, himself, to the spinster, and being accepted, resolves their dilemma. During the revelation of the elder cleric's saving grace, Finlay delightfully exclaims, "if you have anything to tell me of importance, for God's sake begin at the end," to which Drummond announces his "cutting out" of his young colleague.[19] The travails of honour are thus overcome by the impishly dishonourable action of Dr. Drummond. The propriety of responsible restraint displayed by Hugh and Advena is deflated by impulsive abandon. In spite of new obstacles arising to replace the old–Hugh has now been "jilted"; Advena is now an adventuress–they thenceforth follow the dictates of visceral rather than cerebral convention and marry.

The other consuming passion of a romantic nature in the novel is Lorne's dog-eyed devotion to Dora Milburn. Dora is a fey coquette whom the author clearly finds as distasteful a creation as she finds Lorne appealing. Yet such is the truth of her wit, the honesty of her compassion, that when Lorne loses Dora to Hesketh, after being cruelly led on by her, a sympathetic response is generated rather than the expected sense of relief. The very steadfastness of Lorne's affection blinded him to the abusive treatment he had been receiving: "One feels a certain sorrow for the lover on his homeward way, squaring his shoulders against the foolish perversity of the feminine mind, resolutely guarding his heart from any hint of real reprobation."[20] With appropriate irony, considering the alternative to his unrequited passion, Lorne's disastrous infatuation, which is born of his single-minded strength of character, is blocked by the insidious opportunism of the morally cretinous Hesketh. Dora and Hesketh deservedly win each other's marital company. Lorne, his illusions shattered, is freed of them both and of what they represent to him.

Hesketh is typical of England without the advantage of Empire, ignorant of Imperialist necessity:

> Lorne Murchison had never met anyone of Hesketh's age in Hesketh's condition before. Affluence and age he knew, in honourable retirement; poverty and youth he knew, embarked in the struggle; indolence and youth he also knew, as it cumbered the ground; but youth and a competence, equipped with education, industry, and vigour, searching vainly in fields empty of opportunity, was to him a new spectacle.[21]

Hesketh's presence is not unlike the vision of England with which Lorne returns to Canada–an old nation reduced to youth and rootlessness, so long as she ignores the Imperial role that history and tradition demand she play, yet competent, vigorous, ambitious. More and more, upon his return, Lorne finds her present image contrary to his taste, yet he remains as committed to her economic and political redemption as he is to the gracious forbearance of Hesketh.

Dora, in a more intimate way, objectifies the characteristic quality of Lorne's emotional commitments:

> We know him elsewhere capable of essaying heights, yet we seem to look down upon the drama of his heart. It may be well to remember that the level is not everything in love. He who carefully adjusts an intellectual machine may descry a higher mark; he can construct nothing in a mistress; he is, therefore, able to see the facts and discriminate the desirable. But Lorne loved with all his imagination. This way dares the imitation of the gods,

> by which it improves the quality of the passion, so that such a love stands by itself to be considered, apart from the object, one may say.[22]

This divergence between the emotion and its object accounts as readily for the discrepancy between Lorne's devotion to England and the reality he has witnessed, as to that between his love and his beloved.

Sara Jeannette Duncan fuses the narrative role of her characters with theme and ultimate meaning on all levels of reading. These levels, of course, are not superimposed, one upon the other like a stack of film transparencies through which the reader must peer towards a strong light in order to penetrate the symbolic depths. She is neither a Kafka nor a Woolf. Nor are they arranged as interfacing clusters of significantly associative detail. She is certainly not a James Joyce nor a George Eliot. Rather more in the manner of Henry James, although with broader but less penetrating insight and with language less meticulously deployed but of more engaging warmth and vitality, Miss Duncan's levels of consciousness and of meaning follow one another consecutively. They accumulate to form a whole picture, an inclusive portrait. Like James, like the flickering pinpoint dot of electrons shot upon the screen of a television tube, she paints with small details an entire encapsuled world whose dynamics are not consecutive due to the details themselves, but to what they signify.

Hugh and Advena, and the characters on the periphery of their romance, for example, do not represent anything whatsoever other than individual human beings. Yet they participate in the dynamics of a more inclusive complex world than that of which they are separately conscious. In this respect, Miss Duncan capitalizes on the ironic possibilities implicit to the presence of all fictional characters of functioning simultaneously as created objects and subjective beings. Thus, in the following somewhat self-conscious discourse, much of what Hugh, the newcomer, and Advena, the native-born, say is at odds with what they are and with what they conceive themselves to be. The effect is not intellectual posturing but naive self-revelation conjoined with sophisticated personality analysis:

> "Ah well," he said, as if to himself, "it's something to be in a country where the sun still goes down with a thought of the primeval."

"I think I prefer the sophistication of chimney-pots," she replied. "I've always longed to see a sunset in London, with the fog breaking over Westminster."

"Then you don't care about them for themselves, sunsets?" he asked, with the simplest absence of mind.

" '*I never yet could see the sun go down, but I was angry in my Heart,*' " she said, and this time he looked at her.

"How does it go on?" he said.

"Oh, I don't know. Only those two lines stay with me. I feel it that way, too. It's the seal upon an act of violence, isn't it, a sunset? Something taken from us against our will. It's a hateful reminder, in the midst of our delightful volitions, of how arbitrary every condition of life is."

"The conditions of business are always arbitrary. Life is a business–we have to work at ourselves till it is over. So much cut off and ended it is," he said, glancing at the sky again. "If space is the area of life and time is its opportunity, there goes a measure of opportunity."

"I wonder," said Advena, "where it goes?"

"Into the void behind time?" he suggested, smiling straight at her.

"Into the texture of the future," she answered, smiling back.

"We might bring it to bear very intelligently on the future, at any rate," he returned. "The world is wrapped in destiny and but revolves to roll it out."

"I don't remember that," she said curiously.

"No, you couldn't," he laughed outright. "I haven't thought it good enough to publish."

"And it isn't the sort of thing," she ventured gaily, "you could put in a sermon."

"No, it isn't."[23]

Pretentious, contrived, self-conscious–their conversation is all of these. It is also quite believably the initial conversation of a love that has just begun. During the course of their talk, almost every level, every aspect, of the narrative is touched upon, overtly or by implication–never disguised as something else but spoken of directly. Yet there is a subtle emotionality present. The speakers are more aware of each other, by far, than of the motivational or moral import of what they say.

Formal and thematic elements in *The Imperialist* are fully integrated. Polemics are made, always, to serve the purpose of art. The author's own persuasions, if they are present at all, are present subliminally, in a certain preference shown towards some of her characters, particularly to Lorne in spite of the *hubris* she assigns to him. They are present in the edge of vitality given to some arguments over others; in the underlying assumption of the British "moral advantage." Her characters are not Rassalasian abstractions nor functional representative beings, but flesh-and-blood creations whose various principles are the currency of their separate personalities, some founded on solid reserves, and others, only paper tokens. They are inseparable from the foreground presence of society–*church, family, community*–which is drawn with meticulously detailed affection.

The Presbyterian Church in Elgin has an important social function in relation to which theology provides authority but little direction. It assures the community of a continuity of social values and structures which the transigent nature of their colonial status does not offer. A community so far removed from the mainstream of world affairs and in a state of continual growth, progress, flux, appears to its populace by its very viability to be unstable and remote, a place of exile. The dour, benign personality of the church and its ministers is the ubiquitous, the pervasive, antidote–conceived, by the author, like Imperialism, as an aspect of constructive colonialism. As such, its function is the diametric opposite to that of American protestantism, which is to refine the individual conscience and foster independent action.

In the island-oasis of Elgin, kinship plays the same role that Friday did in relation to Crusoe, that his Swiss family did to Mr. Robinson. Family provides an intimate context within which individuals may be scrutinized without their psyches being violated in a pre-psychoanalytic, pre-Proustian era. Lorne's sisters offer bits of information about his character quite gratuitously. Mrs. Murchison can, and does, continually comment upon Advena's curious affair with Hugh Finlay without being subject to the demands of narrative necessity. In both cases, they are allowed this freedom because they are family, and that itself is justification enough for the revelations they utter. Because of their unforced and unexamined intimacy, they reveal much of one another while maintaining the distances by which they are separated from the reality of outsiders. The spaces of this distancing transform

Lorne, as he traverses them, into Dora's fool-lover, yet also refine his strength of character in public affairs. It is these spaces which must be crossed by Advena, and by Hugh Finlay in the opposite direction in order to understand fully her offering of herself to him. Other families in the novel, apart from the Murchisons, have less overt dramatic functions. For the most part, they are indeterminate groupings of people clustered around various surnames, one of whose number stands out for his narrative role. Secondary relationships like those of Squire Ormiston of Moneida and his son Walter, or Mrs. Crow and her son Elmore, display familial obligation or affection, yet they too form unique nuclei essential to the nature of the communal molecule. Only the Milburns play a family role at all comparable to the Murchisons: they function primarily as the latter's mirror-opposite while being also an indispensable and, in a *whole* community, inevitable complement.

The community is more than these families together, more than their businesses, their births, marriages, and deaths. It is the tensions that bind them in place, the forces that fix their position in relation to the far world outside. The community is also the customs, the affectations, and the manners that are the response of Elgin's present to the past; and the politics, the social plans and social structures that are determined by Elgin's collective anxieties and aspirations in regard to the future. Within this living community, itself an ambivalent molecular organism displaying both the traits of parasitic exile and vigorous colonial independence, the individual characters live separate but related and fully integrated lives. They neither exist to serve the community, nor is it their servant. They are in total harmony with it because it is, in Miss Duncan's vision, what they ultimately are–the different aspects of a corporate self. This shared identity of people with place is a particularly Canadian conception of being, quite alien both to old world humanism and American commercial necessity. In Robertson Davies' Salterton, the only populace existent are those referred to directly by the text. In Elgin, people exist beyond the confines of the novel's boundaries; people unnamed, unspoken of, live their lives in Elgin and we never know them, but we know, implicitly, that they are there.

Apart from the prescience of her insight into the Canadian experience, Sara Jeannette Duncan has achieved a particularly complete and balanced picture of society as a dynamic entity of individual and collective responses that have been transferred through time and transported across vast spaces. The *Imperialist* is a work of art that depends not one bit for its universal truth on being accurate, in this respect, but certainly is not less valid for being so. And certainly, this authenticity provides a sustaining vitality that her novel would otherwise not have.

Lorne Murchison is the primary centre of consciousness in the novel. He does not, in a Jamesian way, occupy or represent the forefront of its social vision. To think so is a simplistic fallacy, comparable to accepting Gulliver's assessment of the Houyhnhnms in Book IV of *Gulliver's Travels* as paragons of behaviour, and miss the point of their spiritual impoverishment, and of Gulliver's, who is taken in by them. Rather, it is Lorne in relation to his community who gives the vision a voice. Through him, the Canadian experience of his time is rhetorically and dramatically dissected, but it is left to the passing statements of other characters, to the incidents of other lives, to define its parts. It is left to the centripetal tensions within the whole work to achieve their synthesis into a coherent art equivalent. Lorne's impassioned and often intemperate socio-political declarations are often ironically ambivalent. Those of others are not, not ever. Thus, inevitably, due to this very lack in a clearly ambivalent world, they are collectively a statement of its ambivalence. Lorne's character, however, cannot be separated from the collective being of the people of Elgin, even though he stands somewhat apart from the others, by personal limitations and inclination, and performs a quite different narrative function.

In response to Lorne's single-minded allegiance to the conflicting principles of the Imperial cause, "People looked at him as if he had developed something they did not understand, and perhaps he had; he was in touch with the idea."[24] For his part, as his father explains, he takes for granted "other folks being like himself.[25] He understands them no better than they do him. Yet together they have a common identity, seen from different perspectives, answering different narrative and didactic needs.

As a case in point, Hugh Finlay and Advena, in one of their most animated conversational trysts, offer the two sides of a double image of Canada. Finlay acclaims the country's "space–elbow room," to which Advena counters, "An empty horizon." She responds to his arguments of opportunity and plenitude with the plaintive cry of colonial despair: "I am to be consoled because apples are cheap?"[26] Advena is a Canadian, born in exile. Hugh is Scots, a newcomer to the colonial vista. Their vision is one of conflicting truths, for they are both honest to their own observations. But Lorne, with no less integrity, is himself doomed to witness both sides of the Canadian experience simultaneously. His response, accordingly, is not a measured set of arguments but grandiloquence which raises him above paradox on a flight of patriotic rhetoric. Inconsistencies resolved by jingo speechifying, of course, have a tendency, like the phoenix, to revive–no matter how well-intentioned or nobly motivated was their utterance–and inevitably, Lorne's world collapses around him.

His great love for England derives, ultimately, from his affection for his native land, his desire to have Canada gain the maximum long-range benefits of its British birthright. As he passionately declaims to Dora:

> We're all right out here, but we're young and thin and weedy. They didn't grow so fast in England, to begin with, and now they're rich with character and strong with conduct and hoary with ideals. I've been reading up the history of our political relations with England. It's astonishing what we've stuck to her through, but you can't help seeing why–it's for the moral advantage.[27]

His intelligence the victim, once again, of his imagination, he concludes: "They've developed the finest human product there is, the cleanest, the most disinterested, and we want to keep up the relationship–it's important."[28] Lorne assures Dora's mother that his pilgrimage to England, as secretary to the head of the deputation from the United Chambers of Commerce of Canada attending the British Government in order to shore up the Empire, will only reinforce his fond attachment for Elgin, Ontario.

His actual experience of the Englishman's London is uncannily similar to that of Richler's Norman Price–that which Norman eventually became conscious of, of dissociation and distaste:

> He did his work unobtrusively as he did it admirably well; and for the rest he was just washed about, carried, hither and thither, generally on the tops of omnibuses, receptive, absorbent, mostly

> silent. He did try once or twice to talk to the bus drivers–he had been told it was the thing to do if you wanted to get hold of the point of view of a particular class; but the thick London idiom defeated him, and he found they grew surly when he asked them too often to repeat their replies. He felt a little surly himself after a while, when they asked him, as they nearly always did, if he wasn't an American.[29]

Perhaps to compensate, he assigns what he conceives to be England's imperilled state to her Imperial disinterest, and becomes all the more intemperately committed to the Cause. His ideology becomes grotesque. When he expounds upon his ideas to Hesketh, the Englishman on his home-ground, his rhetoric verges on the fanatical: "I see England down the future the heart of the Empire, the conscience of the world, and the Mecca of the race."[30] Even allowing for the high status of patriotism at the time, Lorne's is excessive. By the time of his final address to the electorate of South Fox in the Elgin Opera House, he is so thoroughly possessed that he ignores the penultimate tenet of Liberal politics in Canada, to place ideals always at the service of power and to campaign accordingly. The impropriety of his speech is graphically anticipated by the "conspicuous stupidity" of Hesketh's, a few days earlier, to a rural audience in the Jordanville schoolhouse. Lorne, vastly the superior man, speaking to a more sophisticated audience, commits no less a blunder–and of a far more wide-reaching consequence. He demands that the electors of South Fox participate in history. He delivers a lengthy oration, from which the author appears deftly to skim the highlights, creating an appropriately lugubrious staccato of emotionality. His one clear message to his audience is that their votes count in the world beyond Elgin, in the future of nations, in the destiny of empires. Such a reality, of course, is one their collective temperament, conditioned as it is by their colonial heritage, will not allow them to bear. Being Canadian, they are polite, they applaud, they even give Lorne a faint plurality, but ultimately they reject him. As in the past, they find opinion more comfortable to live with than ideology, the passivity of conviction less threatening than actual commitment.

Few in Lorne's audience would have been disturbed by his racist proclamations, distasteful as they are to another age. But the outright comparison of Canada to the United States presumes too much upon both their forbearance of immodesty and their hubristic sense of benign superiority. His statement that " 'The Americans from the beginning went in a spirit of revolt; the seed of disaffection was in every Puritan bosom. We from the beginning went in a spirit of amity, forgetting nothing, disavowing nothing, to plant the flag with our fortunes.' "[31] insists that the two neighbouring countries exist on the same level of reality, a possibility quite offensive to the good taste of a determinedly colonial people. By forcing the residual loyalty of Canadians to the Empire into a rhetorical fusion with their latent anxiety about the United States, Lorne's avowedly nationalist argument takes on a quality of hysteria. Thereby, the truths within it are more readily dismissed with the speaker. His familiar warning of an American economic take-over is applauded for its obvious validity, but not as a basis for political action. Lorne's rhetoric spans decades, as he demands that Canadians:

> keenly watch and actively resist American influence, as it already threatens us through the common channels of life and energy. We often say that we fear no invasion from the south, but the armies of the south have already crossed the border. American enterprise, American capital, is taking rapid possession of our mines and our water power, our oil areas and our timber limits.[32]

His argument is relevant even to the present day, but it does not last as an influence upon his audience in the Elgin opera house the scant few hours until polling day.

In Elgin, the United Empire Loyalists are forgiven the misfortune of their alien origins by virtue of having renewed their British connection through the generations of their residency in Canada. Such is the importance of the British connection. Yet its importance depends upon spatial distance as much as on emotional proximity. For instance, Octavius Milburn, born in Canada, "preferred a fair living under his own flag to a fortune under the Stars and Stripes"[33] and felt himself the obvious victor in the comparisons he was prone to making "between the status and privileges of a subject and a citizen."[34] But what he enjoyed in being British came of his "life in a practical, go-ahead, self-governing colony, far enough from England actually to be disabused of her inherited anachronisms,. . .near enough politically to keep. . .securities up by virtue of her protection."[35]

The relationship between Canada and the Empire, in so far as it bears upon life in Miss Duncan's world of Elgin, Ontario, is sensitively suggested by one description in particular of John Murchison and Dr. Drummond:

> So the two of them came, contemporaries, to add their labour and their lives to the building of this little outpost of Empire. It was the frankest transfer, without thought of return; they were there to spend and be spent within the circumference of the spot they had chosen, with no ambition beyond. In the course of nature, even their bones and their memories would enter into the fabric. The new country filled their eyes; the new town was their opportunity, its destiny their fate. They were altogether occupied with its affairs, and the affairs of the growing Dominion, yet obscure in the heart of each of them ran the undercurrent of the old allegiance. They had gone the length of their tether, but the tether was always there.[36]

In the elder Murchison and Dr. Drummond, the link with the Old World is an actual one, born out of their personal histories. In the next generation it is an imaginary link, a perpetual leap across the abyss of time and of space in an attempt to compensate for the felt inadequacies of colonial exile, whereby apples are cheap at the the expense of an alien birth.

Notes

1. Mordecai Richler, *A Choice of Enemies* (London: André Deutsch, 1957), pp.10-11.
2. Robertson Davies, *A Mixture of Frailities* (New York: Scribner's, 1958), pp.37-38.
3. *Ibid.*, p.133.
4. *Ibid.*, p.272.
5. *Ibid.*, p.36.
6. Malcolm Ross, ed., *Our Sense of Identity* (Toronto: Ryerson, 1954), p.28.
7. Richler, *A Choice of Enemies, op.cit.,* p.156.
8. *Ibid.*, pp.157-58.
9. *Ibid.*, p.158.
10. Sara Jeannette Duncan, *The Imperialist* (Toronto: New Canadian Library, 1961), p.124. (Toronto: Copp Clark, 1904.)

11. *Ibid.*, p.262.
12. *Ibid.*, p.98.
13. *Ibid.*, p.108.
14. *Ibid.*, p.197.
15. *Ibid.*, p.173.
16. *Ibid.*, p.174.
17. *Ibid.*, p.v.
18. *Ibid.*, p.161.
19. *Ibid.*, p.252.
20. *Ibid.*, p.146.
21. *Ibid.*, p.119.
22. *Ibid.*, p.147.
23. *Ibid.*, pp: 70-71.
24. *Ibid.*, p.226.
25. *Ibid.*, p.150.
26. *Ibid.*, p.110.
27. *Ibid.*, p.98.
28. *Ibid.*, p.98.
29. *Ibid.*, p.118.
30. *Ibid.*, p.124.
31. *Ibid.*, p.233.
32. *Ibid.*, p.232.
33. *Ibid.*, p.51.
34. *Ibid.*, p.51.
35. *Ibid.*, p.51.
36. *Ibid.*, p.22.

4.
Immigrant Exile

Canada, unlike its American neighbour, has not been founded by revolution upon ideological principles codified in a Constitution. Canada is not an idea, a dream brought to fruition and vulnerable to the dreamers' awakening to its nightmare potential. Canada is a name to which adheres a complex mosaic of histories and geographies. It is a place, a landscape. Dreams and ideas have always been in the order of what to do with it. Being such a vast space, it has always demanded expansive schemes to make it seem less so. National railroads have packaged it with steel ribbons, national police have kept it orderly, national broadcasting has given it what it sometimes believes is its own voice, its own vision. Immigrants have peopled it.

Unlike immigrants to the United States, which exists by virtue of an historical caesura, newcomers to Canada are neither absolved nor relieved of their participation in the world they left behind. Nor were they originally motivated to leave, as D. H. Lawrence says of the Americans, by revulsion, but rather by the force of circumstance, hunger being the most common. They have come with their memories and they have tried to reconstruct the past, an alien past, as it should have been rather than as it was, and often they have done so without regard for the Canadian place where they have relocated. Thus, an expansive land-scheme has become a cultural conundrum, an ethnic agglomerate strewn across a continent.

Canada's appetite for immigrants is described by Laura Goodman Salverson in her 1923 paean to Icelandic settlers of the West, *The Viking Heart*:

> Canada was in need of immigration. She needed immigrants, as all new countries need them, to rid her lands of timber and destructive beasts, to break her virgin soil and prepare it for

> useful crops. She needed them also to build roads and bridges, to bind her towns more closely together, and to dig ditches and lay sewers that her cities might be habitable. She was in need of them–and appropriated them–to make possible the progress of civilization and to lay the foundation for her coming greatness. Her call went out into the highways and the byways. . . .[1]

Amongst those who answered the call were the fourteen hundred Icelanders who arrived at Fishers Landing, Manitoba, in October 1876, "a bedraggled and sorry company."[2] Miss Salverson focuses on one of them, the girl, Borga. In the archetypal pattern of immigrant fiction in this country, it is only after bitter tragedy that a reconciliation of protagonist with nation takes place. Borga and her husband, Bjørn Lindal, have a son, Thor, who is born and grows to manhood in Canada, and dies at Passchendaele in his country's service. To the Icelandic community, his death "meant not only the loss of a promising countryman, it meant that there was lost to them one other opportunity to prove the merit of Iceland's sons wherever they may be."[3] Assimilation is resisted, even in the meaning to be drawn from a tragic death. Yet the ethnic pride which refuses to consign Thor's sacrifice to the general domain is the same that provides the strength by which his parents endure, and eventually accept the conditions of their life in Canada. Grandiloquently, Miss Salverson describes at the novel's close the result of immigrant courage such as theirs, "to turn one's hand to the plow though the heart be broken":

> For in such strength alone do nations live, have their beginnings and everlasting power. Out of the hearts of men, out of their joys and tears, their toil and tribulation, springs that elusive and holy thing, the Soul of a Nation.
>
> Out of the sore travailing of men and out of their quiet death, spring hope and faith, and that great love which, transcending the grave, revitalizes life and makes a nation indestructible.[4]

The very violence of the penultimate confrontation between immigrant and nation fuses their identities. Violence provides a cathartic relief from the burdens of the past, by which the conditions of exile have been enforced–and endured. Thor's death roots Borga's emotions, finally, in the soil of her son's birthplace. A more sophisticated variation of the same transition is in Abraham's macabre execution of Laiah, in Adele Wiseman's *The Sacrifice,* when he is phantasmally merged in the gushing blood with his dead sons.[5] Abraham's perverse sacrifice is the means by which his grandson, Moses, is ultimately freed upon the promised land. In *Home is the Stranger,* Edward McCourt's novel of Prairie exile, Norah Armstrong, the English war-bride, similarly learns that home is an attitude one holds towards oneself. But her isolation is ended only through adultery, great bitterness, and the death of her son.

In each of these cases, violence has also preceded departure from the old country. Norah lost her father and aunt in an air raid. Her ties are thus effectively obliterated, although not their residual effect. Abraham and Sarah left the Ukraine with their youngest son, Isaac, in the wake of persecutions in which their other sons, Jacob and Moses, were murdered in the town square. In turning from the Old World, Abraham declares that finally they must "stop running from death and from every other insult."[6] The loss of a son marks Einar and Gudrun Halsson's decision to take Borga and leave Iceland for Canada. Fleeing from the murderous volcano, Einar takes to their small boat: "Behind him was a belching furnace, ruined hopes, and death. Ahead lay the open sea and life. What more–he knew not."[7] The pattern is consistent: with an ambivalence that characterizes their immigrant experience, the English girl, the Jewish couple and their son, the Icelandic family, all exchange the blood of their kin for their passage to a new world. The war, the pogroms, the famine and volcano–these are the circumstances of their various departures. But it is much more than that which they leave behind, it is their birthright heritage. They pay their debts to the past in tokens of their blood that bind them more resolutely to it. Ultimately, by violence the violence of their leaving is redeemed, and the past is finally cast adrift in time.

Brian Moore's *The Luck of Ginger Coffey* is a tragi-comic parody of the pattern. Ginger and his family are transported to Canada on the inheritance received from his father's death–itself an inconsequential event in Ginger's life. As might be expected, he loses Vera and Paulie, his wife and daughter, through estrangement. They are his sacrifice to the Canadian experience. But this is not a tragic novel. The act of violence through which actions and emotions are reversed is as poetically conceived as the six-months' suspended sentence Ginger receives for its perpetration: in a darkened office doorway on a deserted Montreal street, late in a winter night, he is caught amongst the shadows, urinating. One of the more exotic consequences of his crime is the discovery that "Love isn't an act, it's a whole life."[8] With that, in part, as consolation, Ginger is finally reconciled with his wife, and with Canada which, consistent with the pattern, means with himself, as well. Moore leaves his Irish-Canadian in Montreal, resignedly content. Sounding like a Celtic Salverson, he explains of Ginger that

> He had tried: he had not won. But oh! what did it matter? He would die in humble circs: it did not matter. There would be no victory for Ginger Coffey, no victory big or little, for there, on the courthouse steps, he had learned the truth. Life was the victory, wasn't it? Going on was the victory. For better for worse, for richer for poorer, in sickness and in health. . .till. . .
>
> He heard her stop outside. He went to join her.[9]

The immigrant as exile in an alien land is one of the most pervasive themes of Canadian prose fiction. The past was not to be shuffled off, here, like a used overcoat as in the United States. More like pigmentation of the skin, it took, and takes, generations to be neutralized to the common tint. Thus, a novel like Rudy Wiebe's *Peace Shall Destroy Many,* about a Saskatchewan Mennonite community struggling to maintain a separate consciousness from the world, defying the levelling effect of time and assimilation and the chaotic events surrounding it, is more typical of Canadian experience than might at first be realized. Only by maintaining the conditions of exile in their collective life can Wiebe's Mennonites endure the present-tense Canadian Prairies duringWorld War II. Theirs is a diaspora of choice, for they, unlike the Jews, are a nation that has never had a native land of their own to be driven from. The Jew in Canadian fiction is similarly a perennial exile for whom assimilation is tantamount to annihilation, and who thus remains an immigrant in an alien land, struggling through generations of change to maintain some semblance of the past in his present life. Mordecai Richler's Montreal is such a Jewish world as this, and Adele Wiseman, in *The Sacrifice,* relentlessly exposes the Jewry of Winnipeg to the same end. The exile of a nation within a nation provides a clear impression emblematic of the more diffused experience of other immigrants. But the isolation imposed by the confrontation between established and alien orders is not limited to any particular ethnic or religious segment.

The anxieties generated by this confrontation are magnified by its characteristic ambiguity. The problem of which order is the established and which the alien–Canadian or immigrant–is ultimately open to question. In *The Sacrifice,* for instance, Adele Wiseman effectively fluctuates the focus of her vision, in this respect; arousing sympathy one minute and empathy the next. In the end, the tragedy of Abraham's crime makes the problem of opposing orders irrelevant to the point where it ceases to exist.

Broadly speaking, Canadian literature of national exile may be separated into that of the English-speaking and that of the European immigrant. In the Anglophone group, the confrontation explored is primarily one of sensibility. Language, laws, culture, religion, values, customs, manners are similar to, derivatives of, those the immigrant has left behind. Their Canadian adaptation tends to appear as barbarous distortion, parody, ignorance, or contempt. His exile is further aggravated by the apparent indifference of the resident populace to the degeneration of values and desecration of ideals, as he sees them. He is continually torn by the conflict between appearance, with its intimations of the world he has left behind, and reality, which rejects that world as impractical or irrelevant. Rejection occurs even while the Canadians continue to venerate the symbols of Old World impracticality, its functional irrelevance –the Monarchy and other ceremonial British traditions, the Constitution and other facile American documents. The Anglophone exile is anticipated by Susanna Moodie in *Roughing It in the Bush.* He is exploited in the portrait of Ginger Coffey by Brian Moore. He is, perhaps, best typified by the ubiquitous remittance man.

Mrs. Moodie's *Roughing It in the Bush* has recently found acceptance as a novel, and with good reason. In spite of its non-fictional subject matter, it bears all the formal characteristics of a work of the imagination–certainly as much so as other non-fiction novels such as Truman Capote's *In Cold Blood* and Brian Moore's *The Revolution Script.* It tells the author's story as an English immigrant to Upper Canada in the 1830's. The format combines the intimacy of a commonplace book with the continuity and retrospective insight of a first-person narrative account. The result of this creative fusion places the stamp of art on a type of prose reporting quite proliferate in the last century. Books had been written, some of them exceedingly well and many with more imagination than sincerity, advising settlers or warning them away, extolling or explaining or exploiting the Canadian experience awaiting the British immigrant. But *Roughing It in the Bush* rises above the handbook-bias implicit in its type, as do few of the others. It is relevant, today, not as a pleasing artifact like Anna Brownell Jameson's *Winter Studies and Summer Rambles in Canada,* 1838, nor as an enchanting trove of pioneer lore, like Catherine Parr Traill's *The Backwoods of Canada,* 1836. Unlike the revelations by her sister, Mrs. Traill, of the pioneer sensibility, Mrs. Moodie explores the conflict not only between memory and experience but between appearance and reality. Because her work follows the dictates of the imagination and not of a preconceived verisimilitude, she is able to manipulate the world that is of her creation into an authentic and thereby universal possibility. Thus, for instance, her British consciousness of class, precipitously decried by Ronald Sutherland in *Second Image* as racist,[10] is a characteristic of the created being who has her author's name and, more important, is essential to the thematic and narrative structure of her novel. In this context, whether the author herself is a racist or merely a disoriented immigrant with a predisposition to snobbery, is utterly irrelevant.

Mrs. Moodie's so-called racism is a thoroughly integrated part of her fiction. Describing the "vulgar pretentions" of the working-class of Canada in not showing servile deference to their betters, the narrator explains with an ironic lack of detachment:

> But from this folly the native-born Canadian is exempt; it is only practised by the low-born Yankee, or the Yankeefied British peasantry and mechanics. It originates in the enormous reaction springing out of a sudden emancipation from a state of utter dependance into one of unrestrained liberty. As such, I not only excuse, but forgive it, for the principle is founded in nature; and, however disgusting and distasteful to those accustomed to different treatment from their inferiors, it is better than a hollow profession of duty and attachment urged upon us by a false and unnatural position. Still, it is very irksome until you think more deeply upon it; and then it serves to answer rather than to irritate.[11]

Clearly, in this passage, the author is aware of the ironies of her narrator's condescension towards what she maintains are natural principles. She plays upon these ironies in having her Mrs. Moodie-character struggle to appear correct through the affectation of bemused indifference. The controlling consciousness is the author's, who is at a considerably greater distance from her novel's action than she is from her leading character.

By exploiting the tensions between present experience and the impositions of the past upon present perceptions, Mrs. Moodie manipulates the action of her novel in order ultimately to achieve the peculiarly British victory of benign resignation that is her novel's most delightful attribute. Even the flamboyantly sincere closing paragraph which is flung out at the reader is by its very sincerity reduced to an ironic gesture, as it is elevated by the narrative that has preceded it into a defiant farewell salute to the homeland that has become alien, that she has finally and irrevocably left behind. A subtle reversal has occurred. Her warning, with its implicit pride in her ability to endure–only here do narrator and author finally merge–patronizes that class of English gentlefolk to which she has belonged:

> If these sketches should prove the means of deterring one family from sinking their property, and shipwrecking all their hopes, by going to reside in the backwoods of Canada, I shall consider myself amply repaid for revealing the secrets of the prison-house, and feel that I have not toiled and suffered in the wilderness in vain.[12]

It is as if, perhaps, Susanna Moodie has cast back through her own experience in Canada and drawn a created surrogate of herself forward to the present, fusing memories with aesthetic consciousness to create a reality which is both a novel and the means of her conciliation with herself and with her exiled state.

This is not to say that assimilation has taken place. English-speaking immigrants did not commit themselves to the melting pot any more readily than did their European counterparts. Witness the continuing existence of the Imperial Order of the Daughters of the Empire. Or the fact that the subjects of John Kenneth Galbraith's *The Scotch* dwelt in southwestern Ontario communities within seeing-distance of exclusively Irish towns such as Lucan where the Black Donnellys, described by Orlo Miller and by at least one other writer, maintained their terrible domain. My own grandmother, Isabel Cameron, remembered as a girl in the Scotch community of Granton in the 1870's, seeing barns burning on the horizon under the Donnelly torch with an appalling regularity. Just how appalling could be perceived in the Presbyterian glint to her eye as she described these rites of the neighbouring Irish. Her sister Jess left Granton to work in a Lucan store, in a different world just over the horizon. It was as if she had traversed the Irish Sea rather than crossed over a few concessions along the Biddulph line on a farmer's wagon.

The Englishman who was most truly in exile in this country was the remittance man, particularly in the Canadian West. Primarily a phenomenon of the later Victorian era when the Prairies were being opened for settlement, the remittance man from England was as familiar a part of the Canadian scene in years past as his American equivalent is at the present time. Many English families were able to send their prodigals off to the colonies on stipends sufficiently enticing or meagre to assure their continued absence. The Prairies were an ideal host for such maladaptives. Whereas the American West was opened "by" settlers, the preposition "for" is more appropriate to Canada, as commerce, law, and transportation–the Hudson's Bay Company, Royal Canadian Mounted Police and Canadian Pacific Railway–preceded the influx of population. Thus the remittance man was sufficiently encouraged to resist assimilation, sufficiently coddled by an institutionalized frontier to avoid incentives for survival. Though much of the stereotype in our literature is apocryphal, the remittance man is portrayed with certain consistent characteristics that perhaps arise from the relatively ephemeral possibilities of his historical role. Inconsequential in himself, he nevertheless represents the clash between British heritage and American dream that has typified the consciousness of the Canadian West to the present day. He is, therefore, effete, a snob, dangerously charming with women and disliked, generally, by men, indolent, a wastrel, wanton. Or, he is cultivated, charming, a thinker, a man of independent spirit, a lover of living more than of life. The ultimate point of the remittance man, of course, is that his literary presence satisfies the requirements of all these epithets, on both sides of the scale, with emphasis according to narrative necessity. Alfred Hesketh in *The Imperialist* is a relatively rare Ontario version of the breed who, nevertheless, satisfies its ambivalent requirements. He is both insufferable as a friend and a charming cad. In the Prairie trilogy by Arthur Stringer, however, and in the pot-boilers of Robert Stead, the remittance man comes into his own as the villain, hero, or fool, but always the outsider, even amongst an immigrant populace. Perhaps he is most disarming as Reginald Brown, in William Henry Pope Jarvis's 1907 epistolary curiosity called *A Remittance Man's Letters to His Mother.*

Young Brown is nothing short of a fool with both money and friends, losing the former to the latter with dismaying abandon. This is the price he is made to pay for his overbearing British attitudes; this, and being sprayed by skunks after catching one of them by the tail on the suggestion of his Canadian friends, and being reduced to destitution, drunkenness, and Salvation Army dinners. He is the deserving and impervious butt of cruel jokes, insufferable and abused and yet oddly sensitive to the sociology of his experience. He is resilient and happily naive. When two of his fellow farm-hands torment him, he responds with a characteristic air:

> Today, as I was working about the yard, one of the fellows who were employed near me said: 'Ho, Sam, did you ever hear a remittance man's description of farming in Manitoba?'
>
> 'No,' replied Sam.
>
> 'It is this: " 'Tis nice upon the wintah's morning to get up and look out upon the open prairies, and see the little buttahflies making buttah and the grawshoppahs making graws.' "
>
> This was said so that I could overhear it–it was intended I should overhear it. How ridiculous! Butterflies don't make butter, nor do grasshoppers make grass.[13]

Reginald's unintentionally ingenious deflation of his tormentors' joke marks him as a rather likeable fool but, simultaneously, as the tool of a more subtle irony on the part of the author. Jarvis manipulates his remittance man towards an eventual marriage with Lieutenant Jones of the Salvation Army and redemption as "a successful land speculator, or what you will."[14] But his good fortune comes only after a tragi-comedy of errors which culminates in his finally giving up that last vestige of his former English attitudes, his riding-breeches, or "bellows pants" as the Canadians derisively call them. Reginald is not a fool redeemed by a change of trousers, however, but an Englishman transformed from foreign exile to landed immigrant by a conscious act of obeisance to the sensibilities of his adopted home.

On a more anguished level of reality is the sophisticated conception of the remittance man by Edward McCourt in *Music at the Close.* There are, in fact, two of them in this novel, both representative of

Neil Fraser's lack of engagement, his lack of commitment, continuously at odds with his aggressive sensitivity and his loneliness. At the age of twelve, in 1918, Neil is orphaned and brought to live with his Uncle Matt and Aunt Em on their Prairie farm. He makes best friends with school-mate Gil Reardon, but his idol is Charlie Steele, the remittance man whose affair with Gil's sister ends in murder and suicide. Charlie reads, thinks, feels. He is different and therefore alone. Neil identifies with him. Yet in contrast to Charlie's passionate love affair, for instance, Neil nurtures his own love for Moira Glenn through years of passive bitterness. In contrast to Charlie's self-willed determination, Neil is easily dissuaded from his purpose, whether to succeed at University, which he quits, or with his uncle's farm, which he inherits and quickly brings to ruin. When Neil eventually does marry Moira, after Gil, her first husband, significantly dies for a cause in the vanguard of organized labour, he is again effectively paired with a remittance man, George Meeker. This time the affair is between the Englishman and Neil's own wife, and it is sordid and mean; not romantic. Meeker, named as appropriately as was Steele, is dull, insensitive, and, like Steele, an outsider. Neil identifies with him as well and, while his marriage endures, he is a broken man. At his approaching death on the Normandy beach, he experiences only relief at knowing that the world will not be diminished by his absence. He is a remittance man of the mind, a pathetic parody of the real thing, who finally comes to terms with his exile within himself and, accepting the consequence, dies, free.

Literature of immigration tends naturally to follow in the wake of history, like that of the frontier, rather than to participate in it, like literature of the garrison and colony. The visions of novels like *The History of Emily Montague* and *The Imperialist* are formulated in socio-political, psychological, and moral patterns of possibility. They draw from the garrison and the colonial experience and project the implications of that experience into an aesthetic world that is contained by the limitations of the author's imagination and not by the past. Mrs. Brooke knew intuitively that the garrison was a matter of perspective rather than of ramparts. Much of her novel's characteristic irony is sustained by the way she has capitalized on the ambiguous possibilities of her characters' fickle but graphic observations about what they think they are seeing. Authenticity becomes only a highlight of a vision which, in its own restrictive way, is socially and morally prophetic. Sara Duncan's sophisticated insight into Elgin and the Empire–while tempered by a sometimes ponderous manipulation of her characters' behaviour–is adroitly synthesized into a fictional reality whose potential is clearly defined, whose future is, in effect, known and inevitable. Yet, in a very real sense, nothing whatsoever is resolved in *The Imperialist.* Lorne returns from his flight to the United States because his ideals have been demolished and he is thereby able to participate in the liberal establishment through which the future is to be manipulated. In the world of Miss Duncan's creation, alternatives for the future do not really exist. Her colonial sensibility at work, she fully defines the past, contains the present, and reduces the future to options whose differences are indiscernible, inconsequential, and irrelevant. Far from being prophetic, her vision suggests the precognitive experience of a patriotic clairvoyant determinist. A novel like *Wacousta,* on the other hand, leaves the future to its own devices and attempts to manipulate the past. Frontier fiction, like that of the immigrant, is inevitably concerned with the interactions of established and alien orders, one of which is actually present and the other, present in memory or conditioned response, whether enshrined by religious law, as in *The Sacrifice,* or by socio-historical traditions, as in Richardson's novel. Everything in *Wacousta* either happened, or might have happened. Characters and events are arranged, presented, in such a way as to make the past a tableau, to give it form and meaning whether as historical romance, as in this case, or as, for instance, an existential confrontation like that of *But We Are Exiles. The Sacrifice* is a much more intense and anguished work than *Wacousta,* a work which, rather than structuring history, consumes it in an aesthetic inferno. The historical persecution of the Jews literally becomes Abraham's memory of his murdered sons; the diaspora is embodied in Abraham's knowledge of the seemingly perpetual exile he endures in the Winnipeg ghetto; the physical and psychic horror of the murder of Laiah becomes the violence of the Jew's relations with his God; the reality of Zion is found in Abraham's madness transcended in the mountain asylum by Moses' vision of a joyous continuity. While the future, in Moses, holds promise, it is no more clearly defined here than in the Pentateuch. What Miss Wiseman has done is to define the past as it is residually, ambivalently, ever present in the forefront of her novel's created world.

Novels such as *The Sacrifice* and *Wacousta,* novels of national or frontier exile, have an historical immediacy that those of garrison and colonial exile lack. They achieve an aesthetic consolidation of impressions rather than diffusing them through detailed passages which are either not fully integrated or only of peripheral significance. While *The History of Emily Montague* is laden with observations of the landscape and of society, these exemplify the various themes, or reinforce or substantiate them, but they do not represent their equivalents, they do not articulate the themes in a type of sign language. *The Imperialist* appears to be even more consciously a construction of interlocking details which articulate the themes without being them. But, in the case of *Wacousta,* themes are inseparable from the touchstones of authenticity out of which its plot, with the violence to actual events that characterizes the historical romance, has been structured. *The Sacrifice* is an arrangement of themes which are manifest in the novel's entire contained reality, likewise inseparable from character or event or the perception of either. Perhaps it is for this identity of internal reality with the external world that *Wacousta* and *The Sacrifice,* at least superficially so dissimilar, seem to have an obvious universality that the novels by Brooke and Duncan only imply. The former are both rooted in historical experience and exploit its literary possibilities, rather than glean from it only those factors, however numerous, however perceptive, which help to define its limits and prescribe its future.

Wacousta and *But We Are Exiles* are both frontier novels set on the line dividing order from chaos, physically as well as metaphorically. However, *The History of Emily Montague* and *Self Condemned* describe garrisons that are primarily of the mind, and *A Mixture of Frailties,* like *The Imperialist,* is a response to a colonial attitude rather than the actual conditions of colonial life. *The Sacrifice* and other novels of immigrant experience, however, relate literally to the confrontation of opposing orders of reality which characterizes exile in the nation-state.

As emphasis on immigration moved westward in actuality, immigrant fiction followed suit. As the British influx was largely supplanted by the continental European, the nature of the confrontation changed. No longer was it the irritating abrasion of two factions within the Empire at odds with one another. It became the violent, often explosive collision of different, incompatible worlds. These new aliens faced an unintelligible language, strange customs and stranger laws; an apparent cultural vacuum. And despite the newness of such society as there was awaiting them, it was not open-ended or unformed or elastic. The host society was not still perceptibly evolving. It was established from the outset as an extension of neo-British Upper Canada. Changes in it away from this displaced norm were largely beyond the newcomer's ability to appreciate. There was no impetus for the non-English-speaking immigrant to participate in a common dream and, in many cases, he was actively committed to oppose assimilation of any sort. He learned the language and the laws of his new place–not in order to adopt them but to adapt to them where necessary to protect his alien status.

Perhaps the best examples of fiction which in the west did the duty that Mrs. Moodie's *Roughing It in the Bush* or John Galt's earlier novel, *Bogle Corbet,* had both done over a century before in Ontario, or that Moore's *The Luck of Ginger Coffey* was doing contemporaneously, in Montreal, are the novels of Rudy Wiebe. The Maritimes had produced little fiction of immigration. When Julia Beckwith Hart's *St. Ursula's Convent,* English Canada's first domestic novel, appeared in 1825, the Atlantic provinces already had a relatively established, stable population. More cosmopolitan by far than it is at the present time, the Maritime populace–the Indians, the generations of Acadians, the New Englanders and the smattering of old country transplants, and at least one generation of United Empire Loyalists for whom the status of immigrant was an inadmissible affront to their self-sacrificing allegiance to the British crown–was composed of succeeding layers of homogeneous settlement, each of which adapted those previous to suit its characteristic needs. For the Maritimes, becoming part of a nation was a major step away from its cosmopolitan, if somewhat rustic, heritage–a step towards a rather moribund provincialism in which immigrants have since found little to attract them. Ontario in this century has been sufficiently established to overwhelm the newcomer's resistance to at least partial assimilation. The Ontario immigrant has been conceived by novelists as being the occupant of a garrison of bitter self-indulgence, like Wyndham Lewis's René Harding, or being naively taken in like Jacob Grossman, the Jewish tailor in Henry Kreisel's *The Rich Man* (1948). Kreisel ironically forces a confrontation of opposing value systems not in the New World, Toronto, but in the Old, Vienna, when Grossman returns in

1935 to the country he had left, thirty years earlier. The Jewish tailor is painfully crushed between the two realities, which are the ominous past and the tenuous present of himself and his people.

The theme of being forced to account for oneself by an accumulation of one's personal and collective history is universal. John Stedmond's introductory comment in the New Canadian Library edition, that *The Rich Man* "had dated remarkably little, partially because it does not stress details of historical background but concentrates on the human beings in the foreground,"[15] is, of course, absurd. It is the very historicity of the book that gives its universal theme such an immediate impact, that gives it the authenticity of individual human experience. Apart from this novel, and a few other exceptions which are only peripherally concerned with immigrant experience, Ontario has generated little fiction of this sort in the post-Victorian era. But in Western Canada, particularly the Prairies, the established order has not even yet sunk its roots so deeply that alternatives are entirely overshadowed, suffocated into the consciousness of a collective past. Wiebe's Mennonite stories, with meticulous precision, draw the problem into microcosmic focus. Adele Wiseman's *The Sacrifice* commits it to public vivisection.

In *The Blue Mountains of China,* Wiebe's vision of a people in perpetual flight is inexorably reduced, by the keenness of his perception, to the picture of one man's soul as the young Mennonite, John Reimer, struggles towards self-reconciliation. Reimer's despair is captured in the pilgrimage that, significantly, he intends should lead to no place and have no purpose: "I am not going anywhere; at least not in Canada.. . .I am a human being, walking. That's all. . . .Just a tired, dying human being, walking the land."[16] Reimer, like Thom Wiens in Wiebe's first novel, *Peace Shall Destroy Many,* honours the Mennonite admonition to "obey, pray, work, and wait in terror for God's wrath,"[17] and yet his awareness of himself and the surrounding world instils in him the confusion and doubt through which he is finally allowed the dignity and the personal integrity that the community has withheld. Both Reimer and Wiens suffer from an excess of consciousness which is the arena of their conflicting experiences. Out of the battle within, Thom Wiens ultimately assumes the moral responsibility for the whole Mennonite community of Wapiti, Saskatchewan, and by implication, for the entire sect, and, ultimately, for humanity. He is not, however, the popular prophet that Deacon Block had been.

Rather, in a violent, aggressive egalitarian age, Thom is made to realize (concerning the conflagration in Europe impinging on their rustic Canadian life, on their moral and social struggle for survival) "That two wars did not confront him, only one's own two faces."[18] The violence of threatening communal disintegration forces the knowledge on him that it will not be by suppression or avoidance but by pushing ahead, by aggressive love, that the Christian way can be achieved and be morally and practically exonerated from the pressures of its temporal futility.

In Wiebe's second novel, *The First and Vital Candle,* Sally Howell dies when she goes to offer her Easter prayers in the wilderness. Much as this might seem, out of context, a cynical commentary on reclusive religion, Wiebe actually uses the incident to exemplify the commitment of self through faith. *Peace Shall Destroy Many,* with a more expansive but similar irony, casts doubt violently upon beliefs, but likewise affirms the validity of faith, finally, in mundane isolation, worldly retreat. The exile of the Mennonites is a self-imposed necessity. They are therefore as liable to self-destruction as to outside persecution or imposition. As the schoolteacher disconcertingly explains to Thom, of their response to Hitlerism:

> "Though Mennonites, because of their training, naturally abhor violence, yet they faintly admire it somehow, in someone who without thought 'hews to it'! And if Germans are involved, this unconscious admiration is even bolstered a bit by our almost nationalistic interest in Germany. After all, we are displaced Germans, at least ethnically, and because we haven't had a true home for 400 years, we subconsciously long for one."[19]

Despite his rather ponderous intellectual pretensions, the teacher has accurately expressed at least two Mennonite characteristics–pride in a collective identity and a fascination with violence. They share these inclinations with the rest of humanity, but they have actively denied them and repeatedly fled their consequences rather than exorcising them. Both violence and pride are eventually confronted by Thom. Not in flight or denial but in "the heat of this battle lay God's peace."[20] This is the revelation of his desperate struggle to endure.

The experience of Thom's father is typical of all Wapiti: the past is an illusion; the present an endless threat.

> Forty years before, Wiens had been Thom's age, unstooped and husky, serenely at ease in the Mennonite community life of Central Russia. The upheavals of Russian life after 1917 that drove him to America with his family had wrenched him from his roots. He had lived his lifetime in Russia: his sons built the farm in Canada. For him, the Canadian bush disrupted the whole order of things, for though one could succeed with some Russian Mennonite farming methods, most past standards seemed barely authoritative.[21]

In the land of his new displacement, Deacon Block has been for Wiens as for the whole community the "one rock in the whirlpool."[22] But Block's strength is in the moral tyranny that lies beneath his moral righteousness. When his daughter Elizabeth redeems her "squandered womanhood"[23] with the half-breed, Louis, and becomes pregnant, she is hounded to death by her father's dogmas. From the dead girl's grave where he has lept, like Laertes, Thom sees Block–whose first name, appropriately is Peter–as a "granite form."[24] His feet on Elizabeth's coffin-box, Thom perceives their whole community from a new perspective. To this point he has unconsciously provided continuity for the subservience of his father and his forebears to arbitrary authority. The struggle now begins in earnest, deep within him, which has been going on for some time at a surface level, and by which his own roots are established within the Canadian soil. Thom's experience begins to replace his father's as being typical of their entire community. In a larger sense, it marks the end of their immigrant exile. As with Moses, at the close of *The Sacrifice,* in Thom Wiens the past and the present are finally and forcefully reconciled.

Adele Wiseman's *The Sacrifice* is a strange and powerful novel. It begins with Abraham, familiarly known as Avrom, and his family totally isolated, separated from the surrounding world. Abraham tries in four languages to determine where their train is, but the embarrassed conductor speaks neither Ukrainian nor Yiddish nor Polish nor German. There is no understanding between them. As an act of defiance against the anarchy of their confusion, Abraham takes his family off the train in the unnamed city of Winnipeg. Winnipegers tell me that Wiseman's novel offers a very real presentation of their city. Yet, it is a cityscape, a cityscape of the spirit, that she has defined–with its ubiquitous, ambivalent mountain and its ghetto cross-streets and, indistinctly, the heights where the gentiles live, where rich Jews have turned away from their past and pay exorbitantly for seats in their synagogue. It is a graphic, not ethereal, presentation of place, to be sure, but anonymous, detached, dislocated, a refuge taken on a truncated journey to the end of the line.

The novel closes with Abraham's utter isolation in the asylum on the mountain and the family's disintegration through death and Abraham's crime, both finally transcended, redeemed, by the coming of his grandson Moses on Yom Kippur, the Day of Atonement. There is a recognition between them of love that supersedes knowledge and understanding, forgiveness or retribution. As they touch after years apart, young Moishe, as Moses is more familiarly known,

> saw that the hands were not really different in shape, one from the other. And for a moment so conscious was he of his grandfather's hand on his own, of its penetrating warmth, of its very texture, that he felt not as though it merely lay superimposed on his own but that it was becoming one with his hand, nerve of his nerve, sinew of his sinew; that the distinct outlines had disappeared. It was the strangest feeling of awakening that he saw their hands fused together–one hand, the hand of a murderer, hero, artist, the hand of a man.[25]

With this continuity that Moses carries in him and the concept of love taking form in his mind, with the bondage of exile broken, he returns from the mountain to meet his new friend, appropriately named Aaron, in the depot of the anonymous city.

The Sacrifice fuses the story of a Jewish immigrant family from the Ukraine in a New World ghetto with the familiar history of the other Abraham, Sarah, and Isaac, with another Moses, Jacob, Aaron, drawn from the Torah. Adele Wiseman has not tried to retell an ancient story in modern dress. Nor does she construct a universal example of immigrant exile by building upon fragments of the ancient histories. Rather, with a resounding and controlled voice she has told a moral drama, enacted it in the dimensions of her reader's consciousness. She is heiress to Dostoievsky–yet, as she aspires to a greater achievement, she achieves somewhat less. Her perceptions are too controlled by actuality on the one hand, and mythology on the other, to allow for the unrestricted flights of imagination that her attempt to comprehend the moral universe would seem to demand.

Abraham had fled his obscure place in the Ukraine with his wife and surviving son, from the horrors of a pogrom in which his two elder sons were sacrifieced on an Easter Sunday, during the Passover, to satiate the gentile's Christ. This was the beginning of Abraham's exile, an exile not only from home but from God–and therefore an exile which cannot be escaped, even in Winnipeg.

But Abraham creates another God, in his own mind. He has been a proud man, sure of his destiny. As he explains to his friend, Chaim Knopp, when telling him about the tragedy, " 'my mission was my family, to bring up my sons. And what sons they were! What could a great singer and a great scholar have done for our people.' "[26] He declares, on finding them murdered, to have " 'turned in my heart, away from God. I felt that my soul was gone.' "[27] Chaim, the *shoichet* or ritual slaughterer, a holy man, is incredulous, aghast and Abraham, the butcher, assures his friend that his hatred of God has passed. But Abraham's is a profound pride. He explains to Chaim, " 'I have always known that something extraordinary was going to happen in my lifetime. I was born with this feeling, as though it had been promised to me in another place, another lifetime.' "[28] As he declares of himself and his family to his landlady in Canada, " 'we are not just anybody. Let the world laugh at such things. It shows how small people have grown. We will have strange events to distinguish our lives.' "[29] To Chaim, his identity with the ancient Abraham is vaguely defined. In his conversation with Mrs. Plopler, it is quite overt, for their talk began in a discussion with her about the father of the Jews, begetting *his* Isaac when Sarah was ninety-nine years old. Out of this pride and his suffering, Abraham recreates God in the image of his dead sons. It is as the anguished Ruth accuses him: his God is his own tormented consciousness. But whereas the forebearer of his name and race turned the Hebrews from idolatry, setting God free amongst them, Miss Wiseman's Abraham has confined his God to images graven within his mind. There, at least, " 'he was not afraid to climb, to soar, to walk the edge of the ravine,' " says Chaim, " 'But when such a man falls–.' "[30] And of course Abraham falls, for he is a deeply religious man.

Abraham is not, as he has made Isaac, "grimly anchored to the ground."[31] Anticipating the image used by Chaim about himself, Abraham describes Isaac's agnosticism to Laiah, the temptress:

> "It was as though a man who could fly deliberately descended to the earth and declared that he could not really fly, and to prove it henceforth he would walk. And then he would go on to explain things, step by step, as seen through the eyes of a man who has clipped his own wings. But surely what he sees now are only the pores on the earth's surface, and not the deep breathings and gentle swellings of her breast."[32]

Isaac, the unbeliever, dies from burns and a heart ruined while rescuing the Sepher Torah from a burning synagogue. Abraham had made him, too, a part of the Godhead. Isaac is a sacrifice to his father's conception of what he should be. It is as the widowed Ruth accuses the old man, " 'You wanted one son should make up for three.' "[33] Isaac's heart could not endure the burden of expectation, nor the consequences of trying to fulfil it. The God he impetuously serves, as he burns like a "prophet" amidst the flaming synagogue, is Abraham's God, of which Isaac himself is a living piece.

The oneness of Abraham, his sons, and his God, is a monstrous parody of his own account of how God replaced the other Abraham's son with a ram for the sacrificial altar. He explains the story's conclusion to his young grandson, Moses, in lucid terms:

> "In that moment lay the secrets of life and death, in that closed circle with just the three of them, with Abraham offering the whole of the past and the future, and Isaac lying very still, so as not to spoil the sacrifice, and the glint of the knife and the glare of the sun and the terror of the moment burning into his eyes.. . .God himself is bound at that moment, for it is the point of mutual surrender, the one thing He cannot resist, a faith so absolute. You are right when you say that it is like a circle–the completed circle, when the maker of the sacrifice and the sacrifice himself and the Demander who is the Receiver of the sacrifice are poised together, and life flows into eternity, and for a moment all three are one."[34]

The complete circle of divine identity has its nether equivalent, in Abraham's confused mind, as the moment of Laiah's murder approaches:

> Now, now was the time, in the stillness, as he stood once again, terrified, fascinated, on the brink of creation where life and death waver toward each other, reiterating his surrender; now was the time for the circle to close, to enclose him in its safety, in its peace.[35]

He cuts her throat, and his dead sons are seemingly present:

> Life! cried Isaac as the blood gushed from her throat and her frantic fingers gripped first, then relaxed and loosened finally their hold on his beard. Life! pleaded Jacob as Abraham stared, horrified, into her death-glazed eyes. Life! chanted Moses as he smelled, sickened, the hot blood that had spurted onto his beard.[36]

They appear to him together in Laiah's death, and the realization of what he has symbolically if not actually done soon comes to him: "It was plain that in some way he confused the dead woman with his dead children. Sometimes from the way he spoke you could almost believe that he thought he had killed God himself."[37] It is the God of death that he has killed, however, and he has finally, violently, allowed his sons the peace of their own deaths.

This God of Abraham did not spring full-grown into his anguished mind. It grew. As he explains to Chaim after Sarah dies, " 'death is a seed that is sown, like life, inside of a person, and comes to fruition from within.' "[38] After Isaac dies, Abraham becomes disoriented. Still in ritual mourning on the ninth night, he lies asleep on sackcloth "stretched out, an effigy of death, marring the illusion only by the persistent regularity of his breath."[39] His identity with death is almost complete. He talks often about his inexorable growth as a person, but what grows within him is an awareness of "The other part of him–that was empty, unbelieving, the negation of life, the womb of death, the black shadow that yet was clothed in the warm, tantalizing flesh of life," so that in the imminence of the sacrificial murder of Laiah he acknowledges "his oneness with the fruit without seed, with death, his other self."[40] In this context, killing Laiah is appropriate for, despite her flamboyant promiscuity, she had never borne children–in Abraham's mind she "was like a giant overripe fruit without seed, which hung now, long past its season, on the bough.. . .She had denied creation, and to deny is to annihilate."[41] Only after he has murdered her, years later when he is talking to young Moishe, does he articulate what the sacrifice of Laiah made him realize, with compassion, that "In her voice there were voices of children."[42] She, too, had been crying out, as Abraham righteously explains: "When a human being cries out to you, no matter who it is, don't judge him, don't harm him, or you turn away God himself."[43] This also is Abraham's plea to his grandson, his offering of love.

If the God who is merged with Laiah and Abraham's sons and with Abraham, himself, all bound together in her execution, were exclusively the God of death, within the reality of the novel, then the grisly murder would be given a sort of moral sanction that Wiseman clearly does not intend. Her ultimate message, after all, that is carried down from the mountain by Moses, is love, not moral or social anarchy. The murdered God is a God only of Abraham's creation, in Abraham's mind. His destruction sanctifies nothing. The act of His destruction is irredeemable. It is murder. But to Avrom it was sacrifice, and it is this by which the murderer, though not the act, is redeemed, is absolved of his crime.

Wiseman carefully prepares the way for this ritual killing of Laiah. Abraham is a butcher, trained in the old country. His best friend and confidante, Chaim Knopp, is a *shoichet,* educated to perform ritual slaughter for kosher food according to the law of Moses. When Abraham had been a young apprentice, he too had done the *shoichet's* job, but under cruel duress. His master had forced him to it when the *shoichet* who had to come from a neighbouring village had been waylaid, and the local butchers agreed to pay Abraham's master for providing them with meat from animals slaughtered in the ritual method–without questions. Saying the appropriate prayer and handling the knife as if he were doing a holy act, and not debasing it, the master slaughtered two of the cows. He then demanded that Abraham, too, participate in the grim parody and kill the third. The arcane similarity between these deaths and those of his sons–Moses and Jacob murdered in blasphemous obeisance to a profane Christ, Isaac sacrificed to his father's God–is part of the larger pattern.

In this larger pattern, sacrifice, ritual, and slaughter merge, as the expression of man's relations with his universe. It recalls the achievement of the original Abraham in forcing God to surrender Himself to the faith of man and demand no more bloody proof of their mutual bond. Doing the job of the *shoichet,* Abraham recalls that it was

> ". . .as though I were somewhere between living and dying. Not

> until I saw the creature was dead did I realize that I was still alive. I have wondered since if that is what our forefathers felt when they made the sacrifice to renew their wonder and their fear and their belief, before they were forbidden to make them any longer. It is a mystery too deep for man."[44]

The fusion of sacrificer and sacrificed, without also the inclusion of God, profanes the holy and ancient alliance between God and Jew. When eventually Abraham murders Laiah, he is transported in his confused mind to the crime of his apprenticeship and also to the sacred place of the ancient sacrifice where God had first demanded and then stopped the slaughter of the other Abraham's son. His corruption of ritual killing and his knowledge of God's holy ordinance against sacrifice merge in his pride, humiliation, and madness. Laiah becomes one with the slaughtered beast and Avrom's slaughtered sons and the God that he has created from the experience of his life. Her murder is a ritual of expiation, even while it is a heinous completion of the ancient Abraham's original knife-thrust. It is a ritual slaughter in defiance of a corrupted covenant, and a sacrifice by which the original Covenant between God and His Jews is renewed.

Moral vision in *The Sacrifice* quite clearly adheres to the fundamental primacy of hope, compassion, love. In the sense of reality perceived, however, Adele Wiseman's moral vision is an inversion of the ideal relations between man and the divine as prescribed in the Torah. The basis for this inversion is the consciousness of Abraham and of the cluster of characters who surround him. Using the experience of an elderly Jewish immigrant adrift in an alien world which, in itself and in its effect on the remnants of ancient values, is largely unfathomable to him, Wiseman arranges her novel's reality according to the dictates of a moral, not social or psychological, causality. Her characters' behaviour is isolated from the conditions of environment that normally determine the meaning of experience and she is able to concentrate on those details of motivation and event which serve the larger purpose of her story. Without being an allegory, in that it is not a figurative treatment of one moral structure under the guise of another, her novel is a metaphor for the confrontation of moral systems within the psyche of a universal individual. Thus her city is specific but anonymous. Abraham's joys and his despair are known, yet he is never given a family name. Thus the struggle to maintain ancient traditions is counterposed with the struggle–by Isaac, by

Ruth, and by Chaim's thoroughly assimilated son, Ralph–to escape them. A tortuous exile culminates in murder, and is finally brought to an end by the exchange of love and spiritual continuity in an asylum removed from the world.

Wiseman is not intimidated by language. Its power and precision in her hands serve the intent of the novel well. And her humour lends the novel that dimension of humanity which relieves the weight of its moral burden even while complementing it. At times she drops into place an epithetical sneer, as in the following instance which sounds remarkably like Gulliver perusing the Brobdingnagian countenance–"He breathed in deeply, through his nose, of her perfume. His nose twitched slightly at the impact. He could distinguish the grains of powder on her face."[45] This is Abraham, seeing Laiah too closely to recognize the vulnerable being behind the mask. Describing Hymie, the doltish son of Abraham's employer, she tosses off the following gibe, appropriately superficial and trite–"He saw himself with the visionary eye of the inveterate reader of comic books."[46] But Miss Wiseman can also develop a caustic irony at a leisurely pace, as in the sardonic monologues of Mrs. Plopler which reveal more of the speaker and her milieu than she could possibly realize:

> "It's really a very nice little place you've found, even if it's not such a good district. But what can you do? You can afford so much, after all. And it's very nice that people who, after all, have not been in the country so very long, should be able to rent a little house for themselves. It was years before we moved out of our apartment into this house. Of course, we didn't want to move until we found exactly what we wanted. The minute I saw it, I thought how lucky you are. What if there are a lot of bootleggers around there? Of course we can be just as good friends as ever."[47]

Perhaps the most difficult person for the immigrant to deal with is another immigrant who has preceded him. Using Mrs. Plopler to make this point, just as she uses Chaim Knopp to signify the complementary possibility–that the immigrant's most sympathetic friend may be one who has already been through some of what he is presently enduring–Adele Wiseman turns wit as surely to her story's purpose as she does compassion. She does so with a poetic sensitivity for language, with a poetic insight into experience. With meticulous honesty she has described immigrant exile which is exemplary not in the course of its events but in its resounding moral implications.

Notes

1. Laura Goodman Salverson, *The Viking Heart* (Toronto: McClelland & Stewart, 1925), p.22. (New York: 1923.)
2. *Ibid.,* p.21.
3. *Ibid.,* p.316.
4. *Ibid.,* p.326.
5. Adele Wiseman, *The Sacrifice* (Toronto: Macmillan, 1968), p.304. (1956.)
6. *Ibid.,* p.5.
7. Salverson, *op.cit.,* p.21.
8. Brian Moore, *The Luck of Ginger Coffey* (Toronto: New Canadian Library, 1972), p.243. (Boston: Little, Brown, 1960.)
9. *Ibid.,* p.243.
10. Ronald Sutherland, *Second Image* (Toronto: New Press, 1971), pp.35-37.
11. Susanna Moodie, *Roughing It in the Bush* (Toronto: New Canadian Library, 1969), p.140. (London: Bently, 1852.)
12. *Ibid.,* p.234.
13. W.H.P. Jarvis, *A Remittance Man's Letters to his Mother* (Toronto: Musson, 1907), p.52.
14. *Ibid.,* p.110.
15. Henry Kreisel, *The Rich Man* (Toronto: New Canadian Library, 1961), p.viii. (Toronto: McClelland & Stewart, 1948.)
16. Rudy Wiebe, *The Blue Mountains of China* (Toronto: McClelland & Stewart, 1970), p.225.
17. *Ibid.,* p.100.
18. Rudy Wiebe, *Peace Shall Destroy Many* (Toronto: New Canadian Library, 1972), p.238. (Toronto: McClelland & Stewart, 1962.)
19. *Ibid.,* p.30.
20. *Ibid.,* p.238.
21. *Ibid.,* p.21.
22. *Ibid.,* p.21.
23. *Ibid.,* p.25.
24. *Ibid.,* p.157
25. Wiseman, *op. cit.,* p.345.
26. *Ibid.,* p.59.
27. *Ibid.,* p.59.
28. *Ibid.,* p.53.

29. *Ibid.*, p.97.
30. *Ibid.*, p.315.
31. *Ibid.*, p.258.
32. *Ibid.*, p.258.
33. *Ibid.*, p.290.
34. *Ibid.*, p.173.
35. *Ibid.*, p.303.
36. *Ibid.*, p.304.
37. *Ibid.*, p.327.
38. *Ibid.*, p.144.
39. *Ibid.*, p.228.
40. *Ibid.*, p.300.
41. *Ibid.*, p.261.
42. *Ibid.*, p.344.
43. *Ibid.*, p.344.
44. *Ibid.*, p.38.
45. *Ibid.*, p.275.
46. *Ibid.*, p.157.
47. *Ibid.*, p.45.

5.
Indian Lovers

The patterns of exile in Canadian fiction are various. Enough of them, however, correspond to one or another of the four types in my arrangement to warrant examining them from the present perspective. The novels I have used as the prime examples of each type, and the other novels I have clustered around them for a variety of supportive reasons, serve to offer a working definition of the patterns. These patterns in turn seem to have provided an appropriate leaping off point for their explication while also offering some tentative insights into their collective relationships.

Undoubtedly there are as many Canadian novels of exile which defy classification according to type, that resist clarification from relatively fixed perspectives. This does not invalidate my arrangement of patterns. But it does suggest a richness in our literature beyond schematic measure. Certainly a novel such as De Mille's *A Strange Manuscript Found in a Copper Cylinder* gains only marginal insight by being considered as a work of colonial exile. It more properly belongs to the same order as *Erewhon, Brave New World,* and Sir Thomas More's *Utopia,* by virtue of its visionary conception. As a tale of unfettered imagination, it occupies a tenuous alliance with Poe's *The Narrative of Arthur Gordon Pym,* Haggard's *She.* Like *The Clockwork Orange, Knowledge Park,* and *1984,* it is prophetic in the same light. De Mille's colonial genius is of only peripheral concern to an appreciation of his work. Similarly, his manipulation of traditional themes of exile is of interest from a particularly Canadian point of view only as a literary curiosity. The exile of Stacey McAindra in Margaret Laurence's *The Fire-Dwellers* is a housewife's dilemma, culminating in very human resignation to her lot, that owes more, I am sure, to John Updike, or to Doris Lessing, than to anything peculiarly Canadian beyond the author's private experience. The themes of spiritual, moral, social isolation in Morley Callaghan's novels more readily relate to theological principles by far than to patterns of Canadian exile, although the experience of Canada usually provides the narrative means of their expression. Similarly, the novels of Ethel Wilson, particularly *Swamp Angel,* use Canadian geography to define and to exemplify the intensely private isolation of her feminist protagonists. Frederick Philip Grove explores exile in relation to the natural world and the family unit in *Our Daily Bread* but, while the novel is inextricably Canadian, its patterns of exile lend themselves more readily to either universal or regionalist classification.

Other patterns of exile in Canadian fiction are fragmented, elusive, or transcendent of type. Many novels, including Buckler's *The Mountain and the Valley,* with its appropriately named protagonist, David Canaan, Sinclair Ross's haunting evocation of a composite soul cowering before the onslaught of reality, *As For Me and My House,* and Sheila Watson's allusive *The Double Hook* exploit the original exile of man from the Garden, his God, and his fellow creatures in the world around him, leaning heavily on the mythology of our Judeo-Christian culture. But none of these novels is informed by the sustaining presence of exile in attitude, outlook, or structure. They borrow fragments of its previous expression and diffuse them throughout, to other ends.

Some images of exile are, perhaps, uniquely Canadian but do not identify with one type of fiction in my arrangement more than another. Most notable of these is the function of the Indian or half-breed lover as an expression of escape, reconciliation, defiance. In novels that I have tentatively aligned with the frontier impulse, Mazo de la Roche's *Possession* and Ostenso's *Wild Geese,* the Indian lover is a familiar figure. Fawnie embodies, quite literally, the ambivalent sexuality of Derek Vale. She offers his troubled soul some measure of solace, then retribution, and finally a sorrowful peace. Fawnie, of course, is Indian–a free spirit; without guile, without conscience. For Ostenso's Ellen, the half-breed Malcolm insinuates the possibility of freedom for her from Caleb's tyranny which is the tyranny of a distorted, perverted, natural world. Malcolm implicitly represents reintegration of man with nature, Ellen with life. Rudy Wiebe's novel of national exile, *Peace Shall Destroy Many,* similarly provides a Canadian original in the person of the half-breed, Louis, as the alternative for Elizabeth Block to her sterile condition.

The Indian-figure in *Maria Chapdelaine,* Louis Hémon's 1913 paean to the spirit of an indefatigable peasantry, is a clearly defined alternative for Marie to both the brave new world offered by Lorenzo Surprenant, *en route* to the United States, and the old order typified by her eventual husband, Edwige Légaré, the way of her Québécois forebears. Only François Paradis, as his name suggests, provides the possibility of an Edenic return to the natural state, but there is no going back; he dies, and the freedom and harmony of natural principles disappear from Maria's horizon. Indians play a significant role in defining exile in *The History of Emily Montague,* although they are an environmental factor without romantic pretentions. They occupy the milieu of *But We Are Exiles,* but do not dominate it. The covert affair in *Wacousta,* however, between Frederick De Haldimar and Oucanasta, the Indian girl, exploits the Indian's inherent identity with the primeval surrounding world. Wacousta, himself, of course, is virtually a half-breed. Richardson parallels his demonic madness with his participation in the savage wilderness, incarnate in the murderous Ottawas. Like the half-breed Tay John's love for Ardith in Howard O'Hagan's novel, *Tay John,* his transcendent love for Clara Beverley can only be sustained by an outcast condition. However, where Wacousta's miscegenous devotion grimly parodies the romantic ideal, Tay John's exploits its metaphorical potential as an image of romantic integration–of races, of spirit and the physical world.

The most striking presence of Canadian Indians in contemporary fiction is in Rudy Wiebe's brilliant innovative short story, "Where Is the Voice Coming From," which tells of a people ostracized in their own land, through the futile defiance of an Indian martyr. Margaret Laurence's Canadian novels sustain the spectre presence of the Tonnerres, an Indian family from her fictional town of Manawaka, on the periphery of their action. In *The Fire-Dwellers,* one of the Tonnerre girls, utterly degraded, plays the significant role as unlikely liaison between Stacey's present despair and her childhood past, and, I believe, the novel Mrs. Laurence is presently working on focuses in large part on the Tonnerres. For Laurence, the Indian seems not to embody freedom or defiance but our collective guilt which we continue to generate through our treatment of them. Fred Bodsworth's *The Strange One* tells of an amorous exile in the Canadian wilderness between Scot and Indian girl, and Yves Thériault's *Agaguk* traces the outcast love of two Eskimos in response to tribal deterioration and spiritual atrophy. Gabrielle Roy's *Windflower* explores the consequences of a sexual encounter between an Eskimo girl and an anonymous American soldier as a point of departure for her haunting threnody to a passing way of life considered redundant because it is integrated with its environment.

So many other novels, English and French Canadian, explore the possibilities of the Indian or half-breed lover, that to continue to name them for the sake of academic satiety is an exercise in futility. The best, the most sophisticated, the most reckless variation, however, may be found in Leonard Cohen's *Beautiful Losers.* Counterpoising the imminent presence of the Indian saint, Catherine Tekakwitha, in the narrator's life, on the one hand, with a detailed phantasmic distortion of her historical role and, on the other, with the narrator's unfaithful Indian wife, Edith, Cohen rips the psyche of the modern *isolato* apart and scours its innards for meaning.

Some patterns of exile transcend all classifications except those of subject-matter. The Indian presence in the Canadian experience provides one such cluster; the landscape provides another; the feminist struggle, the deterioration of family are others; the stories of artists painfully drawing themselves into consciousness yet another. But the major groupings I have made do not depend upon subject-matter. They are arrangements made for critical convenience of more tenuous affinities. They reveal a primary function of the Canadian experience in our literature and they help to account for the process of its development. Other patterns are of significance for other reasons; these, for the reasons given.

PART II
The Geophysical Imagination

> *The distorted, barren landscape makes you feel the meaning of its persistence there. As Paul put it last Sunday when we drove up, it's* Humanity in microcosm. *Faith, ideals, reason–all the things that really are humanity–like Paul you feel them there, their stand against the implacable blunderings of Nature–and suddenly like Paul you begin to think poetry, and strive to utter eloquence.*[1]
>
> –As for Me and My House

The imminence of geophysical reality in relation to the patterns of human isolation evokes a profound response in the Canadian imagination. A great many writers of the Maritimes, the Prairies, and British Columbia have shaped their separate visions out of the common experience of an immense northern landscape, its aggressive climate, and the spare distribution of its populace. Central Canada, in contrast, has engendered relatively few writers with a predilection for authenticity that includes both the natural environment and the affairs of humanity. As might be expected, visions of reciprocity between the two articulate experience in parts of the country that are regionally distinctive, where nature is most in evidence.

Out of the West have come such conspicuously indigenous novels as *Swamp Angel, The Double Hook* and *As For Me and My House.* Beside the authors of these three, Ethel Wilson, Sheila Watson and Sinclair Ross, are ranged such perceptive and responsive novelists as Stead, Ostenso, Stringer, Salverson, Wiebe, Kroetsch and Laurence. From the Maritimes have emerged novels like *The Channel Shore* by Charles Bruce, Thomas Raddall's *The Nymph and the Lamp,* and works by a great many others who similarly perceive a fundamental correspondence between the worlds of nature and of man. These include Buckler, Nowlan, Horwood, Montgomery, and Charles G.D. Roberts. By comparison, the offerings of Ontario and Quebec to the formulation of the Canadian imagination, in this respect, are relatively meagre–in English, at least. Mazo de la Roche treats natural phenomena in passing, while Raymond Knister, for example, in *White Narcissus* bends an indifferent landscape too much to his literary purpose for it to remain also a natural world in emotional or moral convergence with humanity; rather, with analytic precision he deploys the southern Ontario farmlands as props in a drama set primarily in the urbanized mind of his protagonist. The majority of novelists writing from our two most populous provinces–Bodsworth being, perhaps, the most notable exception–fastidiously avoid confrontations with nature except to universalize brief statements of thematic significance. Hugh Hood's various forays to the city's edge in pursuit of elusive affirmation provide one such set of examples. Another example, in *They Shall Inherit the Earth,* reveals Morley Callaghan's conception of natural justice in a tableau of frozen deer slaughtered by wolves in the snow, their carcasses left to replenish the she-wolf and her cubs in the coming spring.

Isolation amidst the conditions of our northern geography and climate is not necessarily the correlative of being alone, apart from other people, or being exiled, away from some other place. Those patterns of isolation in our fiction which are shaped by the geophysical presence are essentially moral, revealing the transcendent unity and immediacy of two quite distinct orders of reality as they converge in immediate experience. Such a convergence can more readily occur, it would seem, within the environs of a small Canadian town than in wilderness solitude. The urban experience, where the landscape is laid out by city planners and the seasons are measured by sporting events, almost by definition precludes the intimacy between man and the natural world essential for the revelation of a moral design that is apparently universal rather than a construct of social conventions. Thinkers who talk of how cityscapes dwarf their inhabitants should consider the effect on the imagination of an ocean, the prairies, a mountain range, a snow storm raging across flat open fields. The writers of Canadian fiction who confront nature directly of necessity retreat to the interpersonal configurations of rural communities where the impact of the surrounding environment is dissipated to analogical proportions, without losing its authenticity as an imminent presence. For Bruce and for Ross, in the novels I have mentioned, these are communities settled on the intersection of time, as measured by their inhabitants, and geophysical continuity. Raddall and Wilson both conceive their aesthetic visions amidst communities that are merely clusters of several individuals remote from the mainstream of contemporary society yet subject to its invidious influence. Sheila Watson envisions an equally remote gathering locus of peoples' lives, but one that owes more to symbolic imperatives than to the patterns of actual experience. Each perceives the apparently essential necessity of placing characters in a manageable human context in order to relate their separate lives to geophysical reality in a way that will reveal the similar conditions of both.

Nature is a pervasive and determining factor in much of the Canadian experience. However, there is a popular myth in our literary criticism that the natural world participates in some cosmic consciousness, that it exhibits motivated behaviour, that it harbours imponderable intentions towards those who live in its midst. As emphatically as I possibly can, I would reject all such anthropocentric notions. Nowhere in our literature, that I can see, is adequate support to be found for these obtrusive assumptions. With few exceptions, Canadian writers have perceived nature itself to be amoral, impassive, indifferent. The landscape and its seasons have no ethics, no consciousness. Nature is neither wilful nor benign, malevolent nor beneficent. Some of our writers respond to it with hostility, some with reverence, or hope, or fear, but the emotion is in their response–neither emotion nor conscious design is apparent in nature itself.

The response, however, may be dramatic, allusive. E.J. Pratt's "The Titanic" thrusts the engine of man's pride against the indomitability of his environment, but the iceberg and the Atlantic do not attack the mighty ship. They merely confront her with implacable passivity, ultimately reflecting the "grey paleolithic face" of the age-old struggle of man to subdue nature. The *Titanic* itself is the struggle's inevitable victim. "David," the powerful narrative poem by Earle Birney, displays the shifting response of man to nature according to the immediate events of his life. Before ascending the Finger, the landscape is familiar, beckoning, suggesting death only in fragmented images. After David's fall, the mountains loom ominously, the natural world takes on a hostile mien, horror pervades. In neither poem does nature attack; nor does it change. In the first, it is itself attacked and, in the second, it is the narrator's perceptions that change. Objective reality is not confused with subjective response. The moral drama in both poems is in the tensions between the two, between nature and man, object and subject. The primary attribute of nature in either case is that it exists, it endures–anatomical imagery notwithstanding.

These tensions and their moral implications are perversely apparent in Frederick Philip Grove's well-known short story, "Snow." There appears in this story to be an almost nihilistic malevolence to the determinism of a natural world that would murder Redcliff because he is the hope of his in-laws, the father of six small children, and a good man committed to the land. Yet Grove's description of Redcliff in death is touched with compassion, as well as horror:

> And there, in the hollow, lay the man's body as if he were sleeping, a quiet expression, as of painless rest, on his face. His eyes were closed; a couple of bags were wrapped about his shoulders. Apparently he had not even tried to walk! Already chilled to the bone, he had given in to that desire for rest, for shelter at any price, which overcomes him who is doomed to freeze.[2]

Redcliff is the victim of nature, perhaps, but he is also its beneficiary. And he is as much the victim of social as of natural circumstance, in any case. His death participates in a natural process that is as indifferent to sorrow as to the irony of our presence within it. His mother-in-law's dour judgment, "God's will be done!" is both absurdly inadequate to the human events and utterly appropriate as a description of the way things are, inexorable in retrospect. The story's immense power lies in this terrible ambivalence between occurrence and response. Nature is not manipulated by the authorial imagination. It is observed and its impassivity recorded, its effect on human affairs is lamented, and always it is respected for its power, its beauty, and its indifference.

In this story, as in the separate journeys described in *Over Prairie Trails,* Grove studies the course of nature with a meticulous regard, even when it is most virulent. Abe Carroll sees beneath the surface of things, points "to a fold in the flank of the snow-drift which indicated that the present drift had been superimposed on a lower one whose longitudinal axis ran to the north-east."[3] Grove's clinical detachment from natural phenomena, combined with his acute perception of it, together become Carroll's own knowledge that leads him to Redcliff's body but stifles his outward response to a tragedy that is, ultimately, a natural event. In *Over Prairie Trails,* Grove describes himself whiling away the hours of his winter journeys by observing exact movements of individual snowflakes, tracing their swirled progress with obsessive precision, as he turns the mundane into a cosmic dance that is all the more exhilarating because it is mindless, disinterested, despite the implicit threat to his safety. Nowhere in Grove's writing, apart from *Consider Her Ways* which is a utopian fable featuring ants, are the elements of nature personified or given to conscious intent. Yet nature is demanding, imposing conditions on the lives of those who live close to it. In *Our Daily Bread,* for example, he declares that the land must be cultivated with responsibility shown towards its needs: it provides or impoverishes accordingly. The Elliotts participate in a process whose balance and continuity are vulnerable. As John Elliott's offspring move away from the land or abuse it, the process excludes them. The land and the people are wasted. Yet the natural world, in Grove's vision, is the source of a poetic justice at best. It is an environment the autobiographical traveller confronts with civility and is rewarded by gaining safe passage. For Redcliff there is nothing beyond being an object of its implacable indifference as he lies dead in the snow, whatever the redeeming implications of Carroll's response, of his mother-in-law's, of the whole.

Death by freezing is appropriate to the tragic side of Canadian experience. Both dying and the hard winter driving upon us are brought into fresh consciousness with each exaggerated revolution of the seasonal cycle. Their impact on the creative imagination is evident in the image of death in the snow that is repeatedly encountered in Canadian fiction as the terrible completion of a moral vision that reflects the physical conditions of our existence. In no case is such a death the effect of a personalist Nature. As in Grove's "Snow," it is one possible consequence of man's intimacy with the natural world, an intimacy imposed upon us by the great untrammeled contours of the Canadian landscape, by the dramatic seasons and the wilderness ever there at the edges of each cultivated enclosure of the civilized presence. Death in the snow is a fundamental possibility of the Canadian experience. It is fixed profoundly in the Canadian imagination.

One of the most alarming short stories in the English language, "The Painted Door" by Sinclair Ross, closes with the discovery of the cuckold's corpse frozen grotesquely in a standing position against the fence of his own pasture. John and Ann had been married seven years, farming their prairie homestead. She never learns to accept the isolation, cannot conceive the distant farms on the horizon "as a testimony of human hardihood and endurance. Rather they seemed futile, lost, to cower before the implacability of the snow-swept earth and clear pale sun-chilled sky."[4] Such is her response to their life, generating a "brooding stillness in her face as if she recognized this mastery of snow and cold."[5] John, as he prepares to travel through the raw weather to help with his father's chores, five miles away, vows to return to her by nightfall and comforts her with the memories of his fidelity during their courtship when, twice a week through blizzards and all, he never failed her. Such is his response to their life, convinced that travail sanctifies and nature serves man's duty.

When, in the eye of the blistering winter's storm, Ann beds for the night with their neighbour, Steven, who has come to look in on her, she sleeps fitfully. A shadow seems to loom over her and, "though it never reached her still she cowered, feeling that gathered there was all the frozen wilderness, its heart of terror and invincibility."[6] The shadow recedes, drawing her into wakefulness. She is contrite, determined to make amends. But John had been doggedly true in his devotion. The shadow was his and he has walked out into the night, to his death. The winter landscape fulfils Ann's expectation of it, reproaching her by its possession of her husband's body, both metaphorically, as he is the looming shadow, and literally, as he stands frozen rigid against the fence. The frozen prairie also satisfies John's stolid expectations, offering in the intolerable storm, where he blends almost surrealistically with the shrieking winds and twisting shadows that embody his wife's betrayal, the medium for the expiation of his dogged fidelity. Only nature is constant, giving him without compromise the death he asks of it. The prairie storm provides for their moral turpitude, their moral carelessness, an appropriately dynamic context which dominates their lives, ironically without forcing on them an awareness of motivation or responsibility.

Ross deploys the natural world as a vast indifferent context that gives the human drama an ironic impact of cosmic proportions. Nature is no more responsible to man, in this story, nor concerned for his lot, than in "Not By Rain Alone," where Eleanor dies giving birth after Will's futile struggle against a ruinous winter snow. There is a profound irony in life that is revealed by nature, but it not consciously engendered. Rather, the natural world is the condition of human existence. This is Ross's conception of it–the way he has allowed it to function–in his short stories, in *As For Me and My House,* to a lesser extent in *The Well,* and only in the fragmented memories of Sonny's boyhood in *Whir of Gold.* Their convergence is typified by John's frozen corpse in "The Painted Door" as the mordant symbol of misplaced responsibility. Similarly, the two horses that Philip discovered, in *As For Me and My House,* frozen on their feet against a fence, their backsides to the wind, suggests much about the Bentleys' moribund union, turned from each other, from adversity, engulfed by the implications of their geophysical environment.

A short story in a much less intuitive vein is Dave Godfrey's "The Winter Stiffs." Godfrey shows men living close to nature as being apparently crude and reckless, familiar only with two fundamentals of life, breeding women–to use his image–and dying. Finn recounts how, as a young lad, he had found three frozen corpses in the snow. He mocks their deaths, jokes of stacking them on the bulldozer and taking them to the blacksmith's shop to thaw–one of them, whom he had run over, broken in pieces "like cordwood, neat as could be."[7] Suddenly in the story, three paragraphs from the end, Godfrey shifts to Toronto, to an old woman possessively feeding pigeons, possessed by the fifty pound egg-symbol of Manufacturers Life by which her own death is insured. Godfrey has first described a grotesque scene of death as a natural event, a mockery of human vanity. In alarming contrast, he then shows a civilized world where communion with nature has been reduced to feeding parasitic pigeons near an old Eaton's mansion and death is confronted with an accumulation of money, the antidote to a manufactured life. In retrospect, Finn's story seems ennobling. Three drunks frozen stiff in the snow, found and flung contemptuously against a wall to thaw like so much dead meat, belching obscenely as their stomachs swell–this is the honour that death deserves. Contempt for it is the only viable response for the living. But in the world removed from nature, in Toronto, death is an event to be banked against, saved for; an event to which living bodies are chained, as if it were a fifty pound gold egg and not a metamorphosis from lust and appetite to frozen flesh.

Somewhere between Finn's response to death as a natural phenomenon and the old lady's distortion of life as the prelude to mortal impoverishment, is William's reaction to his mother's corpse in Sheila Watson's *The Double Hook.* William does not fear the presence of death but neither is he indifferent to it. As he explains, "I've seen men die in winter stowed away in trees until spring thawed the ground soft enough for digging. In summer a man can't wait."[8] It is something to be endured as much as is necessary, put out of mind as soon as is possible.

Death in the snow eliminates François Paradis as a marital possibility for Maria Chapdelaine. Hémon could not more fittingly have destroyed the embodiment of natural impulse. In this and other French Canadian novels, snow and death are contiguous. Yves Thériault's *Agaguk* and Marie-Claire Blais' *Mad Shadows* both set murder amidst the swarming winter's waste. Roch Carrier's brilliant novel, *La Guerre, Yes Sir!,* surrounds the warm enclave close to Corriveau's encoffined corpse with a ruthless winter. In Ringuet's *Thirty Acres,* winter is the season of death. But winter is always the season of death in the natural cycle and fiction that attempts an authentic vision of man in the natural world is obliged to perceive how closely the two are related.

Graeme Gibson's variation of the affinity between mortal demise and the climatic nadir is given resounding dimension by his peculiarly fragmented style. His protagonist in *Communion,* Felix Oswald, tries to set free a dying husky, driving him from his cage into the snow. But the dog will not take his freedom and, instead, cringes close to Felix, choosing inevitable death. The snow becomes merely an extension of the human cruelty the dog has already endured, rather than the natural habitat that it is for such a breed. Felix, nevertheless, commits him to it. Felix is a compassionate voyeur and the closest he can come to participation in life is to force another being into it. Over and over, Gibson defines the course of their mortal struggle, advancing bit by bit towards its completion.

Like the husky, Felix has no place in the world where he can go, no place to which he belongs. There is nothing for him beyond himself except death which he lives with as his sole possession. He flees the Canadian winter and is immolated in Detroit–surely a nationalist statement. His murderers are casually shot by the grotesque Ritson who has emerged from the nightmare shadows of a society that Felix could not reach or touch. For Gibson, the natural world is an almost hallucinagenic setting where "All possibilities exist at the same time, in space like a tapestry."[9] But away from it, from Felix's ravine and the winter snow, there is chaos, anarchy. The external world is constant. Perceptions of it are ephemeral, amorphous, as in a dream, and as profoundly affecting.

What is probably the most famous fictional encounter with death in the Canadian winter appears, somewhat incongruously, in Morley Callaghan's *They Shall Inherit the Earth.* In a brief glimpse of nature, Callaghan perceives the moral design of the living universe: "the deer and the wolf have their place in the pattern, and they know justice when they conform to the pattern.. . .And there would be a justice for all things in terms of the things themselves."[10] He counterbalances the lurid slaughter of deer by wolves with the possibility of the frozen flesh providing sustenance for a she-wolf and her litter when spring comes and hunting is hard. The carcasses frozen stiff in the snow, preserved until the thaw, only their tenderloins torn away, represent the hard facts of self-preservation for the wolves and not merely wanton carnage. Callaghan describes the pattern:

> The sun had vanished from the sky and a vast shadow fell upon the earth, over the rocky ridges and the desolate bush, and over the frozen carcasses stuck in the snow; the snow was driven hard against their faces as they leaned into it, and it covered the deer paths, and fell on the wolves, and the lynx and the rabbit and the bear and the multiplicity of life that was preserved in the winter. The wolves had their time and their seasons, and the deer fled and fattened and died in their own time, too, and when the snow had gone and the warm weather came, their carcasses lay there and rotted, and carrion picked at them, and beasts that were hungry tore at the old bones, but still there was a little left for the she wolf and her litter.[11]

There is neither crime nor guilt in Callaghan's conception, his understanding, of the course of natural events. This is in sharp relief to the novel's predominating themes of remorse and absolution in the life of the protagonist, Michael Aikenhead. It is as if Callaghan is clearly establishing the vast spiritual gap between the world of nature and the world men have made for themselves.

In allowing their father to bear the blame for his step-brother's death, Michael dreadfully compounds his original crime of letting David drown. He tries to evade his moral responsibility through his love for Anna Prychoda, for he finds no surcease from his guilt in religion or cynicism or revolution. Ironically, Anna offers Michael a pattern of living that is the exact replica of the natural pattern he perceived in the winter drama of wolf and deer, but with the addition of a spiritual presence, of redeeming consciousness and the absolution of acceptance:

> She went on from day to day, living and loving and exposing the fulness and wholeness of herself to the life around her. If to be poor in spirit meant to be without false pride, to be humble enough to forget oneself, then she was poor in spirit, for she gave herself to everything that touched her, she lost herself in the fulness of the world, and in losing herself she found the world, and she possessed her own soul. People like her could have everything. They could inherit the earth.[12]

The novel's moral dynamics, as is often the case in Callaghan's novels, are not entirely sustained by its plot dynamics. Structurally, the story seems to drift downwards, in a drowning movement, to despair, and then surge in the end to the surface on a bubble of authorial conviction. Michael's debilitating moral evasions are precipitously resolved when his child is born and, asking his father's forgiveness, he once again becomes a son, a part of the pattern extending beyond himself.

David Canaan, in Ernest Buckler's *The Mountain and the Valley,* finally achieves a vantage point atop the mountain and sees the possibility of absolving those he loves, even the dead, of "all the hurts they gave themselves and each other,"[13] through the creative reconstruction of their lives, through writing. But the outcome of the confrontation of David's peculiar introspective genius with immutable reality is inevitable. Collapsing in the snow, he experiences "the blackness turned to grey and then to white: an absolute white, made of all the other colours but of no colour itself at all."[14] His life cannot sustain his vision which is too much a burden upon it. Together, life and vision fade:

> The snowflakes fell on David's face and caught in his eyelashes and melted. They caught in the strands of hair that escaped beneath his thrown-back cap and melted. They melted in the

> corners of his mouth. They clung to the wool of his jacket and the wool of his mittens without melting.
>
> And then they clung, without melting, to his eyelashes and his hair. And then they did not melt on his eyelids.. . .[15]

The transition is complete: animate becomes inanimate, the living becomes frozen in death, and the snow continues to fall. Nature is passive, the winding sheet that David wraps about his life.

In Robert Harlow's *Scann,* nature appears, by contrast, to be active, virulent, oppressive. But ultimately these are human characteristics, reflected in the harsh indifference of the natural world, reflecting the moral violence of Thrain and Linden's struggle against the frozen winter of their souls, the disfigurement and dismembering of their bodies. In this strange, brooding, powerful novel, the release offered by death in the frozen waste seems diabolically to be withheld from either of the two antagonists. Nature's only demand upon them is that they struggle. They cannot submit. Harlow is not manipulating an ominous bush-presence but only the lives of the men within it, to lay bare their moral anatomies. The wolverine, who embodies natural impulse, is determined to consume them, even when it is dead and is consuming Linden's dead flesh, not wilfully but with the inexorability of an unknowing force, an indifferent continuum beyond man's power to withstand or fully comprehend.

Rural interludes traditionally represent an awakening to consciousness of urban characters: Alexandre Chenevert in Gabrielle Roy's *The Cashier* when confronted by his boring, uninspired self at Lac Vert and Michael Aikenhead's impressions of natural justice while visiting his sister and her husband north of Toronto, are two notable examples. In neither case, however, is a corresponding moral awakening the immediate consequence of their rural experience. Both Roy and Callaghan save the completion of their moral visions until their closing pages. Human and geophysical realities do not converge. There is no reciprocity, no mutual illumination of complementary conditions. Instead, there is the residual effect of opposing conditions, where one acts as a spotlight on some particular aspect of the other.

The converse, moral deterioration of rural characters transposed to an urban scene, is not common in Canadian fiction. Surprisingly few have tried to exploit its possibilities–most notably, in English, Sinclair Ross's *Whir of Gold* and, in French, Roch Carrier's *Is It the Sun,*

Philibert? Neither of these novels is outstanding in respect to its vision of the inherent conflict in this type of displacement. Inevitably, Ross's Sonny and Mad are urban losers and Carrier's Philibert a hapless victim. But Ross cannot visualize the urban experience with anything approaching the same intensity that he evokes in the few brief fragments of Sonny's childhood on the Prairies. Both Sonny and Mad are merely pathetic; their common condition lacks the distinctiveness required to touch their plight with an element of tragedy. Carrier's Montreal is real enough, a tangible experience, but its effect is dissipated in a metaphysical superstructure that his vision of it cannot sustain. Philibert dies in a car crash where a spinning tire merges with his perception of the sun–too obvious, too contrived as an overlay upon the very ordinary experience of poor Philibert, adrift in the city.

For authenticity of external reality in closest conjunction with acute perceptions of the human condition, the Canadian imagination seems to demand a rural setting. Most of our urban novels make little attempt to envision their characters' environment as the correlative of their experience. Instead, as in the novels of Callaghan, MacLennan, Margaret Laurence's *The Fire-Dwellers,* or Wiseman's *The Sacrifice,* they exploit the narrative implications of the city without ever moving it into the foreground of their characters' lives. It is a convenient, often causative, setting. Hugh Garner's Toronto novels, *Cabbagetown* and *Silence on the Shore* in particular, and John Buell's Montreal novels, *Four Days,* for example, are, perhaps, exceptions. Garner's characters are inseparable from their experience of city life. Ken Tilling does not embody Cabbagetown but he is its product and, in many ways, its equivalent. The people in Mrs. Hill's rooming house are similarly shaped by their environment, their behaviour determined by the urban process. For Buell, the city breeds violence, discontent, and dreams of futile escape from the conditions it imposes on its inhabitants. The boy in *Four Days,* for example, is damned by the impress of the city ethic and the texture of city life. From the beginning, his rural sojourn, waiting for his brother who has been killed in a bank robbery, is doomed. But he has learned from the city that he can only wait and then die. He has no concept of continuity, nor of redemption, nor of the need for either.

Nature is seen by the Canadian writer to be without motive or ethic, the fundamental state of existence from which man continually attempts to insulate himself with social and religious conventions, with technological and political sophistication, with the accoutrements of cultural and material progress. Nature is at best a dumb witness of man's troubled movement away from its principles. Often, nature is the witless accomplice of man's fall from its indifferent grace. Occasionally, it is the implement of his self-destruction. If these possibilities are negative, it is because life at the level of man's intercourse with the natural world, where human and natural conditions converge, is profoundly tragic. Humans are cursed, and blessed, with the capacity to remember and to anticipate. In the natural world, both memory and anticipation hold tragedy foremost in the conscious mind.

Even when the natural world embodies innocence, as in Ethel Wilson's *Swamp Angel,* and *Hetty Dorval,* or in Bodsworth's novels, it is a tragic innocence. Wilson's image, in *Swamp Angel,* of the eagle and the osprey–the latter killing and the former stealing the kill–typifies her vision of a natural world, where justice is not in mercy but in survival, and beauty is in the capacity to endure. This is much the same, in concept, as the meaning Callaghan gives to the slaughter of deer by wolves in the snow. Tragic innocence is at the core of all of Bodsworth's novels. *The Last of the Curlews,* a bird book beside which *Jonathan Livingston Seagull* weighs as insubstantially, in my opinion, as Kahlil Gibran beside the writings of Saint Paul, traces the uncomprehending demise of a straggling member of a vanishing species. The curlew is innocent not because he does not understand his plight, however, but because he follows instinct with a trust that, ironically, leads to his destruction. Through the malevolent interference of man, who has shot his species from the air by the hundreds and hundreds of thousands, the curlew approaches extinction. His natural resources are inadequate to overcome the obstacles to breeding, to surviving, engendered by his decimation. Natural innocence in all of Bodsworth's novels is diametrically opposed to the acquired characteristics of civilized man. In this respect, Bodsworth's view is perversely romantic, were it not that such innocence is also available to man if only he would shed the unnatural ways of aggression and exploitation and the struggle to subjugate his own and all other species to his will, ways that he has taught himself for collective survival at the cost of personal freedom. Farley Mowat's writings of whales and wolves nurture a quite similar anthrophobia, not so much directed against man as at what he has made of himself. Both Mowat and Bodsworth, like Charles G.D. Roberts, Ernest Seton, and Grey Owl before them, perceive in the natural process an innocence that has nothing to do with specious Edens of human dreams. Natural innocence, rather, such as I believe each of these quite different writers conceives it to be, is for all of them a working process, a dynamic pattern, as Callaghan describes it, of integrated function and unified being.

It is not a moral state, no more than natural corruption–aging, death, decay–is a moral state. Both are conditions of existence. In the process of nature, neither life nor death is wasted, except in the eyes of the beholder; neither life nor death is astonishing, except in the eyes of the beholder. The possibility of perceiving joy or tragedy is contained by both.

The imminent presence of nature, in fiction where it is an authentic experience, provides the context for a moral vision without determining it. In other words, quite the contrary to a popular idea that the Canadian geography moulds moral precepts in our fiction and absorbs personality, its opposite, in my opinion, is true. The conditions of the Canadian geography reflect rather than determine moral vision, are informed by it while forming and not dissipating individual and collective personality. Obviously, the distinction is considerable. What I am suggesting is that Canadian fiction in which the geophysical presence is at the forefront of consciousness is essentially moral, that the vision of man in a natural world is a moral vision.

This is immediately apparent in the works which I have identified as exploiting the image of death in the snow. Clearly, *They Shall Inherit the Earth* uses the wilderness interlude to provide a key to the moral structure of the whole work, and to Michael Aikenhead's own moral dilemma. Godfrey's story concludes on a dissonant note such as one finds at the conclusion of fable, aesthetically jarring but morally instructive. With more subtlety, Grove defines a larger moral vision of mankind confronted by the cosmic machinery of his environment, while Ross so meticulously integrates landscape and personality that human events themselves assume cosmic proportion. Buckler's novel is intensely moral–psychological, as the author apparently claims, only in that it is interior–but it is not the psyche, not behavioural motivation, that Buckler explores and defines; it is the impact of events and the responses they stimulate, the judgments based upon them, that are the substance of the novel. *Scann* is a particularly moral conception of reality, more so in the wilderness segments, however grotesque, than in the hilariously obscene religio-political fantasy that is overtly more laden with metaphysics and meaning. Gibson's *Communion* grapples with principles of expiation through commitment, absolution through involvement, through communing with externals as readily as with the self, even when that communion is self-consuming. This, at least, would seem to be the moral basis of the major fragmented episode about freeing the husky to be destroyed in the snow, and of the eventual aftermath in which Felix is burnt to death in Detroit.

The vision of man in the natural world as a moral vision is most clearly evidenced in what is conventionally called the regional idyll. Ralph Connor's Glengarry novels, of which I find *The Man from Glengarry* to be the best as both literature and historical document, greatly simplify the pioneer past while displaying fidelity to what must be the author's own earliest memories of the Ottawa Valley. They provide a latitude for preachment amidst rousing entertainment which a less honest, more accurate, account would not sustain. Connor's Prairie novels even more clearly betray the identity, behind the pseudonym, of the Reverend Presbyterian, Charles William Gordon. Like Arthur Stringer's Prairie fiction, but with a more distinctly wholesome evangelical bias, Connor's offer a melodramatic and intensely sentimental transmutation of man's struggle amidst nature into the struggle within man between virtue and depravity. Stringer's cumbersome realism suggests that depravity or, at least, deprivation prevails. Connor, of course, idyllizes reality and virtue invariably triumphs.

Regional idylls as flimsy as Theodore Goodridge Roberts' *The Harbourmaster* or as rigid as Nellie McClung's autobiographical *Clearing in the West* or the first of her three Pearl Watson novels, *Sowing Seeds in Danny,* are at heart moral treatises. Roberts' novel of exploitation, intrigue, and improbable love in a Newfoundland outport has no more depth or subtlety than a contemporary comic strip and, like the comics, its self-righteous message is exuberantly clear and simple. This is no less than might be expected of a novel apparently conceived from the beginning as a colourful pot-boiler. McClung, by comparison, was a social activist. Her autobiographical writing is polemical rather than aesthetic, translating her childhood experience of the Prairies into fodder for the growth of social justice and self-righteousness. The Pearl Watson novels are blatantly moralistic, distorting life and the natural world to their rhetorical purpose.

The most famous of Canadian regional idylls, Lucy Maud Montgomery's *Anne of Green Gables,* integrates moral precepts with the story in a mixture of subtle delicacy and good-humoured bombast that makes it endearing even when it seems most self-satisfied. Whether, in fact, *Anne of Green Gables* is a regional idyll or not is open to question. It is indeed set thoroughly on Prince Edward Island–its setting is geographically and emotionally authentic, distorted often in Anne's imagination but never, in the objective reality of the novel, for the sake of extra-literary intent. The moral vision of Montgomery's book, such as it is, is not imposed upon the landscape as in the regional idylls mentioned above but, rather, is reflected in Anne's intimate relations with her rural island setting.

In contrast, the best-known of Canadian romances, the saga of the Whiteoaks of Jalna, is not usually thought to be a regional idyll but a good case could be made that it is. De la Roche displays an intimate understanding of authentic southern Ontario experience, that of the landed gentry who still perpetuate their own mythology, as did the Whiteoaks, in the Hunt Clubs and Horse Shows and rambling agricultural estates on the edges of Toronto and London. She writes with affectionate familiarity of the landscape on the northern shore of Lake Ontario west of the provincial capital. The woodlots and orchards and fine old homes around Clarkson, Ontario, as they grew out of the past and were slowly engulfed by suburbia, are detailed with a fine eye for their romantic implications, and these she exploits with a remarkable aptitude for meeting the demands of conventional contemporary taste. Her vision is idyllic, however, for its perception of authentic experience from a highly romantic perspective, rather than for the imposition of moral premises which her fiction, in any case, could not readily sustain.

Perhaps regional fiction may be called idyllic when parallel conditions between human life and the surrounding environment are exploited without being contextually integrated. When they are not aesthetically convergent, then art does not universalize. Fiction that remains local, parochial, in meaning as well as in subject-matter, tends to convey a moral vision that is over clear, often an embarrassing affectation. Such works I would include in the category of regional idyll.

The correspondence in Canadian fiction between the geophysical and human conditions is subject to the vagaries and red-herrings of what seems to me is critical irresponsibility with regard to the concept of regionalism. Just as the term "mosaic" insinuates its way into discussions of Canadian social patterns, "region" is the epithet most common to explorations of the natural world in Canadian experience. Exile is the cement that binds the mosaic together, and separates each fragment from the others. In exile there is the isolation of distance–from the homeland, from the past, from the surrounding presence. Regional isolation, however, is a matter of place, rather than distance. Like that of exile, it generates a dual vision in our fiction, but one which is primarily moral rather than social or sociological. The duality of this vision is born out of the resolution upon a single plane–like the adjusting of binocular cones to a single image–of authenticity and imminence. By that, I am referring to the convergence in our fiction of the natural world as an authentic condition of objective reality and as an imminent complement to the subjective conditions of human experience. Such a convergence is characteristic of the best of our regional literature–which, to a great extent, is our literature's best.

Canada is a vast landscape and the context of innumerable regions. Its geography and climate impose an isolation of place, of many places, upon the consciousness of its populace. They separate community from community, and link them together. The unrestrained immediacy and indifference of the landscape is a condition, as well, of individual experience that debilitates or exhilarates or sustains individual personality. The Canadian landscape provides the possibility for the creative imagination of a vision encompassing the widest diversity of behaviour set in the midst of the most compliant of optional settings.

Because there is only the barest imprint of civilization here and there in clusters across an expansive and imposing surface, regions in Canada are largely self-defining. They are uncertain measures of the human eye, which has not yet learned to perceive the nation whole, nor yet seen a vision of its own imposed upon it with any sort of ordering conviction. Tentatively, I would define a region as the dimensions of our response to the imminence of a particular landscape. In a country that displays such a diverse geography as Canada, there are bound to be many such responses, many and diverse regions. Each, in effect, is a pattern of consciousness, a focal pattern. To some extent, regions are determined by geophysical phenomena and the whims of historical necessity, but it is in the imminence, in the insistent presence, of their natural characteristics in human experience that they achieve definition. Each has a geography at once characteristic and continuous beyond its limits, a native history inseparable from the larger history of its national context, from the smaller ones within it. Regions are determined as much by point of view, by quality and breadth of vision, as by inherent or acquired characteristics of their own. Writers who focus on geophysical conditions in relation to the events of their characters' lives are regional, not because a particular region defines what they write, but because their writing defines a particular region.

I realize that such an observation is both self-evident and highly contentious. Perhaps this paradox can be resolved by considering the possibility that all fiction writers are, in one sense at least, regionalistic. A writer inevitably circumscribes reality in one way or another. He appropriates a region, as it were, from conscious experience and he works within its limitations, transmuting by creative force a segment of the objective world into a region of the creative mind. Hardy devised Wessex and Faulkner, Yoknapatawpha, not from their imaginations, but through their imaginations from the aspects of a continuous external world most appropriate to their separate visions. Proust similarly made a region of his memories; Kafka, of his dream-fears. Faulkner is a Southern novelist because the South is the lateral dimension he placed upon the scope of his imagination. Proust writes memories because the past is the actuality he perceived to be the most appropriate coefficient of his immediate perceptions. The past does not define Proust, but he, the remembrance of things past. Mississippi does not define Faulkner, but offers the materials for its definition as a unique and a universal experience. Both, and Hardy and Kafka as well, are regional writers, mapping out regions of the imagination that conform to designs implicit in external reality.

Regionalism is a response to the actual, where response and actuality are dual aspects of the same experience. In Canadian fiction, as for the most part elsewhere, it is usually a characteristic of works in which the human and geophysical worlds converge. A novel such as Charles Bruce's *The Channel Shore* merges the landscape with consciousness in a manner not unlike that of Thomas Hardy, although Hardy does so with resounding drama and Bruce with sensitive precision. In Sheila Watson's *The Double Hook,* the land is an interior experience, disembodied from a specific geography, yet specific, concrete, actual–providing the touchstones of a more cerebral universe. While the implicit aesthetic and moral aspirations of her novel are nothing like those of Kafka, there is a close similarity in their manner of merging animate and inanimate worlds, and of making the real unreal and the unreal real. *As For Me and My House*, by comparison, explores the confrontation, the collision, of two quite separate regions–one, the prairie setting, and the other, the Bentleys' conjugal psyche. With Proustian exploitation of detail and something of Proust's capacity to make impersonal factors–things, conditions, time–primary events in the human drama, Ross draws his characters and their environment together to a pitch of brooding intensity much as Proust manages to fuse past and present into a sustaining emotional balance of renewal and irretrievable loss. Ethel Wilson's *Swamp Angel* is regional in a quite different way. She uses the British Columbian interior as both metaphor and analgesic for Maggie's changing emotional state. In common with Faulkner, a writer whom she could not be more unlike in respect to prose style or metaphysics, she conceives the environment to be not only an imminent presence in her characters' lives but an extension of their lives as well. In Faulkner's world, this association is enervating, related to social and moral collapse. Wilson, however, sees in it a more positive effect–an alternative to destructive social conventions, the resolution of the conflicting moral responsibilities to the past and the present. *The Nymph and the Lamp*, different again, projects the intense isolation of Marina (Sable Island) into the lives of its characters, and exploits the intimacy between man and nature in terms of the common conditions each imposes upon the other. In Raddall's conception, man places demands upon his environment as surely as it imposes its own on him. This correlation implies something of Hardy in terms of the pathetic fallacy that it narrowly avoids and in the powerful shape it gives to the novel's moral universe, but it is more akin to the romantic determinism of William Faulkner in the extent to which the characters submit to its effect on their lives. In any case, each of these writers, Canadian and foreign, is a regional writer in terms of the authenticity of his vision, the imminence of the reality perceived.

In the five Canadian novels to be discussed, which I believe are among the best of our regional fiction, imminence and authenticity of the geophysical presence are inseparable from the isolation of individual experience and that of the community. I do not, however, mean to suggest that the moral visions implicit in these novels are conceived by conscious design. Rather, they are shaped by the patterns of converging realities. *The Nymph and the Lamp* and *Swamp Angel, As For Me and My House, The Double Hook* and *The Channel Shore,* from different perspectives, indicate the impact on the Canadian imagination of our geophysical context. With the observations I have made about the nature of this impact in mind, it seems to me that critical analysis within the implicit perimeters of each might reveal much about the Canadian experience and about the novels themselves. My intention is not to offer definitive interpretations but rather to identify the particular patterns in each work which are apparently generated by what might be called the geophysical imagination.

Notes

1. Sinclair Ross, *As For Me and My House* (Toronto: New Canadian Library,.1969), p.80. (New York: Reynal, 1941.)
2. Frederick Philip Grove, "Snow," in *Canadian Short Stories,* ed. Robert Weaver (Toronto: Oxford, 1970), p.61.
3. *Ibid.,* p.60.
4. Sinclair Ross, "The Painted Door," in *The Lamp at Noon and Other Stories* (Toronto: New Canadian Library, 1968), p.100.
5. *Ibid.,* p. 100.
6. *Ibid.,* p.115.
7. Dave Godfrey, "The Winter Stiffs," in *Death Goes Better with Coca-Cola* (Toronto: Anansi, 1967), p.23.
8. Sheila Watson, *The Double Hook* (Toronto: New Canadian Library, 1969), p.53. (Toronto: McClelland & Stewart, 1959.)
9. Graeme Gibson, *Communion* (Toronto: Anansi, 1971), p.66.
10. Morley Callaghan, *They Shall Inherit the Earth* (Toronto: New Canadian Library, 1969), p.197. (Toronto: Macmillan, 1935.)
11. *Ibid.,* p.197.
12. *Ibid.,* p.242.
13. Ernest Buckler, *The Mountain and the Valley* (Toronto: New Canadian Library, 1969), p.300. (New York: Holt, 1952.)
14. *Ibid.,* p.300.
15. *Ibid.,* p.301.

1.
The Nymph and the Lamp and *Swamp Angel*

The main body of *The Nymph and the Lamp* is set on an island off the coast of Nova Scotia, called Marina, but presumably the replica of Sable Island where Raddall spent some time, like Matthew Carney, as a wireless operator. It is remote, austere, the appropriate context for a story of love and self-discovery emerging into consciousness, residual effects of behaviour engendered by the conditions of individual being. From the extreme opposite side of the continent, Ethel Wilson begins Maggie Lloyd's quest, in *Swamp Angel,* into the interior of a vast land mass and of her solitary state. Life on Raddall's Marina is continuous with the rest of humanity, as suggested by the wireless and lifeboat operations, but intensified, penetrated by the haunting solitude, and shaped by the surrounding elements. In Maggie's environment at Three Loon Lake, human identity is obscured and its integrity dissipated by the surrounding wilderness, so long as the external world is perceived as a refuge from reality rather than reality itself, continuous with the rest of experience. The essential link between the interior and the outside is evident in Maggie's ultimate reconciliation with the ghosts of her distant past. It is apparent in her correspondence with Nell Severance, and her eventual service *vis à vis* the swamp angel, as well as in the presence at the lake of the Chinese boy, the brother of the unabashedly urban cabbie who helped her escape. Neither interior nor island are the contexts of separate realities. Yet they are remarkably accommodating to the separate visions that these novels convey. Both Raddall and Wilson exploit the characteristics of remote settings to evoke the universality of individual experience, and to circumscribe its uniqueness.

The structure of Raddall's novel insists that Isabel Jardine is the major protagonist, although she is not presented until the novel is well under way. Emerging from obscurity in Halifax, she is forced to recognize the dimensions of her personality on Marina, and is reconciled to them in the valley town of Kingsbridge or, rather, in her solitary retreat outside the community. Inevitably, she returns, whole, to Marina. Maggie, too, becomes whole, but in a quite different way. For her there is no revelation, as there is for Isabel. There is only the gradual accumulation of insight. She, too, was stifled by life in an urban environment–in this case, Vancouver–but her journey into the natural world, initially at least, represents escape into anonymity, into the solace of oblivion, rather than into identity. Only after she comes to terms with herself, under the influence of examples from nature, do body and soul or, in the terms of the novel, substance and essence, converge into a whole personality that she can comfortably live with. While Isabel moves from a known world into an entirely alien environment, then back to her source in the Annapolis Valley, and again to the alien, newly perceived as beneficent, Maggie travels in a single geographical direction from centre of despair to expiating circumference in surroundings such as she knew through childhood. For each, however, the chapel perilous is contained by solitude and the insistent presence of the natural world. Their internal wastelands are restored by their errant quests into external reality.

This is not to suggest that their lives are redeemed solely by natural influence. Maggie becomes entangled in the Gunnarsen's lives. Only as she takes the initiative to extricate herself is she freed to serve their mutual needs. Their interdependence has been enervating for all concerned, but the strength she gathers from the wilderness, the insight and compassion, directs them all onto a more constructive course. Self-reliance ultimately serves communal stability. In a similar pattern, when Isabel returns to Marina it is with a determination to serve the island's resident community as well as to devote herself to Carney. Through her previous stay she had been continually annoyed by the islanders' apparent obsession with finding "something to do." Now she perceives their predatory, acquisitive or frivolous pursuits as armaments against their extreme isolation, indicative as much of defiance as of moral deterioration. Equally defiant, she returns with the promise of materials to start a school. She comprehends the necessity, for survival, of having something to do.

Picking up the metaphor of the fisher-king, if the geophysical contexts of the novels are the chapels perilous, then the old man in each is the threatening visionary, offering temptations of riches and refuge.

After tending old Mr. Cunningham as he recovers from near demise, Maggie is invited to manage his private lodge as a munificent reward. Isabel is confronted by a similar enticement from Mr. Markham, the superannuated entrepreneur in Kingsbridge whom she serves with alarming efficiency. The difference is that Isabel is freed of responsibility to Markham by his financial ruin; Maggie acquires a renewed sense of responsibility in her rejection of Cunningham's offer. The effect, however, is much the same. Cunningham's proposition would place Maggie in bondage within her beloved wilderness. Markham's promise of worldly security proves to be precariously founded on potential bankruptcy. Both old men provide a spiritual limbo of sorts which could be soul destroying. But they are both rejected as impotent old men offering sterile salvation, as objects of compassion and unacceptable alternatives. Maggie and Isabel choose the courses of responsible sacrifice–Maggie to be a lamp for Carney's blindness; Isabel to participate in a sustaining relationship with the Gunnarsens at Three Loon Lake.

In *Swamp Angel,* as in *The Nymph and the Lamp,* people are important to the self-determining perceptions of the main protagonists, although the natural environment is contiguous with their relationships. Nowhere is this more apparent than at the most intimate level of human intercourse, the sexual, which is described by Wilson as well as by Raddall in sharp relief to the geophysical setting, yet in harmony with its often ambivalent imminence.

Isabel Jardine is an incipient spinster of twenty-nine, taunted by the memory of a chorus-girl stripped naked in the hallway of Mrs. Paradee's boarding house and arrested for sportive indecency. Sometimes her impressions of the event would turn "to nightmares in which Miss Jardine herself stood naked on the stairs.. . .At such times she awoke in a clammy stupor, groping feverishly for things to say or do in this frightful situation and wishing to die."[1] When such an unlikely event actually does occur, she responds "with a cunning quite foreign to her natural self, in fact in outrage to her virginal instincts."[2] She turns for solace to Matt Carney, himself a virgin of forty-six. The cumbersome course of their ensuing sexual relationship precipitates much of the strain between them and many of the complications of their union. What it does not cause, it highlights. Yet the fact that it is a confused and unhappy relationship is due in no small part to their external surroundings. The hotel, the violent sea, the oppressive isolation of

Marina, the sand dunes, the storms, the awesome weather, each helps to shape their responses towards each other, towards themselves.

For Maggie Lloyd, sexuality is at once less intensely perverse and more innocently deviant than for Isabel. Deserting her second husband, Edward Vardoe, for the interior, she discovers there that the "tormented nights of humiliation between four small walls and in the compass of a double bed were gone, washed away by this air, this freedom, this joy, this singleness and forgetfulness."[3] Maggie exchanges the indignities of her marital bed for self-reliant union with the natural world and the sufferings and joys it engenders. She sublimates in the immediacy of the external present the longings that were satisfied only in the irretrievable past. The sterility of her relationship with Vardoe is replaced by more fruitful communion found through solitude.

Maggie lost her little girl, Molly, to polio and her regenerative instincts have atrophied, although the maternal necessity continues to haunt her. She lost her beloved first husband, Tom Lloyd, in the War and sexual relations with Vardoe are an abrasive to her memories, although she still craves communion beyond words or understanding. Given these conditions, it is inevitable that her relationship with Vardoe, who is unimaginative and demanding, would extinguish the possibility of her reconciliation with the conventional role of wife, mother, subservient and submissive woman. She flees to the more promising fulfilment offered by her role as *major-domo* of the lodge at Three Loon Lake, in the heart of the regenerative wilderness, where communion is with no man but with the entirety of existence.

Sexuality is somewhat more explicit in *The Nymph and the Lamp* and less the universal equivalent of the relation between all things. It does not invite the Freudian fallacy of imposing extra-contextual sexual schemes such as might be sustained by MacLennan's novels with their allusions to multiple father-figures and the ambiguous identities of lovers and sons, or by Laurence's with the analytic sexual ruminations of Rachel or Stacey or even Hagar. Nevertheless, Raddall's novel is overtly structured to conform with the evolving sexual relations of its characters. These, however, are explicitly accounted for within context, growing out of personalities in relation to external conditions. Matthew's virginity and sexual naiveté are simply explained: "as the years and the voyages rolled by Carney had withdrawn into himself, too clean to wallow, too bashful and too proud to beg, until at last he had a shell that nothing could break down."[4] Isabel, more conventionally, lost her only lover to the War and another woman, and has attracted no other, until Carney. Gregory Skane, the third side of their triangle, is somewhat of a brooding satyr whom tragedy has set adrift for solace on Marina's barren waste. Their formative backgrounds, however, are relatively unimportant to the intensity and the complexity of their interpersonal relations, which seem to a more considerable extent to be determined by the conditions of their environment.

The Nymph and the Lamp is a story of love, rather than a love story. The austerity of Marina and its continuity with the outside world, its immediacy as both graveyard and beacon, give the assurance that this is no Prospero's isle of ethereal delights, but the context of fundamental human experience. That experience is conceived primarily in terms of love and sexuality. Out of its imperious complexity, an aging young woman comes into fullness of consciousness, the mark and the reward of maturity. Isabel Jardine is both the nymph of the title and the lamp. As she emerges from blindness herself, of a moral nature, she is impelled to bring light to the darkness that is closing around Carney, her vision giving sanction to their renewed relations. She is the figurehead nymph, Clélie, in the photograph of Skane and Carney beside the wreck of a French barque. Skane identifies the figurehead with Mademoiselle de Scudéry's heroine caught in the flowing "River of Inclination."[5] But later, after she has left Marina, Isabel sees "herself in Clélie's place between the two men, with Skane's face turned to hers in a whimsical smile and Matthew squinting against the sun."[6] The photograph is an appropriate emblem of the situation into which their mutual inclinations carried them. But Isabel grows from her experience and becomes a different sort of nymph, more in keeping with Carney's appearance on her return akin to "those Norse kings, right out of the Heinskringla!"[7] In Norse mythology, a nymph "shaped in the image of the woman he'd most desired on earth"[8] awaited the drowned sailor in the caves at the ocean's floor. Such is Isabel's role in saving Carney from the terrors, the indignities, of oblivion as blindness encroaches, and as his telegraphist function becomes historically redundant, and Marina threatens to close around him like the walls of a cave.

The novel moves towards Isabel's achievement of these roles rather than to the culmination or climax of her affair with Carney. She is introduced as a nondescript character impinging mildly on Carney's life–a plain office-girl who attracts him on his first shore-leave in a decade. By the novel's end, she is a powerful and engaging presence whose behaviour is endorsed by a sense of the inexorable, while Matthew has been faded out until he is merely the spectral object of her discovered capacity to live. As a love story, the structure of the novel is precarious. But as the story of a woman emerging into identity, it is flawlessly conceived.

Isabel has been alone much of her life, in her childhood near Kingsbridge and then in Halifax. On the wastes of Marina she is drawn into a community for whom assimilation with setting has meant apparent moral sterility, spiritual aridity. Visiting the quarters of the lifeboat crew, she ruminates–on the verge of insight but still carrying the burden of reticence, of her isolated past.

> There was something about them, something that made her skin feel strange as if she stood unclothed in a hot wind off the sands. As she turned to leave it came to her that the crew house was a little monastery, and she had come into their seclusion, a strange young woman, presumably desirable, and had brought them an awareness of the great lack in their lives. The next thought amused her. She had a vision of Miss Benson. It was a situation that Miss Benson would have loved. But her final reflection was a sober one. All these men, even Matthew and Skane and that shy boy Sargent, were castaways really, condemned to a womanless existence in terms of the most deadly monotony; and this sexual and mental starvation gave them their callous attitude toward all other life (and death) about them, and created the eternal need for "something to do." She seemed to hear the echo of Matthew's voice in that phrase she so detested on the lips of McBain. And again she had that uncomfortable notion of herself as the Eve who had robbed Carney of his innocence, the innocence that alone had made this solitude endurable.[9]

In this passage, if any one passage can be singled out, is the key to Isabel Jardine, to the action and the vision of which she is at the centre. In the transposition of her maidenly fantasy at Mrs. Paradee's to the midst of this masculine world, she is titillated, but racked with guilt. She dissociates herself from the former, identifying it with the coquettish Miss Benson back in Halifax. The guilt, at feeling that she has stirred up lust that they have learned to live with, she bears herself. In her conception, Marina is a place of innocence, particularly for Carney. She has disrupted that state–which exists, of course, more in her mind than in fact. She determines to make amends, beginning by inviting Carney back to her bed. Her misunderstanding of the men's attitudes towards living and death–thinking their apparent indifference is the result of moral atrophy rather than the means by which they combat an austere environment and, for Carney, at least, a moral triumph of sorts–imposes on them all the burden of innocence that her relations with them cannot support. Calamity follows and continues to follow, but she has begun the transition into a world of larger consciousness. When eventually she realizes the imperfectability, the frailty, of Matthew and of Skane, and has learned that evasion of her sexuality, or guilt because of it, or escape within it are all equally divisive, the transition is complete. It is a self-reliant, self-determining woman who returns to Marina; knowing herself fully and no longer alone.

At the time of her visit to the lifeboat crew she had already begun to regret keeping Carney from her bed: "Time and again in the small hours, weary, the prey of longings insistent like hunger that melted away her resolution and all thought of pride,"[10] she yearned for him to come to her. The "cold indignation" that was the residue of their disastrous night at sea fades with her recognition that she has created a need that only she can satisfy.[11] In an uncanny coincidence of sexuality and natural imagery, she draws him to her:

> In an April storm of tears and kisses he carried her to the bed. Outside, the gale blew on. The building shook; it seemed to blench before the stronger gusts, and the keening in the arials rose to a witches chorus as if all the ghosts of Marina had found voice about the mast. It was a fit night for passion. Within the walls, in the warm dark of the bedroom, their own storm rose and fell, renewed itself in sleep, and wakened to new gusts and further calms.[12]

Isabel conceives of herself as Eve who, having taken Carney's innocence from him, offers herself as compensation. Their only other sexual encounter, in the Halifax hotel, had resulted in both shame and ecstasy–"She wondered if this bearded Adam would reproach her as she now reproached her own quenched and lazy flesh."[13] She clearly perceived her body as a thing apart from herself and this distortion allowed both remorse and joy to dissipate. She overrules her guilt and decides to use Carney as an escape from all the forces of her age and sex and situation which are threatening her. Inevitably, she sees Carney, and all the men of her refuge on Marina, as innocents. The humiliation of her body aboard the *Lord Elgin,* when from beguiling nymph she becomes a wretchedly pathetic seasick derelict, collapses her resolve to give Carney his due, to uphold her end of their mutual quest for escape from the rigours of loneliness. They had not been married by law and, as if this were her cue, she withholds herself, body and soul, from Carney's affections. However, while visiting the crew's quarters with McBain she realizes her rejection of responsibility in having disrupted the tenuous constructs by which the islanders endure reality and draws solace from it. Discovering this is a joyous but short-lived release of herself into their community, into sexual communion with Carney.

Isabel remains blind to the complexities of moral responsibility. Her assumptions of their innocence cannot be sustained, for, in making no demands on the others, she makes no allowances for their frailties. She accepts the onslaught of winter as a personal affront, a reproach for her inadequacy. As a consequence of her inability to see the reciprocity of human relations, she inspires no confidence in Matthew to share the secret of his impending blindness. Responsive to her as always, he turns away from her and wraps himself in mystery:

> Even as a lover he had been swayed and governed always by her own impulses; and if now, in the strange aloofness that had come upon him with the onset of winter, he seemed less of a lover and more of a recluse, she knew that sexually at least she had become as withdrawn as he. After that ecstacy in the autumn their passion had drifted into a sort of hibernation, as if it were subject to the weather like everything else on Marina.[14]

She has not yet the insight to impose her own understanding upon their relationship, and it withers. She turns to Skane, presupposing in him the universal innocence she has perceived amongst all of them. With Matthew, her expectations had not been met. But with Skane, they are perversely, disastrously satisfied.

From the first time she sees Gregory Skane, Isabel is intensely aware of him as a man. His projected virility is an irritating threat to her moral complacency, to the sexual repression by which her arid life has been recently shaped. Skane is a dark and brooding and ubiquitous presence in Isabel's life on Marina. He is inseparable from Carney and, indeed, is jealous of her displacement of him in Carney's intimate world. He offers enticement for her as an alternative to Matthew, taking an interest in her isolated condition, teaching her the secrets of telegraphy, of a specialized disembodied type of communication. He displays to her, in his musical accomplishment, another kind of communication, one on an ethereal plane from which Carney is necessarily excluded. Gradually, he insinuates himself into her loneliness and ultimately offers her intercourse on a more basic level. But in their sexual relations, as with telegraphy and music, communion is restricted only to the dimension of its accomplishment. Skane's innocence, of course, is purely an illusion, as Isabel finally discovers at Kingsbridge where he is revealed as crass and somewhat bland, typical of the outside world.

In the winter of her sexual-spiritual discontent, after Matthew has turned away from her, Isabel feels herself more and more the victim of primal forces around her, "a primitive creature in a lost corner of the world, the prey of phantoms, a prisoner of the weather and the sea–and of the dark."[15] Unable, in her moral blindness, to rise above these isolating pressures, she attempts to compensate with surcease sought at the same level of reality. She is possessed by fantasy-memories of Skane naked at the pump as she had seen him, unobserved, at work on a hot September night. With the coming of spring, she submits to him in fact:

> Her one conscious thought was that the long frustration of the winter months had led in some mysterious way to this encounter and this moment, and now that it had come to crisis she might find relief.. . .There came a moment when she felt the sun's warmth on her thighs and then she was caught up in Skane's passion and her own wild longing for oblivion.[16]

Bodily relief without spiritual communion is divisive, however, and the abuse of her sexuality as a channel of escape is bound to bring ruin. With appropriate irony, she is wounded by a juvenile rival for Skane's affections, and forced to leave Marina, and leave Matthew, with her illusions of innocence shattered and her loneliness still intact. But she has gained the essential strength of character, seen body and soul pathetically reintegrated into a unified being, and learned to live with herself–the precondition, in Raddall's vision, of living with another.

Isabel makes love with Skane on the warm spring sands of Marina after a cold and brutal winter. On her voyage there she had been turned from sex by the violence of nature, and when their love brought her together again for a time with Carney, the renewal of their passion is marked by the elements storming around them. Raddall clearly weds the natural world with the sexual and corresponding emotional and moral development of his novel. When Isabel leaves Marina and insulates herself from the realities of moral responsibility at Kingsbridge, she becomes obsessively absorbed in the commercial aspects of her work as Markham's secretary, in responsibilities clearly defined. But periodically, she slips away from Kingsbridge to a small private place–long grass, alders, and a rushing stream in the wilderness–to be alone with herself in a larger world. There she strips naked to soak in the sun and cure the wounds of her love and dishonour. It is there that Skane reveals to her the mystery of Carney's approaching blindness that had come between them, and drawn her to Skane. In this setting, where the natural and commercial realities are contained one within the other, she sees her brooding lover in a different light, "no more like the shabby and savage Skane of Marina than this torrent in the woods resembled the quiet pool amongst the dunes" beside which they had made love.[17] Just as the forest clearing and its running waters are a refuge from reality, so Skane had been for Isabel on Marina. And as she is impelled to turn away from Skane, when he is seen as continuous with all that has oppressed her in contemporary society, she is drawn back to Marina, not as an escape from herself, this time, but as a world continuous with the whole of her experience.

Her immersion in the commercial life of the valley community and the small place of her escape from it, both are revealed as no more than diversions from the central moral dilemma of her life. Innocence, human frailty, and responsibility converge in her vision as concomitant conditions of joyous being and she returns to Carney, to the possibility of love. Isabel travels the full course of a moral quest. The landscape and the elements have been more than a setting. They have provided the external conditions of her journey towards personal completeness, towards acceptance of herself as a unified being in relation to others and the world around her.

Ethel Wilson places Maggie at the centre of a more integrated vision; one which does not grow with the changing circumstances and changing environment, but is gradually revealed as a whole, implicit in external reality. As Edward Vardoe's wife, Maggie sees the natural world through the front room window of their house at the edge of Vancouver. It is an ephemeral world, passing her by on the periphery of experience like the brown birds that fly past and out of sight in the opening sentence of the novel. Nature, in Maggie's cloistered experience, seems no more than a function of time, the measure of her excruciating endurance of Vardoe. She determines to escape "the night's hateful assaults and the day's wakings in a passing of time where daily and nightly repetition marked no passing of time."[18] The vision of the novel becomes clear in the course of her retreat, her quest into the nature of being, her discovery of herself.

Tasting the first of her freedom on the banks of the Similkameen River, she begins to perceive the intimations of change:

> Something had happened, she thought as she lay there, to her sense of smell. It had become vitiated. But now her breath drank and drank again the scent of firs and pines and juniper. Time dissolved, and space dissolved, and she smelt again the pinewoods of New Brunswick, one with these woods, a continent away, and she was all but a child again. No, she was nothing. No thought, no memories occupied her. The clouds, that drifted across the blue, drifted through her mind as she lay idle.[19]

Away from Vardoe, with Vancouver and the Pacific Ocean "disproportionately remote,"[20] her identity is almost immediately immersed in the natural world. Sexuality is no longer a humiliating threat and time is a dimension, a context, of living. The transformation is detailed in the description of her fishing the Similkameen before moving on, deeper, to the interior past Kamloops:

> Maggie continued to cast. In the pleasure of casting over this lovely stream she forgot–as always when she was fishing–her own existence. Suddenly came a strike, and the line ran out, there was a quick radiance and splashing above the water downstream. At the moment of the strike, Maggie became a co-ordinating creature of wrists and fingers and reel and rod and line and tension and the small trout, leaping, darting, leaping. She landed the fish,

> took out the hook, slipped in her thumb, broke back the small neck, and the leaping rainbow thing was dead. A thought as thin and cruel as a pipe fish cut through her mind. The pipe fish slid through and away. It would return.[21]

Making flies to sell at Thorpe and Spencer's for other fishermen brought her the price of physical escape. Inevitably, fishing, for Maggie, represents integration with the natural world. But, as the passage just quoted suggests, she is to be haunted for some time yet by a "thin and cruel" thought.

In deserting Vardoe, she has escaped the humiliation of his sexual aggression. He remains with her, however, as a coarse intruder amidst the bitter-sweet memories of her first husband, Tom Lloyd, and their daughter, Molly, both of whom are dead, and of her dead father, as well. In avoiding the brutality of passing time as manifest in her life with Vardoe, she avoids the essential confrontation with change and death that alone can lead to acceptance, to a reconciliation with the past, rather than merely to sustained resignation. Before Maggie Lloyd can be at peace, she must learn first to accept both herself as a woman, life-giving and compassionate, and as a changing, growing, dying thing.

Maggie's flight to the interior is a journey into substance, from being a picture-window voyeur, vestigial to the natural world, to being a part of it. Like the sedentary Nell Severance, who as a young woman gave herself wholly to the passionate embrace of her husband and, fifty years later, lives more confortably with her memories of their love than with Hilda, their daughter, Maggie's emotions are restrained, distorted, although her commitments are strong and, in contrast, humane. To those whom she has irretrievably lost, who no longer have substance, she remains devoted. She nurtures not only the memories of her husband and father and daughter but the conditions of emotional reticence their deaths have imposed upon her. As she becomes immersed in the actual world she is unable to cope as an individual with the immediacy of her past and must merge her identity with nature and with the pursuits of others. The Gunnarsen's lodge at Three Loon Lake provides the ideal refuge. There, she can be committed to others without suffering reciprocation, and the emotions whose human objects have gone from her can be exercised without fears such as Vardoe aroused and the sedentary life in Vancouver sustained–both, at the price of annihiliation of self.

Swamp Angel is not a novel of flight but of discovery. Its moral complexity arises from the journey into consciousness which continues for Maggie long after she has arrived at the Lake. As she gradually regains her identity through the conditions and examples of her natural environment, the counterpoised story of the Severances reveals the meaning of her clarified vision. Nell Severance is a wilful and rather cranky old woman, a former juggler gone to fat, who shows penetrating insight into the souls of others, and a lust for life that only death or loss of pride can extinguish. She can manipulate people but her understanding of them is more intuitive than rational. She has no idea, for example, of the suffering she has caused her daughter Hilda, and yet she fully recognizes the ambivalence of her daughter's feelings towards her. She has a great heart, it might be said, in that she commands Vardoe to abjure his consuming self-pity; in that she releases Hilda from the bonds of vengeance and guilt, affection and distaste, by which they are held together; in that both Alberto and Albert are her emotional beneficiaries; and Maggie, who, she says, has not the gift of the "wholly feminine joys of communication, the déshabillé of conversation,"[22] she has made her confidante. But Nell Severance is motivated by pride and the love of power. She offers Vardoe "salvation." She determines the course of her daughter's escape from their mutual bondage and the course of Edward's marital destiny. She relishes Alberto's flamboyant funeral rites. Only Maggie is above her contempt and only while she holds her emotions in reserve, for when Maggie chooses the Gunnarsens over Mr. Cunningham's munificent offer, she too bears the scorn of Nell Severance.[23]

The swamp angel, the pearl-handled revolver that had been part of Nell's juggling act, is her perfect objective equivalent. It is a symbol to her of the living past. When she realizes the imminence of her death, she discards it. It is a symbol, too, of the tremendous barriers between Nell and Hilda and, with it discarded–the barriers acknowledged–Hilda is set upon the course of her own life. It is to Maggie that Nell sends the angel for keeping until she dies, when it is to be thrown into the lake and oblivion. Nell wants it to be spared the indignities of indifferent ownership. Even when she relinquishes it, she wants assurance that its disposition is not ignominious, as a derelict curiosity such as she has become. Maggie recognizes the significance of the act, and, even when Nell relents and asks for it back, she insists on honouring the original behest. In this, Wilson makes the revolver a symbol of her larger vision, beyond the understanding of her characters. To Maggie, it is a symbol of Nell Severance's submission to her own humanity, but it is, in effect, also a symbol of Maggie's deliberate acceptance of life and death, angel and swamp, as complementary conditions of being. The revolver does not generate insight. Rather, its narrative function is to reveal the metaphysical similarity between Nell and Maggie, to act as a bond between them essential to the articulation of the moral vision which they inhabit.

Before trying to abstract that vision from its context, it seems to me critically necessary to draw attention back to what I have described as Maggie's journey of discovery into a full and mature consciousness. Maggie is, on this journey, a representative being. But she is also highly individual, and a woman. Whereas Isabel Jardine's achievement as a woman is the consummation of love (her creator is male, of course, but the implications of this will, with critical discretion, be disregarded), Maggie's triumph is in learning to live with the profound solitude of metaphysical self-reliance and responsible interdependence with other people. Her progress is impeded, however, by the continuing frustrations of being a woman whose feminine instincts, as Wilson perceives them, have been abused by the cruelest circumstances of death and a precipitous escape from the isolation it imposed on her. In marrying Vardoe she only became further isolated–from others and the outside world and, most of all, from herself. On leaving Vardoe, she is haunted by the memories of his nocturnal demands. Children who enter her experience, whether casually like the little girl of the bus, or intimately, like Alan Gunnarsen, stir ambivalent feelings of bitterness and affection.

Others respond to Maggie as a sexual being. Joey, the young Chinese-Canadian taxi driver appeals to her with his "swagger, a downtown arrogance in his movements,"[24] and he later confides his suspicion of her designs on him to his family. Despite Maggie's asexual pursuit of oblivion, others respond to her very much as a woman and she, as she increasingly comes to know herself, responds to them as a woman. While Gunnarsen first sees her as "strong and plain and sensible.. . .Vera Gunnarsen had a feeling that the woman was beautiful" and a potential rival.[25] Within minutes of their meeting, Haldar, too, is stirred by her femininity; a condition that continues through much of their relationship, mistaken by Vera for a sexual rather than a maternal attraction. Even old Mr. Cunningham, rescued from the brink of death, rhapsodizes to himself about her "bountiful figure" as well as her goodness.[26] A young city-man from Chinatown, a proud cripple, and a lonely old man–none of them can possibly supplant the pervasive memory of her beloved first husband, just as no child can take Molly's place in her life. The author's imperative, then, is that Maggie must learn to accept her loss and her lack without self-extinction, without committing herself to nonentity, in the attempt.

Once she has arrived at the place of her interior journey, at Three Loon Lake, the process of Maggie's education begins in earnest. It explicitly derives from her response to the natural world and is developed, by Mrs. Wilson, on two distinct levels. On the one hand is the growing recognition by Maggie of the complementary relations between man and nature, and, on the other, are the intimations of a dichotomy between actuality and essence, substance and its meaning or residual effect. Ultimately, through the convergence of both levels or dimensions in Maggie's experience, there is a resolution of the novel's metaphysical complexity. Unlike *The Nymph and the Lamp,* Wilson's vision does not resolve narrative complexity, determining the novel's ultimate structure. Instead, it arises out of the narrative, the result of its structure. Raddall gives Isabel the moral insight of his fiction and shows its effects upon her character and actions as it gradually takes shape and then springs into consciousness. Wilson speaks more directly to the reader, exposing the moral vision of her novel in the whole of her protagonist's cumulative experience.

Maggie Lloyd's is not a moral drama, like Isabel's, but a quest with moral dimensions. As I have suggested, its progress occurs on two distinct levels. On the level of metaphysical awareness–and that is not so pretentious a phrase as it might at first seem–Wilson introduces her concepts of the appearance and reality dichotomy quite impersonally:

> A first meeting. A meeting in the desert, a meeting at sea, meeting in the city, meeting at night, meeting at a grave, meeting in the sunshine beside the forest, beside water. Human beings meet, yet the meetings are not the same. Meeting partakes in its very essence not only of the persons but of the place of meeting. And that essence of place remains, and colours, faintly, the association, perhaps for ever.[27]

Essence is the residual experience of physical and emotional factors melded inextricably together. When Maggie applauds Nell's parting with the angel, she offers the consolation that "our ability to throw away the substance, to lose all yet keep the essence is very important."[28] As she assimilates this knowledge, applying it haphazardly, for example, to her English earthenware that "assumed a living entity which even its destruction would not destroy,"[29] Maggie learns to cope with her ghosts. Her final act in the novel, appropriately in this context, is to throw the revolver into the lake. As she does so, she wonders about the nature of memories and the death of things: "Does the essence of all custom and virtue perish?"[30] Her knowledge is tentative. There has been no epiphany for Maggie Lloyd. She has learned to accept and has perceived in the essence of the past a justification for approaching the future with confidence.

Maggie displayed moral courage in leaving Vardoe but it is the quiet strength which continues to sustain her that is most important to her psychological survival and moral growth. First of all, she endures. That in itself is important. Like the swimmer in her favourite analogy for life, she is submerged in the elements and when obstacles appear she swims around them. When she does go swimming, in actuality, she senses that out there in the water she is merged with the creature world and divinity, moving like a woman who is both seal and god. The choice for Maggie, then, is between immersion as part of the chain of being in an element that "If she could not swim, ah. . .then. . .it would no doubt kill her and think nothing of it,"[31] and removal to the dry land, to be isolated from the rest of creation. Maggie has chosen, in deserting Vardoe, to be a swimmer, and she endures. Gradually, she comes to realize that the water in which she swims is an indifferent host to the process of her life or to death.

In one of the finest and most famous descriptions of the natural process, which is the closest thing Maggie experiences to epiphany, Mrs. Wilson offers the episode of the osprey and the eagle. After the osprey lifted his quarry, the fish, into the air, "From invisibility came the eagle," which, beating its wings, forced the osprey to drop its prey–

> Down swooped the eagle. He caught the fish in mid-air and rose. His wings beat slowly and calmly, all crisis over. Maggie looked for the osprey, but the sky was empty. Did a bird's rage or a bird's acceptance possess him? There was nothing he could do. The

> eagle disappeared into the blue which at the horizon was veil-like, mist-like, carrying the fish, pontoon-wise. Maggie returned to her reality.[32]

The keynote of this short episode is that "there was nothing he could do." The response in nature to defeat as to victory is acceptance. This Maggie learns from the creature world, but she also participates in the divine. Not only does she endure, she prevails. Mrs. Wilson insists on this possibility of higher being in an easily overlooked passage that follows immediately after the battle described:

> There is a beautiful action. It has an operative grace. It is when one, seeing some uneasy sleeper cold and without a cover, goes away, finds and brings a blanket, bends down, and covers the sleeper because the sleeper is a living being and is cold. He then returns to his work, forgetting that he has performed this small act of compassion. He will receive neither praise nor thanks. It does not matter who the sleeper may be. That is a beautiful action which is divine and human in posture and intention and self-forgetfulness.[33]

In a simple and lyrical observation, the grace of man, which is compassion, is revealed with arresting precision.

The author continues the above paragraph to question Maggie's capacity for continuing selflessness despite Vera's misapprehensions of her intent. The whole structure of the novel, however, suggests that the implication of this query is not that Maggie is all too human, but that she is somewhat too divine. Similarly, Maggie's response to the osprey's acceptance of what he cannot control implies too close a kinship with the natural world, too much a denial of her humanity. Maggie, the creature-goddess, is not enough a woman. She is essence, on the one hand; substance, on the other. As the two become integrated, the consciousness of Maggie, the woman, emerges. The novel's moral complexity is resolved in the simple act of her return to Three Loon Lake, neither for escape nor self-righteous sacrifice but for the human pleasure of company and service and solitude, and in her disposing of the swamp angel and, with it, the ambivalence it represents in regard to life, time, and death.

Both *Swamp Angel* and *The Nymph and the Lamp* set their characters' evolving perceptions in contexts in which death is as imminent as the natural world surrounding them. Maggie, on her way to the interior, pauses for a three day sojourn in limbo, beside the Similkameen, for a respite like that which "comes to the soul after death." The poignancy of her community with the trees and the wind, the "pine-made earth," the river, and her own solitude "brought tears to her eyes. I am on a margin of life, she thought. . .that margin of a world. . .powerful and close."[34] Travelling along the banks of the Fraser, she sees three rustic crosses on the hillside and ruminates on the seasons passing pleasantly around them and does not think, then, of her own three, her husband and daughter and father, who are dead. But after she arrives at Three Loon Lake–the haunting cry of loons, the cry of their three souls by which, in her memory, she is possessed –beyond Kamloops, much of what she sees in the natural world is coloured by her perspective from the margin of life and of death. On the one hand, she watches the fawn and the kitten play innocently and, on the other, the eagle vanquish the osprey. She learns from the process of natural life to accept death, and draws back from the precipice. The three loons and the water which is her element no longer entice her to oblivion, but provide solace and strength.

Death, on Marina, is a more casual affair than that of Maggie's acquaintance. And, unlike Maggie, Isabel's response is more to the attitudes it inspires than to death itself. Isabel is disturbed by the callousness of Carney and Skane in their duck-hunting, revolted by their complicity in the barbaric export of the island ponies. But the very sands of Marina contain death, the bones of innumerable lost sailors. The presence of death in her experience corresponds quite directly to the course of her sexual affairs which in turn correspond to her painful growth into consciousness. The relationship is not causal, but thematically appropriate. Shortly after Isabel is told that the preserved remnants of the past are often bared by the wind shifting the dunes, she tells Matthew she wants no further intimacy. Immediately before her distorted revelation at the crew-quarters which sends her back to his embrace, she is shocked by the row of skulls casually stored on a shelf in the rocket house. Just before she gives herself up to Skane, she becomes aware of "the cold clutch of Marina itself, the evil sea-monster with its belly full of wrecks and dead men's bones and still unsatisfied."[35] And finally, on her return to Marina, she is likened to the nymph awaiting drowned sailors in the caves at the bottom of the sea. Sexuality and death are inextricably bound, in Raddall's vision (for reasons quite different from those of the Metaphysical poets) because they are complementary conditions of existence. The one represents choice and regeneration but, in abuse, can be the context of divisiveness. The other represents inexorable change but implies continuity as well.

There is a movement in *The Nymph and the Lamp* from accident to responsibility in the affairs of man. From being the victim of someone else's drunken impulse at Mrs. Paradee's, Maggie becomes determinedly self-willed in Kingsbridge and, with decisive control of her destiny, returns to Marina. The movement in *Swamp Angel* is from determinism through flight to acceptance. In the former, it is the nature of innocence that is ultimately explored. Matthew Carney is a sort of fool-saint in the tradition of Prince Myshkin and Billy Budd, and Isabel is both his scourge and his salvation from the ignominy that awaits such beings. *Swamp Angel* illuminates more the nature of experience, of existence. Maggie Lloyd is not morally blind, like Isabel, nor innocent in the impending darkness, like Carney. She sees only too well, the darkness as well as the light. Ultimately, she reconciles the two.

The geophysical factors in Raddall's novel, as in Wilson's, have integral narrative functions not only revealing their quite different visions but in shaping them as well. Authenticity accompanies moral integrity and coherence, but it also allies external reality inseparably with interior experience. Marina, like Three Loon Lake, is a place in which the patterns of human isolation and the visions they engender are made tangibly specific, profoundly universal.

Notes

1. Thomas Raddall, *The Nymph and the Lamp* (Toronto: New Canadian Library, 1965), p.43. (Boston: Little, Brown, 1950.)
2. *Ibid.,* p.73.
3. Ethel Wilson, *Swamp Angel,* (Toronto: New Canadian Library, 1962), p.96. (Toronto: Macmillan, 1954.)
4. Raddall, *op.cit.,* p.26.
5. *Ibid.,* p.175.
6. *Ibid.,* p.245.
7. *Ibid.,* p.328.
8. *Ibid.,* p.326.

9. *Ibid.,* p.136.
10. *Ibid.,* p.124.
11. *Ibid.,* p.116.
12. *Ibid.,* p.142.
13. *Ibid.,* p.77.
14. *Ibid.,* p.191.
15. *Ibid.,* p.192.
16. *Ibid.,* pp.208-9.
17. *Ibid.,* p.303.
18. Wilson, *op.cit.,* p.23.
19. *Ibid.,* p.38.
20. *Ibid.,* p.36.
21. *Ibid.,* p.38.
22. *Ibid.,* p.32.
23. *Ibid.,* p.152.
24. *Ibid.,* p.25.
25. *Ibid.,* p.75.
26. *Ibid.,* p.137.
27. *Ibid.,* p.75.
28. *Ibid.,* p.129.
29. *Ibid.,* p.139.
30. *Ibid.,* p.157.
31. *Ibid.,* p.100.
32. *Ibid.,* p.90.
33. *Ibid.,* p.91.
34. *Ibid.,* pp.39-40.
35. Raddall, *op.cit.,* p.207.

2.
As For Me and My House

As For Me and My House is a haunting orchestration of so many of the themes and image and behavioural patterns that are prevalent in our fiction as to seem uncannily prescient of the Canadian experience. It is a laconic novel, tense, terse, concentrated. Ross packs emotion tightly into the explication of simple events. He gives them cosmic dimensions without lifting them out of their mundane context by fusing them with the world of nature around them. Yet the inexorable presence of the elements, and of the endless Prairie landscape, does not obscure the intolerable foibles, the moral restraints, of his characters. With the precise deft strokes of an artist but more with the sensitive variations of fine detail and great flowing movements that a composer might develop into a symphony, Ross creates a compelling vision of the human condition.

But this novel is not another fictional *Symphonie pastorale.* It is a far more subtle interpretation of reality, a more inquisitive and more introspective exploration of the human condition, than is André Gide's achievement. It shows less concern with the underlying principles of behaviour and more with their dynamic patterns, more with the music of experience than with its meaning. Ross orchestrates the facts of a Prairie environment, a small Canadian town, a dingy home, a childless marriage, and the physical, emotional, and spititual impotence, even depravity, of two individuals in a world that they, in part, have made hostile. From these facts comes the melodic progression of his novel, arranged in movements according to the wind, the dust, the sun, the cold, and again, the wind in a cyclic design indeterminately promising either renewal or repetition. The harmonies which give the seasonal movements shape and draw the melody into a symphonic arrangement are discovered in Mrs. Bentley's voice as she articulates her experience. The tension between subjective and objec tive realities provides the novel with much of its ambivalent strength and brooding elusive beauty.

Before definitions of the author's intent or evaluations of his achievement are possible, the harmonic patterns of the novel itself, with some reticence, invite close examination. Such an obvious prelude to critical imposition would seem to be essential, yet it has been somewhat too readily overlooked. *As For Me and My House* is probably the most thoroughly analyzed of Canadian novels, with the possible exception of *The Double Hook,* and on the whole it has received imaginative and intelligent treatment. Nevertheless, it seems to me essential to begin at the beginning, and that is with Mrs. Bentley.

As both character and narrating consciousness, she is an ambiguous personality. Her world is inexorably ironic. She has a waspish sense of humour and little, of proportion. She is at times oppressively vicious but always vulnerable. Her intractable faith in her own inadequacies amounts at times to arrogance. Her dogged compliance brings suffering, and the strength to endure it. She is an intellectual romantic who thinks she is a realist, and her emotions and her husband's are tyrannized accordingly. She is most ingenuous when least trying to be so, most the dissembler when she claims candour. Mrs. Bentley is the victim of a reckless imagination, and subject to the consequent moral and emotional restraints that have cauterized her passionate nature, a nature which only her music and the profound solitude of the Prairie landscape occasionally reveal. She is a woman incredibly alone.

She arouses great sympathy for being human. But as she is human, she is also fallible, self-indulgent, and sometimes mean. This mixture of characteristics makes her a complex engaging character but an unreliable witness. Her periodic submission to the meanness of spirit that perhaps confirms her humanity, undermines her authority as a moral arbiter. An acquiescing reticence combined with exploitive self-dramatization renders her observations of behaviour unbelievable. She displays little insight to match the clarity of her perceptions. The motives and responses of which she is so presciently aware are repeatedly misinterpreted, misunderstood. This is as true of her own as of Philip's. Her vision is acute; her judgment errs.

I have described Mrs. Bentley as being mean of spirit–a notion that runs counter to the over-all empathy she seems to command. But even in the novel's closing pages, when it might be assumed that she has gained some measure of grace as the complement to her newly assertive behaviour–and indeed she claims to have attained insight and compassion such as had previously eluded her more passive condition–she reponds to Judith's death with cynical arrogance, and with desperate relief:

> I sent Philip a telegram this afternoon, telling him that Judith died and that the baby's a boy. He'll be better to learn it away from me, with time to think it out and find himself again.
>
> For me it's easier this way. It's what I've secretly been hoping for all along. I'm glad she's gone–gone–for her sake as much as ours. What was there ahead of her now anyway? If I lost Philip what would there be ahead of me?[1]

The certainty with which she presumes to understand her husband is characteristic of earlier assumptions that have nurtured the misunderstanding between them. Her relief at the morbid turn of events suggests no resolution to the stifling moral complexity of her continuing confrontation with experience, nor does it suggest an end to her marital difficulty. The attitude conveyed, "better her than me," is hardly the stuff of spiritual enlightenment. More than ever, she submits her identity, her integrity, to maintaining a relationship they both desperately want to change. When the following month, in her last entry, she records their departure with the notation that their year in Horizon has run a "wide wheel" and that in Philip's eyes there is "a stillness, a freshness, a vacancy of beginning,"[2] it is indeterminant whether, as I have already suggested, the coming revolution of the wheel offers renewal or repetition. In a cyclic pattern, either one is a beginning. Even the last sentence, "I want it so," suggests both the promise of new expectations and the legacy of a determining wilfulness. Mrs. Bentley is the passive victim of an incomprehensible existence and yet capable of manipulating its significance most assertively in the narrow reality the two of them occupy. The ironies of the Bentleys' story and her telling of it ultimately converge as the moral vision of the novel, raised to the plane of what might be called cosmic irony.

Mrs. Bentley's sporadic ignobility and her humanity are inseparable. They are complementary facets of the same being. Just as she should not be considered a paragon, Mrs. Bentley should not be judged as demonic, or as misanthropic. Her capacity to endure is in fact the result of the same weakness of character which causes her suffering to continue unabated. Meanness is her way of meeting what she cannot fully comprehend. For example, she jealously anticipates the time when Philip will see Steve for what he is–or, at least, what she conceives him to be: "After a while the pity and imagination are going to run out; and there's going to be left just an ordinary, uninspiring boy."[3] She passively awaits a turning of Philip's affections towards herself, a turning to what has never been, but with Steve's presence as a substantive alternative, seems to her more a possibility than ever. In sustaining this delusion, however, she encourages a division between Philip and the boy, insinuating herself between them: "because it had been such a humiliating afternoon I played brilliantly, vindictively, determined to let Philip see how easily if I wanted to I could take the boy away from him."[4] Not that Steve is not an eager accomplice in her assumption of the adversary role between them; not that he is not an opportunist, a manipulator, a rather nasty and superficial boy. But she uses him without sympathy, judges him without understanding, and she is relieved when he is taken away to the orphanage.

She will not let Philip understand her, and suffers the consequence of her conviction that she understands him. Even Steve is sacrificed to her perverse faith in herself:

> Ever since the day he let me see I was less to him than Steve I've been trying to find and live my own life again, but it's empty, unreal. The piano, even–I try, but it's just a tinkle. And that's why I mustn't admit I may have lost him. He's spoiling Steve, hurting him, and I must stand by and let him. He would resent my interference. It would make me one with the town then, hostile, critical, aligned against him. He would resent and even hate me if I did, and I'm too small for that, too cowardly.[5]

She is trying, she says, to find herself again, to be herself. But her quest is empty, unreal, as it is bound to be, because it is based on her desire to possess Philip completely, on the artful sacrifice of Steve's well-being, on hypocrisy and conscious dissembling, on the egocentricity of self-pity–in short, on the denial of her integrity for the assumptions of a misguided faith in her own insight.

Living by the errors of her judgment and enduring the pettiness of her own nature generate a far more devastating hypocrisy than the blatant contradictions of their social function. For example, her plea with Philip to keep the table that Steve surreptitiously removed from his former home is an acknowledged play on their dubious roles in the community, but she is oblivious to the moral compromise by which her argument is concluded:

> taking it back now would amount to declaring Steve a thief, just when it's so important that the town think well of him. After all it's a nice little table, with a drawer and a shelf and not a scratch, and I don't want to give him the one in the living-room that I keep the fuchsia on.[6]

It is the narrowness of her vision, which in itself is often shrewdly acute, imposed on the broadest reaches of their life together, that so distorts her understanding of it. Perhaps the most obvious example of this is in the following commentary on Philip's vocation:

> I don't know what the solution is. Surely there's more than one way for a man like Philip to earn his living. Surely something can be done to make him realize it. Because you're a hypocrite you lose your self-respect, because you lose your self-respect you lose your initiative and self-belief–it's the same vicious circle, every year closing in a little tighter. Already it's making him morose and cynical–smaller than he ought to be. I can't help wondering what he'll be like ten years from now.[7]

Ironically, she does not see herself in the same light. Earlier, she proclaimed that: "Lack of self-respect has meant lack of initiative to try something else–it's been a vicious circle."[8] This, too, was applied exclusively to Philip. Eventually, she accepts responsibility for what being so obtuse has done but, even then, without understanding what has happened between them–"I made up my mind about Philip once–and as a result see what he is today. He was so dark and bitter and lonely, struggling away toward such cold, impossible goals, and I was so sure that my little way of sympathy and devotion was the better way."[9] She acknowledges that she has been wrong, but she has no idea why. Seeing the grand design of their lives from the limits of her perspective, she remains unaware that her bitchiness more than her conscious duplicity has been largely responsible for their individual isolation from each other, from what each of them really is, objectively, and from the world around them.

I have said that Mrs. Bentley is mean, and that she is self-indulgent and fallible. If the case for her meanness may be taken as at least tenuously established, I should, perhaps, sketch in the remainder of her character. Mrs. Bentley cannot indulge herself in physical or social amenities. But emotionally she is self-dramatizing; not only does she savour the bitterness of her isolation on long walks past the edge of Horizon, but enjoys their recollection as she records them with a meticulous recall of external detail. The times when she is truly dramatic, however, fill her with humiliation and remorse. When she is given an ignominious ride back to town on the railway jigger and is dropped off in the midst of the adjourning Ladies Aid meeting she had meant to avoid, her pride demeans her instead of making her defiant. When she stands for hours in the thickening snow outside the Wilsons' house, hoping to spy on Philip's transgressions with Judith, she has none of the righteous dignity of a woman wronged, only the wretched demeanour of a creature lost in the world. Usually, however, upon the small and undramatic incidents of which her life is primarily composed, she asserts a highly refined sense of the dramatic. She approaches the study door any number of times, hesitates, turns back, and creates a rationale for the scenario she has just played. She weeps to herself, heightening the impact of her emotions on her own experience. She play-acts internally with the intimations of numerous encounters with Philip's eyes, with a shrug or a stoop in his shoulders, with the silence so often between them. These are small compensations, perhaps, for her dreary existence, but they are damning as she interprets them. She accepts her responses as if they were reality itself.

Mrs. Bentley's delusion, in this respect, compounded by an autistic narrowness of vision, makes her observations unreliable. Time and again she is fallible, contradictory. She is wrong about the effect of Steve on their marriage, as she is about the effect of his leaving them. She is wrong about Judith's affections for Philip, sure of its futility, and she is wrong about the consequences on all three of them of its consummation. To some extent, such wrongheadedness is the result of her grasping at straws. But more, it seems to me, it rises out of her character rather than her immediate emotional responses.

She is dowdy, fussy, morose. These are not emotions, however. They are justifiable responses, given the conditions of her life. Yet, ironically, they perpetuate the same conditions. She is dowdy because they are impoverished, impoverished because of Philip's complex aversion to his vocation. But his aversion is in part because she chastens him for his failure with her appearance, weakening his capacity to endure, his resolve to escape. The effect is cyclic, centripetal, thrusting them closer together even while it thrusts them apart. Similarly, her being fussy and morose contributes to the futility of their baneful existence.

Mrs. Bentley is a good woman, as well. Philip is as culpable as she for the oppressive gloom of their lives. She is a young woman, in her mid-thirties, but anonymous, care-worn, and vindictive for being so. Her promise as a brilliant pianist has been attenuated by the anxieties of her married life, just as Philip's artistic aspirations have been reduced to interminable sketches of the surrounding still-life metaphors for his private suffering.

She desperately loves her husband. Several times she seems aware of the annihilation of love that is the consequence of possessiveness, yet in manipulating their relationship as she does, she continually attempts to possess, to control him, to subvert his independence to her will. Her most insidious method is by submerging herself in her conception of his personality–causing the additional rift of his resistance to her instrusion. She is forgiving of his petulance, his selfishness, and in so indulging him she perpetuates his weakness, his misery. On the whole, Mrs. Bentley's personality would readily sustain the damning epithet that "she means well." She is an unfortunate creature, with more strength than weakness, more love than animosity, more compassion, more intelligence and imagination, more insight, more integrity than my argument, perhaps, has given her credit for. But my purpose has not been to reveal the whole of her character. Sinclair Ross does that with great subtlety and precision. What I have tried to illuminate in particular are those of her characteristics which create the ironic tension between the subjective and objective functions of her role as recording consciousness. In this context, the strengths and virtues of her personality are less relevant than her foibles and her self-delusions–her creation as the ironic medium of an ironic reality.

It appears to me that Ross has achieved an arrangement of the specific concrete elements of his characters' experience into a spatial, a cosmic, form. This is much like the architectural form of music, generated by its residual and reflexive impact–extending in his novel from the picayune to include the whole of existence. It is an inclusive vision, rather than exclusive like those of Raddall and Wilson. It does not explore a particular aptitude for living such as Maggie Lloyd embodies; nor does it define the progression of a person like Isabel Jardine towards self-recognition and consequent reconciliation with the terms of her life. Nor do I mean to suggest that Ross's vision is temporally inclusive in the disparate ways of *The Channel Shore* and *The Double Hook,* both of which define the perimeters of collective experience while exploring its effects on individuals.

Alone, of the five novels, *As For Me and My House* is written in the first person–and then, the first person reflective, each episode being recollected, structured, evaluated subjectively before the narrator proceeds to the next. The point of view is as intimate as an individual's consciousness, and as I have suggested, subject to the idiosyncrasies of that individual's personality. At the same time, because externals are not imposed omnisciently upon the narrative but arise directly out of the narrator's experience, the effective scope of external perceptions is not limited to either the dramatically relevant or to an abstract thematic form. In this novel, theme is not a superstructure of meaning. In accordance with Mies van der Rohe's architectural dictum, form, in this respect, follows function: theme is content. Dramatic relevance is inseparable from the narrator's perceptions. What has impact on her is what she chooses to present, and the objects of her choice are, in a sense, self-determining. She does not select; she responds.

Her familiarity with the objective, the external, world of the novel allows for its more intensive presence than a less involved observer could possibly achieve, while being more inclusive, by the implications of its impact on the whole of her being, than the necessary discipline of an omniscient observer could effectively allow. Only through the eyes of a reflective participant in the cosmos of the author's vision can the cosmic be seen. Only through the ironic interpretations of a responsive participant can its meaning be translated into communicable experience. These would seem to be the operative principles according to which Ross's vision of cosmic irony achieves articulation. *As For Me and My House* offers the inclusive vision of a dynamic universe occupied at the centre by the single responding consciousness of his narrator, Mrs. Bentley.

It would be difficult to conceive of a greater loneliness than Mrs. Bentley's. The patterns of her isolation incorporate every aspect of her experience. These patterns emanate largely from the clusters of irreducible external facts impinging on her life; the things, places, beings, the geophysical elements, which are rearranged interminably but with compelling intensity through the progressive movements of the novel. Her isolation is spiritual and emotional, as much as it is, more substantively, social or conjugal–more so, in fact, for while she is morally and psychologically bereft of any continuity beyond herself, she is yet able to function, to plan and manipulate, in the physical world. In any case, the various inter-functional dimensions of her isolation all emerge in the arrangement of the external world according to the patterns of her perception of it. Her isolation is the medium of the author's vision rather than its content or meaning.

Ross orchestrates a relatively limited number of facts into tight, almost brittle, variations which move his novel towards completion. These facts have only to be abstracted from the text for the nature of his achievement to be realized. Each immediately suggests a number of separate contexts and also the residual impact of its repeated appearance in the narrative. Their function is more akin to the sound phrases in a musical composition, in this respect, than to the conventional symbol-images of literature. They have been arranged in the text in a sequence of reflexively associated patterns which explore their individual and interrelated potential as objects of response in the limited universe of Mrs. Bentley's perception. They are not objective correlatives but the facts, themselves, of her world and her isolation in it.

Innumerable variations on the interrelated presence of these word-objects in narrative clusters constitute the external world of the novel. If the same abstraction were performed on another novel, on *The Nymph and the Lamp,* for example, conundrums generated by variable functions would be inevitable. So much do the externals of Raddall's novel, of most novels, operate on indeterminately varying planes of narrative reality, that such a list would be of factors rather than facts. Marina, for example, and Clélie, the bones protruding from the sand, and the telegraphy apparatus, all carry symbolic burdens alluding to differing levels of experience. Much as Moby Dick embodies Melville's vision of goodness and of evil, of primal force and of man's determining will, the tangible factors deployed by Raddall through his narrative lead simultaneously in different directions of interrelated meaning. The bones in the sand suggest death, finality, but they also suggest continuity, and their intimations in either direction are related to the sexual dynamics of the novel and the moral vision that emerges into consciousness as a consequence. Similarly, the island itself, the figurehead, the wireless are factors interwoven into the texture, the structure, the meaning of the novel, inextricable, except through analysis that implies synthesis at every turn. Ambiguity in Ross's novel, however, is a function of irony. It is not the cause. The external facts are operative on a single plane of reality. Their impact is simple, subtle, and cumulative. It is because of the response they arouse in the recording consciousness of his narrator that they achieve complexity, ambiguity, that their implicit irony is compounded to pathos and tragic ambivalence. When they are removed from the text, from context, they do not evoke confusion that demands critical resolution; they simply suggest the flow of Mrs. Bentley's response to the world around her.

The following list is neither complete nor definitive, but I believe it will help to reveal the validity of much of what I have said:

music	moths
art	son
words	main street
study	false-fronts
garden	house
train	church
tracks	car
ravine	horizon
elevators	dog
pipe	hat
horse	

An exhaustive explication of the list is impractical but, perhaps, exploring the function of a few examples will clarify what I mean. Trains, for instance, recur a number of times. They are an uncomplicated event in the Bentleys' lives. There is "always the train, roaring away to the world that lay beyond,"[10] a reminder to Philip of "the outside world he hasn't reached,"[11] and to Mrs. Bentley, of his, of their limitations. Unlike the train in *Sons and Lovers* on which D. H. Lawrence transports Paul forward into life, unlike the seemingly ubiquitous locomotives in novels of the North American mid-west, or the trains that appear again and again in the novels of Thomas Wolfe, the Horizon train does not represent escape, continuance, or continuity on a variety of simultaneously present levels of meaning. Nor is it, like these others or like the train in *Cry, the Beloved Country,* for instance, a plot mechanism, forwarding the action. It is not freighted with the significance of the symbolic, the moral or conceptual implications inherent in such a vast machine. It is a simple impinging fact in people's lives, forcing each of them back upon inner resources or deficiencies. For Steve, the train provides compensating excitement for the loss of a precarious stability that he knew as the surrogate son in a union strained intolerably by his presence. It is the vehicle of a self-preserving indifference towards things human. Quite the contrary, for Judith the trains offer tangible, physical, almost sexual, excitement. Her visceral response to them stirs a lust that reaches completion only in the lean-to tryst with Philip while Mrs. Bentley lies sick in the bedroom. They stir a passion for dramatic form in her life that culminates finally in her destruction. In both cases, trains are not also some other thing but are the objects of significant response, and ironic for that reason alone. For the Bentleys, they are recriminating spectres, but trains, nevertheless. Even when a train passes directly overhead at the ravine, it is a penetrating, overwhelming presence rather than an operative conveyance, ironic by the very fact of its being amorphous while generating an indefinably specific response:

> Then the bridge picked up the coming of a train. It was there even while the silence was still intact. At last we heard a distant whistle-blade, then a single point of sound, like one drop of water in a whole sky. It dilated, spread. The sky and silence began imperceptibly to fill with it. We steeled ourselves a little, feeling the pounding onrush in the trestle of the bridge. It quickened, gathered, shook the earth, then swept in an iron roar above us, thundering and dark.
>
> We emerged from it slowly, while the trestle a moment or two sustained the clang and din. I glanced at Philip, then quickly back to the water. A train still makes him wince sometimes. At night, when the whistle's loneliest, he'll toss a moment, then lie still and tense. And in the daytime I've seen his eyes take on a quick, half-eager look, just for a second or two, and then sink flat and cold again.[12]

For Mrs. Bentley, recording the event, the train is an apocalyptic intrusion. For Philip it is also an intrusion, but as a tormenting and deadly irritant.

Even when Mrs. Bentley observes at close hand locomotives out by the grain elevators, her response suggests a ghastly affront to her security more than a vehicle of deliverance. Yet in every case, the narrative effect of trains is simple, ironic. Out of this irony is born a marvelous complexity. Such facts in the novel as the trains cumulate in a resonant progression of reflexively related patterns. They do not cause the turnings of event, but they are facts in their happening, orchestrated so as to make them both dramatically and thematically inevitable. Steve's aroused indifference, for example, creates a lesion in Philip's anxiety which leads to adultery, fatherhood, and perhaps freedom. Judith's sensual longings penetrate the sterile walls of Mrs. Bentley's moral restraint, erupting in the form of betrayal and, possibly, post-dated fulfilment. Philip's anxious recognitions of an alternative life grow tumorously within him, but keep imperceptably alive the possibility of release. His wife's struggle against both the strain of an overbearing presence and the limitations of response it arouses, leads to the reckless manipulation of their mutual restraint towards a positive goal, towards continuity in what she desperately hopes will be more amenable conditions, emotionally, morally, physically. Ross deploys trains strategically throughout the novel without ambiguous possibilities of meaning, yet so that they arouse ambiguous responses in his characters–profoundly so in their cumulative effect, although separately they are of minor importance as facts in the external reality of his created world.

Facts more central to the narrative flow, more significantly a part of the narrative structure, are the ravine, the elevators, the tracks. These are the places of Mrs. Bentley's solitary walks. She takes Judith, Paul, and Philip, separately, with her on a number of occasions. Each is a time of uncharacteristic intimacy. But that this is a rarity is ironically conspicuous, for time and again her walks beyond the town have been periods of solitude. Through their repetitive insistence of her personal isolation, their being shared appears as an unusual deviation from what is accepted as an oppressive norm. Inevitably the intimacies are betrayed. Judith confides her past, her aspirations, to Mrs. Bentley on one of their walks, and the culmination of her confession is the affair with Philip and the birth of his child. With Paul, she experiences a pleasant communion on their walk, and fails later to recognize his dogged devotion to her that, in good part, drives Philip further away. Walking with Philip in the rain and feeling the joy of their being together is the ironic prelude to their increasingly arid relationship. In each case, the shared solitude, in retrospect, is a source of misery. Similarly, Mrs. Bentley's intrusions into Philip's study almost invariably reinforce the extent of his habitual isolation within it. This recurrance of place and of event in a free-form pattern allows Ross great latitude in the orchestration of emotions.

With other facts, the patterns in which they are present are more variable. The son, for example, and the dog have a number of different forms. The son reappears in allusions to the boy the Bentley's never had, and as their stillborn infant; as the Lawson boy who is doomed and whose father looks so much like a rustic and more rugged, resilient, version of Philip; as Steve, of course, who is a surrogate; and as the young Philip in Mrs. Bentley's flashback to his pathetic childhood. Each of these instances is uncomplicated in itself, but they gain dimension through the ironic redundancy by which they are multiplications of each other. The dog-fact, too, has a multiple presence. In this case, with the significant exception of the cur Philip executed because he could not afford its maintenance, it is embodied by a single being, the wolfhound, El Greco. Named for the artist whose distended figures suggest much about the inner lives of the main characters, El Greco is a constantly changing apparition with an appetite. He first appears as a wretched foundling. Later, he is an elegant companion, trotting beside Mrs. Bentley to the butcher's; then, sorrowful without dissemblance at Minnie's departure; finally, the victim of starving coyotes. His only constancy is in the responses he arouses from the people around him. Philip is forbearing; Steve, possessively fickle. Mrs. Bentley finds in him solace, and in Paul he generates disinterested compassion characteristic of the small-town liberal.

Other items on my list and those I have neglected to include operate similarly on a recurring basis within a carefully modulated series of contexts. Some relate primarily to a single person, like the dowdy hat to Mrs. Bentley, the surreptitious pipe to Philip. Yet, like the hat and the pipe, they have reference to the behaviour of others–usually, as in these two examples, quite specifically. Some, like the moths against light, and the false-fronts of Main Street, recur with a seemingly endless variety of narrative implications. All of them are effective, however, on the same level of mundane reality. Where they attain resonance, dimension, and universal proportion, is primarily in the author's determining control of his narrator's consciousness. Like the musical phrases arranged in my persistent analogy of the novel with a symphonic composition, they are presented through an interpreter who is subject to the creator's discipline.

Mrs. Bentley's character is brilliantly conceived. She is a dynamic being within her own context, not entirely under the direct control of the author. Not that she is a free agent, any more than a conductor is free of the symphony which he directs, in which he participates. But she is the medium, as well, of the author's vision, the instruments articulating his arrangement of sounds into meaning. She is therefore allowed sufficient scope to observe, sufficient capacity to perceive and record, according to the implicit dictates of her own personality.

Within context, however, she is subject to more arbitrary measures, the geophysical facts. These inform the movement of her narrative with an organizing principle that is complementary to the behavioural dynamics of her own, anti-determinist vision of reality. The vast Prairie reaches are invariably defined by the prevailing weather, yet remain ominously the same. Looking out from the town in early summer, "The dust is so thick that sky and earth are just a blur. You can scarcely see the elevators at the end of town. One step beyond, you think, and you'd go plunging into space."[13] In a mid-winter description, the perspective has changed from the window to the path from the backhouse, but the impression remains constant: "When you pause a moment to look across the prairie a queer, lost sensation comes over you of being hung aloft in space, so like a floor of clouds does the unbroken whiteness coil and swell to the horizon."[14] Using their presence in the landscape as a metaphor for Philip's brooding recalcitrance, she reveals more of their condition than she intends–"I wish I could reach him, but it's like the wilderness outside of night and sky and prairie, with this one little spot of Horizon hung up lost in its immensity. He's lost, and alone."[15] A small cluster of humanity in the midst of a vast indifferent universe–she does not realize, as perhaps Philip does, that this is the primal condition of existence and all else, in Ross's vision, is reconciliation with this inescapable fact.

The town of Horizon is isolated by the geophysical environment, as its name suggests, and suffocated by it, shabbily sustained in a state of premature senility. After the germinal surge of life in such a town, and the brief period of ingenuous confidence, it quickly recedes into an old age that forces its residents in upon the narrowness of their own memories, which become their only convictions. This state, brought on as much by an implacable landscape and its aggressive seasons as by economic factors, shrivels the soul as well as the body. Mrs. Bentley, with acid whimsy, explains–

> For there's a story that a goddess once, enamored of a mortal, sought for him from the other gods the gift of immortality. But not of youth. The years went on, and her handsome lover grew bald and bleary-eyed. Young and beautiful herself she begged the gods again either to grant him youth or let him die like other men, but this time they were obdurate. And she hardened at last, and found another lover, and to escape the first one changed him into a grasshopper.
>
> They're poor, tumbledown, shabby little towns, but they persist. Even the dry years yield a little wheat, even the little means livelihood for some. I know a town where once it rained all June, and that fall the grain lay in piles outside full granaries. It's an old town now, shabby and decrepit like the others, but it, too, persists. It knows only two years: the year it rained all June, and next year.[16]

The shabby decrepit old town, founded in the recent past, is a particularly Canadian phenomenon. European towns of ten times the age seem less old, by comparison, although their roots are more deeply embedded. American small towns, as shabby and decrepit, inevitably suggest the immediate present, ten years out of date. But any number of Canadian towns, Minto, Deseronto, Drumheller, and the fictional Horizon, conform to the pattern of Mrs. Bentley's description. Probably the cause of such tenuous continuity lies somewhere between the incredible impositions of the geophysical setting and the rapidly changing means by which we exploit it and attempt to transcend its presence. In the case of Horizon, a town increasingly without meaning in a larger context, serving no cultural or economic purpose when that is what its populace demands of it, Ross locates an indigenously Canadian version of universal isolation.

The weather, the active and variable extension of the natural environment corresponding to the variability of human response to an unalterable universe, intrudes insistently on Mrs. Bentley's experience of the world. Again and again there is the wind, clean and then saturated with dust, then the sun, the cold, and again the wind. Each is as enervating as the one preceding, each as intrusive–so much so that changes from one to another are imperceptible, yet oppressively inexorable, inevitable. However, it would be a mistake, I believe, to say that Ross is operating on the level of pathetic fallacy. The weather is not described to correspond with emotions or events. If that were the case, he would have merely achieved a somber deterministic lament. But Ross envisions an indifferent universe to which man, ironically, submits his individual will. The elements, ubiquitous in his character's experience, are not barometric measures of their confrontation with reality. Nor are they, directly, behaviourally causative. Rather, they are cosmic pressures upon the lives of individuals which are met in a variety of ways–in this novel, seldom comic; more ironic than tragic, except perhaps in the case of the Lawson boy and the small community of farmers at Partridge Hill. It is in submitting to the elements as a causative factor in their lives that Mrs. Bentley embodies what I have described as cosmic irony. Instead of recognizing them as process, like the Partridge Hill farmers, and assimilating, accepting them, she takes them as a private affront, often a reproach, insinuating into her most inner life. Acceptance, which might lead to reconciliation with the unalterable conditions of their life, is instead distorted into an intolerably strained resignation and misdirected attempts at control. Such restraints drive the Bentleys farther and farther into the isolation of hypocrisy, of compromise, deeper into themselves and their destructive union than they can humanely endure without it breaking. And it does break: Mrs. Bentley obsessively hoards money and dreams of a new life; Philip, recklessly, turns first to Judith and then to compliance with his wife's dream. With fitting irony, the breaking strain of their union holds the possibility of renewal in balance with that of repetition in new surroundings.

As For Me and My House has a simple plot. There are few diversions, no tangents, from the narrative core. Nonetheless, it is a complex novel. It has spatial form more in the manner of Beethoven's *Symphonie Pastorale* than of Gide's. It occupies space, has dimension, the way music occupies space–fleetingly, reflexively, cumulatively. For this reason, in my opinion, a conventional architectural analysis may be an inadequate and misleading basis for critical exploration. The nature of Ross's vision confounds the principles of structural form, inviting hypotheses derived from disembodied, discontinuous episodes. But the episodes are subservient to a less tangible arrangement than the plot offers or even than the moral complexity of its themes might impose. For this reason, my emphasis has been on the ambiguous presence of the narrating consciousness and the ironic arrangement of objective facts to which it responds–rather than on the dramatic or thematic evolution into being of the whole novel. It is a work of infinite diversity, rewarding the most esoteric of interpretations, or the most simplistic, with substantive confirmation of validity. It is prototypically Canadian, composed out of the patterns of isolation native to Canadian literature, usually in more diluted, less integrated form. Time and again *As For Me and My House* has been called a minor Canadian classic. Surely it is time, and we have achieved sufficient maturity and good taste, for the delimiting adjectives to be dropped.

Notes

1. Sinclair Ross, *As For Me and My House* (Toronto: New Canadian Library, 1969), pp.161-62. (New York: Reynal, 1941.)
2. *Ibid.*, pp.164-65.
3. *Ibid.*, p.53.
4. *Ibid.*, p.47.
5. *Ibid.*, p.75.
6. *Ibid.*, pp.51-52.
7. *Ibid.*, p.85.
8. *Ibid.*, p.67.
9. *Ibid.*, p.150.
10. *Ibid.*, p.32.
11. *Ibid.*, p.33.
12. *Ibid.*, p.29.
13. *Ibid.*, p.73.
14. *Ibid.*, p.150.
15. *Ibid.*, p.25.
16. *Ibid.*, p.97.

3.
The Double Hook and *The Channel Shore*

Setting, in *The Double Hook,* is as anonymous and specific as a wasp sting or a wild flower. As if she were stripping an insulated wire from the middle, so that the covering is bunched at the ends and the bare metal strand is pulled taut between them, Sheila Watson divides the landscape, revealing a tense surrealist tale of human isolation and the moral imperatives which compel humans to endure or perish. On one side is the natural world as universal presence and on the other, as corporeal being. Her sensuous evocations of both as they impinge on the experience of her characters have the effect of reducing the most dramatic events of their lives to the commonplace while magnifying their moral implications beyond contextual significance. The universal is implicit in the pervasive presence of the primal elements, earth, air, fire, and water, and at the opposite extremity are Coyote and the characteristics of anatomy assigned to the land. Between the two, a small community tucked in the folds of the landscape struggles towards renewal, the integration of body and soul, of individual and collective being. Over the whole is an unobtrusive God.

Charles Bruce, in *The Channel Shore,* reveals an intricate web of time and event sustained by the continuity of landscape. In the farms and the bushlands that slope to the sea, bearing the names and the imprint of passing generations, continually summoning intimations of the past into imperious presence, are the shapes of people's lives. The people of the Shore are caught up in the gyring patterns of geneology that extend beyond their separate realities. Their history is set upon the contours of the Shore and takes the form of the land and forms their response to the land as well. Through the passing of time, the land and the events by which it is known to its people merge inseparably. Change has become process; the intense isolation of individuals, fragments of community experience. Bruce envisions in this context a universal pattern of responsibility and compromise, perceives its design in the lives of the Channel Shore.

Bruce and Watson are vastly different in style and vision. The geophysical world of *The Double Hook* is derived from a particular setting–the Cariboo country in the British Columbia Interior, I would imagine, where Mrs. Watson has spent several years–but it coheres in a separate reality of symbol and myth, pared clean of encumbering allusions to regional antecedents. In *The Channel Shore,* Bruce plots the Nova Scotian locale with astronomical precision in relation to the world continuous with its perimeters and fills it out with such specific detail that it is as real as a remembered place revisited. The effect is of actual experience met straight on with a penetrating eye, recorded with meticulous fidelity, with meaning implicit–realism turned magic-realism by the author's devotion to a profound verisimilitude extending in time and emotion beyond representational necessity. Bruce manipulates perceptions as well as responses. Sheila Watson manipulates reality. Subscribing to the symbolist's prerogative of arranging stimuli according to supra-contextual meaning rather than to the literal imperatives of their presence, she bends the mundane, the temporal, to a more fundamental and universal reality than they inherently imply. Yet with a genius for increasing their impact she roots her vision firmly in the common ground of actuality, effectively bridging the gulf between substance and essence that she has imposed upon them.

Sheila Watson populates, makes tangible, a moral universe. The structure of *The Double Hook* is an attempt to articulate that universe, to give it form. It is this that she communicates: form, rather than meaning. I believe that Mrs. Watson is not so arrogant as to assume prior knowledge of matters that have confounded understanding since man became conscious of his own existence. I find a singular humility in her vision; the kind of humility one associates, for example, with St. Augustine, for all his prophetic brilliance and earthly wisdom. Her purpose seems to be the revelation of universal reality; explication rather than explanation. By the meticulous arrangement of character, relationships, and factors of the physical world, and by the elimination of all emotions, feelings, and details extraneous to her purpose, she reveals an idealized structural basis from which the human condition for all its diversity is ultimately derived. Consistent with the apparently symbolic purpose of her novel, she arranges tangible experience according to the abstract allusions its presence is made to infer. She is, in a sense, a Platonist, struggling towards the realization of ideality in aesthetic form. Bruce, in the same sense, is Aristotelian. No more than Watson does he presume to understand the ineffable, but rather than attempting to reveal its form through symbolic abstraction, he explores its mundane presence, implicit in the particular representational events experienced in a particular place through a particular sequence of time. It is an inductive conception of reality, whereas Sheila Watson's is essentially one of aesthetic deduction. He describes interpenetrating worlds of consciousness, within which the trivial and the universal are relevant in relation to actuality. By arranging time, place, and personality in a structure informed by his perceptions of them and not of an abstract universe, by studious fidelity to the patterns of life on the Channel Shore, he reveals the operative principles of existence, as he sees them, within the experience of people's lives.

The three families in *The Double Hook* who, along with Theophil and Kip, make up the small community in the hills, are occupants of an island in time. Unlike those of the Marshalls and Gordons and McKees, whose lives constitute the central design of *The Channel Shore,* the interrelationships of people in Watson's novel are determined by logical necessity rather than by a complex of free will, coincidence, and chance. They are isolated in a brief segment of time but there is nothing spontaneous about their behaviour. Their motives are singular, uncomplicated, determined exclusively by immediate circumstance. Even at the most significant turning point of the novel, when Felicia's hooker, Lilly, steals James' escape money and he is forced back upon the resources of the community he has deserted, the effect is redemption, but the cause, beyond planning. The complexity of this particular event arises not out of an individual psyche but from the form of the novel itself. On crossing the bridge into the town "he saw the dark figure of his mother playing her line out into the full flood" of the river.[1] But she is dead: he killed her. As to the others, her apparition is revealed to him, fishing. Here, however, in the valley, the water flows with force, the land is not arid, and the air is cooler, the sun, benevolent. But the people he has fallen in with are corrupt. Even their fish are imported, pickled. The primal elements of his village in the hills are drained here of their ambivalent power and "For the first time in his life he felt quite alone." Responding to the sounds of the river flowing through the dark night outside Felicia's, he goes "Looking for something," as he says, that "I hope is lost."[2] His mother is not there, of course; she was an illusion of what he is obliged to escape. His money spent–for, allowing it to be stolen is a form of spending–he must return to the community in the folds of the hills. His simple change in direction, then, carries the explicit and associative burden of the novel's major symbols for life, death, renewal. Their astounding complexity, however, is revealed not in James but through him, in Watson's manipulation of her materials. In a similar fashion, the other characters provide focal points for the patterns of symbol and myth from which the novel is shaped.

It is these patterns, I believe, which invite such diverse interpretations and various quests for the source of allusions as *The Double Hook* has sustained. And here I return to an earlier premise, that her vision is one of form rather than of meaning. If this is the case, and I think that I can fairly argue that it is, then her novel is, in effect, a repository for as many interpretations as are plausible–none of which are definitive. The very strength of the work is that while it invites interpretation, it resists definition. In this context, of course, *The Double Hook* is not a novel at all but an eclectic form of poetry. Critical analysis should first seek to reveal the structure of its vision before proceeding to the extra-contextual resolution of the meaning of its allusory fragments. The myth of the Fisher King, or the whole of the *Golden Bough,* for that matter, provides only limited insight into *The Waste Land* if the poem itself, within its contextual limits, is not first examined as a structural entity, a complete design that either fails or succeeds according to its formal integrity and cohesiveness. Similarly, *The Double Hook* must first be formally considered before the Amerindian, Celtic, Biblical or Classical allusions, or the transliteral symbolic patterns can effectively reveal more than the eclectic nature of the author's mind. Not that poetry is more inviolable than the novel–but its parts consort in a more delicate harmony of aesthetic rather than conceptually causative logic and their contextual relations must at least be acknowledged before being usurped by critical projection. Because of the unusual form of Mrs. Watson's novel–for I would still persist in calling it that–I am inclined to consider it primarily as a structural unit within the context of my discussion and forgo esoteric interpretations of meaning beyond what is implicitly revealed in such an approach.

Duality, as suggested by the title and reiterated by the fish hook imprint at the beginning of every section, is the keynote of *The Double Hook.* Somewhere between the glory and the darkness, hope and fear, spiritual essence and corporeal being, is the natural condition of man. The form of the whole of Sheila Watson's vision is an ironic movement for her characters from one barb to the other of a hook bound in the middle by their mortal being. In the beginning, an old woman, Mrs. Potter, dies at the hands of her own offspring, James, and the other individuals of the community are each beset by residual visions of her still in their midst, fishing in the stream that runs through their lives. In the end, a child is born to Lenchen, and James has returned to accept responsibility for them both. Clearly there is a progression from death to birth, from the illusions of fear to joyous awakening. But Coyote, under whose eyes this progress transpires, has the last word, crying through Ara, the childless and ugly daughter-in-law of the dead Mrs. Potter:

> I have set his feet on soft ground;
> I have set his feet on the sloping shoulders
> of the world.[3]

The baby, the prospects of renewal, are bound to precarious mortality. With life have come the conditions of inevitable death; with hope, the conditions of fear. The child will need a strong back, as Angel says, "to carry round what the world will load on his shoulders."[4]

There has been no transformation of reality–only a change of perspective. Coyote is still an integral presence in the lives of the community although it suffers less, now, under his dispensation. Whatever he signifies, he is still there, at the edge of consciousness, emphasizing the essential sameness of things. James, who is overtly responsible for life and death being manifest in the community, is the bridge between the two possibilities, the shank of the double hook. The others fall into place as a functioning chorus whose words and actions highlight the futility and the grace which define his role as protagonist in the grim comedy of moral existence.

The others exist, however, in their own right within the confines of the text. In the pendulum's swing from fear and divisiveness to hope and community, they are existentialist measures of the breadth of its arc. Greta, for example, covets the house but has been unable of her own will to do anything to possess it. With her mother gone, she does so, fiercely, bitterly, and is literally consumed by it. Stripped naked, rebelling against the warning of her mother's apparition, she lights the kerosene: "Greta had inherited destruction like a section surveyed and fenced. She had lived no longer than the old lady's shadow left its stain on the ground. She sat in her mother's doom as she sat in her chair."[5] For Greta there was never choice, only wilful response. The alternatives offered by knowledge of the universal duality are beyond her wretched capacity to understand. Felix Prosper, by comparison, intuitively knows both the glory and the darkness but he is incapable of action that would reconcile the two. The best he can accomplish is to still the pendulum and benignly endure:

> He went back to the table and gathered up the bones that lay around his plate. He stood with a fish spine in his hand. Flesh mountainous contemplating. Saint Felix with a death's head meditating.
>
> At last he threw the bones into the stove. The heat from the stove, the heat crept in from the day outside, anointed his face. Blest, he sat down again in the rocker, and the boards creaked and groaned as he fiddled.[6]

He is the passive complement to James, "like a round world all centred in on himself," as the Widow's boy describes him;[7] waiting, knowing, enduring until Angel returns, until the child is born, until glory prevails. Kip is the messenger, the servant of Coyote, who envisions the glory and rises to pull it down from the sky. He tries to possess it. Analogous to his impositions on Lenchen, about which he declares "I wanted a man's girl. . .I'd seen enough to buy her,"[8] he covets what cannot be had. James says of his greed, "Kip had been playing around with the glory of the world."[9] As a consequence, he is blinded. He is contrite, but his vision, however myopic, is gone and he becomes an integrated part of the community rather than its ominous prophet. William, the link with an outside world, and Ara, his barren wife, Theophil, the Widow and the Widow's boy, Heinrich, Angel and Lenchen, each in their separate ways similar to Kip and Felix, fill out the gap between darkness and the glory. Yet none of them reconcile the two or embody their reconciliation. Even James does not do that, but rather moves from one perspective to the other, carrying the rest along with him. Nothing happens in the novel that is not an extension of James' activities. They are each caught up alone in the existentialist vacuum between substance and essence; all but James who intuitively rebels, who, murdering his mother, lacerating Kip, flees to another reality where he is confronted with the impracticability of escaping himself; returns with humility, freed, as he says, from freedom,[10] to accept his moral obligations in the community.

James is not an existentialist protagonist. The novel is not a Sartrian conundrum of existentialist despair. Through the carefully modulated duality of her vision, Mrs. Watson declares the possibility of moral triumph in an amoral universe. The fact that the community is, in a sense, eventually healed, reconciled to the darkness, with hope for the glory, is in itself the mark of grace. Existentialist conditions of moral and social isolation that each character endures prove to be self-imposed, the result of allowing the ubiquitous Coyote to displace in their experience the possibilities of universal continuity, of hope and glory. Still within the arc of the pendulum, they nevertheless are moved to acceptance and to the freedom of moral responsibility which they had previously been denied by their separate fears. Fear is divisive; hope draws them together. In the overall form of the novel, the human characters occupy the span that lies between two extremities of being. They are subject to the knowledge that each implies the opposite. Knowing that the opposing extremes are not mutually exclusive, they perceive them, respond to them, not as complementary conditions but as irreconcilably coexistent. In the novel's beginning, they are separately bound to physical mortality. By the novel's end, they have been drawn together in the common knowledge that spirituality might prevail. In the total vision of the novel, however, they have learned to participate in no more than the freedom of hope, of communal responsibility. They have not escaped their mortal condition; but they have learned to rise above its divisive and terrible imposition on their lives. Through James, they are reconciled to duality although it is not resolved and cannot be.

The shape of this movement, which is one of moral perception more than of action, conforms to the dualism it exhibits. It is a form derived throughout from the counterpoised presence of the corporeal world, on the one hand, and the universal, elemental, world, on the other. But these worlds are not singular, either. Corporeal being in itself holds the potential of renewal as well as destruction. Earth, air, fire, and water are the stuff of spontaneous existence as well as eternity. In exploiting these ambivalent possibilities on simultaneous planes of visceral and intellectual response, Sheila Watson builds a dualist edifice as clear and as complex as existence itself. The external realities of her novel, and there are no others, for her characters never ruminate without objectifying their feelings in terms of the physical environment, are as anonymous as they are specific. They are structural in effect, enclosing her vision in an objective world that has perimeters, but endless dimension.

The primal elements are deployed in imagery that makes quite evident their ambivalence, their universality, and their intimate consequence to individual existence. Air, the host of light and of darkness, in the following passage is both reproach and perverse benediction, and provides tangible evidence for the clarity of James' new vision with which he has turned homewards:

> James' horse still brought him on. Night had shrunk into the long shadows of the trees, into slender shadows of the grass, into the flitting shadow of birds. Light defined the world. It picked out the shattered rock, the bleached and pitted bone.
>
> It would edge the empty bottle on Felicia's table, James thought. It would lie congealed in the unwashed plates. It would polish the yellow on Traff's head and count the streaked tears under Lilly's eyes.
>
> It would shine in his own empty mangers. On Kip's face. On Greta's bleak reproach. On the loose stones William had piled on his mother's grave.[11]

Air is the medium of the glory, shining with the sun. It also sustains the aridness of their communal lives. Air is the medium of darkness, of fear. Paradoxically, it carries the penetrating cold light of the moon: "He was alone under the moon in the white shed of the world,"[12] refers to an outcast Kip, and some of this same vulnerability is cast upon Lenchen who, waiting for James, felt "Fear flooding her body as the moonlight flooded the hills. Exposed in the white light like a hawk pulled out and pinned up on a barn door for all to see."[13] Earth, too, is a medium of continuity and of destruction. Combined, in the following discourse between the Widow Wagner and her son, with other elements, it suggests both:

> How would you know? his mother asked. You've not loved.
> No, he said. But he thought of light blazed into a branch of

> fire. How could he say that the earth scorched his foot. That he must become ash and be born into a light which burned but did not destroy.[14]

Similarly, potatoes that "baked in the shallow soil" are paradoxically associated through the presence of Felix with "the vertical glory of the July sun."[15]

Water and fire are symbolically employed with less economy and more clarity, perhaps, than the passive elements, the earth and the air. Time and again, images of water intrude on the consciousness of Mrs. Watson's characters. It is a life force but it carries death in its flow:

> The water was running low in the creek. Except in the pools, it would be hardly up to the ankle. Yet as she watched the old lady, Ara felt death leaking through from the centre of the earth. Death rising to the knee. Death rising to the loin.
>
> She raised her chin to unseat the thought. No such thing could happen. The water was drying away. It lay only in deep pools.[16]

For Ara, as for the others,, water is simultaneously appropriate to the present conditions of her life–she is barren and she is receptive to the old woman's spectral embodiment of death, yet she is determinedly wilful–and to the universal conditions of existence. In water are the fish that sustain Felix but, also, the nameless fears that drew Mrs. Potter to fish without satisfaction for the ineffable. The fourth element, fire, the element that consumes Greta, warms the chilled spirit of the solitary Felix. Fire, inseparable from light, as all the elements are ultimately inseparable from each other, is in the lamp that old Mrs. Potter burns like Diogenes in broad daylight, searching for the indefinable consequence of existence. It actively characterizes the effect of the other three elements in Heinrich's attempts to perceive the same elusive mysteries:

> In the sky above darkness had overlaid light. But the boy knew as well as he knew anything that until the hills fell on him or the ground sucked him in the light would come again. He had tried to hold darkness to him, but it grew thin and formless and took shape as something else. He could keep his eyes shut after the night, but it would be light he knew. Light would be flaming off

> the bay mare's coat. Light would be kindling on the fish in the dark pools.[17]

Unlike the old woman, an apparition already past the brink of death, the Widow's boy cannot elude the fire, the glory, even when he is most consciously determined to do so. In his particular sphere of being, fire is as beneficent an element as it is destructive in the sphere occupied by Greta, as it is ambivalent in that of Felix, who is anointed with characteristic passivity by the sweat on his face from the heat of the stove and of the day outside.

However the ubiquitous Coyote might conform to schemes of Indian or Celtic or Judaic mythology, in context it seems to me that Coyote is first and foremost the simple embodiment of corporeal existence. The elements air and earth are inert and, like fire and water, without form. They are universal tangibles which extend from specific perceptions to the conditions of universal being. But the setting of *The Double Hook* is contiguous with human experience and not just an elemental equivalent. It has physical, anatomical, form–usually expressed in images of desiccation or decay:

> Overhead the sky with tight as rawhide. About them the bars of the earth darkened. The flat ribs of the hills.[18]
>
> Ara looked up too. For a minute she saw the light. Then only the raw skin of the sky drawn over them like a sack.[19]
>
> Twigs cracking like bone.[20]
>
> Must the whole world suffer because Greta had been wronged? Must the creek dry up forever and the hills be pegged like tanned skin to the rack of their own bones?[21]

These and similar images lend to the landscape an aura of stasis, while having diverse narrative and symbolic significance in their separate contexts. Ara's perception in the sample above, for instance, conforms to her notion of thunder as a bull-whip in the paragraph following this one, an image which emerges later as the characteristic implement of her notion of God in confrontation with recalcitrant humanity. She is several times overwhelmed by the possibility of mortal subjugation to a profligate Lord. The raw skin closed over the community carries the lash-marks of its collective suffering. Conversely, the image in the last example I quoted, which James associates with Greta, offers intimations of an opposite state. That James questions the necessity of such misery implies the possibility of avoiding it. Recognition of his past moral deprivation in the paragraph preceding this one lends such a reading credibility, makes the image an ironic emblem of hope. Accepting moral responsibility, James has determined to return, to "stand silent in their cry of hate. Whatever the world said, whatever the girl said, he'd find her. Out of his corruption life had leafed and he'd stepped on it carelessly with a man steps on spring shoots."[22] With the introduction of vegetative imagery, the hide of the world stretched for curing comes to represent a rejected state of existence, of moribund passivity, from which the community has already begun to emerge.

The anatomical form of the physical setting, revealed in the images of bodily death, is the habitat of Coyote. He is everywhere alive in the depths of the rocks and the folds of the hills and as the embodiment of fear in the minds of the community. Only Theophil is close-minded and wilful enough to regard Coyote as merely an animal. To the others he is an ominous presence in animal form, the elusive imponderable purveyor of death:

> Above on the hills
> Coyote's voice rose among the rocks:
> In my mouth is forgetting
> In my darkness is rest.[23]
>
> To gather briars and thorns,
> said Coyote.
> To go down into the holes of the rock
> and into the caves of the earth.
> In my name is peace.[24]

His is the voice of living death, the condition of mortal being. By resigning to the primacy of substance, of material reality, the characters of the novel have given themselves over to Coyote's domain. Each of them is really alive only to his own physical presence. Each is isolated from the others, haunted by inexorable death in the apparition of old Mrs. Potter, consumed with fear. By the novel's close, they are freed of Coyote's grasp on their lives, yet, as I have already suggested, he cannot be entirely denied. The liberation of souls from individual stagnation to spiritual community rests on a renewal of vision rather than of actual being. Lenchen's baby, like the others, is mortal. None can entirely evade the reach of Coyote, least of all Theophil who, in not recognizing him as an object of justifiable fear, is unable to escape his grasp and remains outside the community, alone.

Coyote, Kip, the Old Woman, and the act of fishing are explicitly interrelated throughout the text. Coyote's presence inevitably coincides with a consciousness of death. He is the darkness of the soul that fear of death brings into individual lives. He is the pervasive embodiment of that fear. The old woman is the seeker of meaning in the darkness. Her lamp at high noon is the tangible symbol of her quest and her fishing, its analogous activity. The others who see her still fishing after her death were unnerved by her apparent behaviour because they have accepted the darkness, the imminence of death, without question–all but James who understands that it is not something to be sought after, whatever it is that she seeks, and kills her. In doing so, the first step is taken unwittingly towards the light. Kip is Coyote's servant. He can see the glory and he reaches out to possess it. Doing the work of Coyote within the community, he shows it to be unattainable. Only when he is blinded by James, by the whip that, in Ara's perception at least, is akin to an instrument of God's vengeance, does the glory become possible as something that is each man's due, along with the darkness, rather than being a radiance beyond his reach or his realm of being.

Coyote's power in the conscious lives of the community diminishes as it is drawn together by compassion and the possibility of renewal. The world of substance is reduced by the change in the moral perspective and the world of essence, of hope and commitment, is given ascendency. The ambiguities of elemental reality which is the universal context, however, are not resolved, for life is a double hook and without the body, there is no soul, without responsibility there is no freedom, without the darkness there is no glory.

This dualism, out of which the form of the novel emerges, implies the continuing presence of a God in whom the extremities of substance and essence, of corporeal and universal being, are both possible. Such a God as there is, portrayed in this novel, is somewhat of a mystery. Like the God of the faithful, he is known yet obscure. He is context rather than presence, form rather than being. The darkness of Coyote's realm is contained within him, in spite of Ara's assertion to the contrary–

> Even God's eye could not spy out the men lost here already, Ara thought. He had looked mercifully on the people of Nineveh though they did not know their right hand and their left. But there were not enough people here to attract his attention. The cattle were scrub cattle. The men like sift in the cracks of the earth.[25]

If this were so, there would have been no possibility of redemption. And clearly, in context, Ara is shown to be wrong. Nor is he returned as a Saviour to their midst, despite such an event being envisioned, for example, through the humility of Felix:

> His eyelids dropped. His flesh melted. He rose from the bed on soft owl wings. And below he saw his old body crouched down like an ox by the manger.[26]

If this were so, all the acts of responsibility–the Widow's knitting a singlet, for example, and the submission of Angel to her husband's plaintive request for help–would signify community with God and not with humanity. They would be gestures of obeisance rather than positive acts of reconciliation with the conditions of life. Allusions to a Second Coming are aptly countered by the closing words of Coyote which proclaim the infant's mortality. It seems to me that there is a God in *The Double Hook* who occupies neither of the extremities of being, but includes both. He is the context of dual reality rather than a redemptive or ignorant or malevolent presence within it. Ultimately, he is the form of the moral universe that Mrs. Watson has revealed in the poetic arrangement of physical imminence and spiritual grace that is the vision of *The Double Hook.*

God, in *The Double Hook,* exists as a logical and structural implication, if he can be said to exist at all. *The Channel Shore* contains no such circumscribing and elusive being. The metaphysical implications in Bruce's novel derive consistently from the patterns of moral complexity which repeat themselves through the continuum of human experience. Bruce maintains a penetrating focus on a single, lateral, plane of reality. As with the magic-realist painters, meaning is revealed in form, and form derives from actuality. As in the paintings of Tom Forrestall and Alex Colville, Maritimers, or Ken Danby or the American, Andrew Wyeth, the design of *The Channel Shore* grows out of the shapes and the details of ordinary experience in a representational relationship. Such a design has no room for a Supreme Being from another dimension of reality. However, while God does not make an appearance in the form of divine providence or divine retribution, he is manifest in the religious castes of the Shore. As a consequence, his presence is dissipated through the channels of Roman Catholic and Methodist social conventions and sectarian dogmas. The Godhead in itself is a negligible force except as a moral justification counterpoised with the real needs of the characters for moral, for spiritual, guidance and comfort.

The Channel Shore is not a novel of religion, however. Nor is it prophetic. Quite the opposite to Sheila Watson's achievement, Bruce envisions a world of moral complexity in a dynamic social context in which faith and revelation are functions of personal knowledge rather than transcendent intuition. The differing dispositions of certain common factors reinforce the opposition of their visions, although their vastly different scales of representation and focal perspective leave little doubt of their dissimilarity.

Each novel deals with a small community in an isolated setting. Each concentrates on three families. But in *The Channel Shore,* these are contiguous with a larger community on the Shore, which in turn extends throughout a broad spectrum of time and place. This is Bill Graham's conclusion, for instance, as he leaves for Ontario, in the final paragraphs of the novel:

> And the essence of the Shore was that you couldn't foresee anything. All you could see were the following waves of time.
>
> Nothing is ever finished.
>
> He let it go. He watched the gulf shore slide by, then woods and hilly pastures as the train swung inland. But even though he had turned his thought from plans and problems and speculations, back into dreamlike communion with the living Shore, he could not keep his mind away from people.
>
> For he was one of them. One of the thousands who had taken this road away. To Boston, to Montreal, to the western prairies. To Denver and Winnipeg. To Dawson City and San Francisco. To Vimy and Dieppe and Caen.[27]

In contrast, Mrs. Watson's community is self-contained, self-limiting. When James leaves, it is to a separate reality, a descent into the outside world conforming to archetypal preludes to ascension. Only

William, his brother, lives in continuing intercourse between the two realms in his function as postal agent and rational, although uninspired, link with the outside, the other, the unreal world of actuality. Bruce also makes use of the rural postal service, but as a means of continuity and community, rather than as the reminder of isolation that is William Potter's role. The Post Office in Currie Head is in the McKee's kitchen and there, through the three generations that the novel includes, the people gather and gossip and participate in their common experience. Even when Anse returns after World War II, he is given tacit acceptance by the McKees, despite his complicity in their daughter's death a generation earlier. Their house is a reception centre for the community and, for good or bad, Anse is a part of the Shore and must be allowed re-entry into their midst. But it is Adam Falt, the mail driver along the Shore through the same period of time that the novel covers, whose personality and vocation connect Currie Head with the rest of the world. His mode of conveyance changes with the times, his schedule becomes concentrated, but inevitably his presence suggests continuity, spatially and in time. He is a constant:

> Adam spent most of his time behind his horses, on the road. The variety of people who lived along it was wide enough to satisfy his interest and every one of them he knew by name.
>
> Most days there was nothing new. The same men and boys, harrowing and seeding in the spring, making hay in late July and August, digging potatoes in October, ploughing in October and November, working in the woods when the snow fell. The same women, seen against a background of blowing sheets on distant clothes-lines, or swinging hand-rakes in a sweeping motion behind the hay rack.
>
> The same weather, cold and windy in March, bright with sun under tall clouds or overcast with brooding rain, from June to fall; frosty or wet or white with snow in winter.
>
> In all these usual things there was something to interest a man.[28]

At this point he had been on the route for nine years. A generation later, now driving a Chevrolet, he arouses in Bill Graham "a small interesting thought. This was, that a man of forty-odd, seen by a boy of thirteen, never gets any older. Adam Falt was just as he had been, on this platform, twenty-seven years ago. Just as he had been a year ago, in the timeless land of memory."[29]

There are other common factors between the novels which similarly have quite different functions. Felix Prosper, for example, is in many ways the same as Richard McKee. People come to both of them for definition of their private isolation. Yet both are benign characters offering more by their company than by their advice or example. However, where Felix embodies benevolent resignation in the community's midst, Richard offers a dour indefatigability against the rush of time and the anxieties of moral dilemma. Both have a positive effect. But Richard's influence is direct, not passive, ennobling rather than being, like that of Felix, demeaning even when it is most operative. And Richard is not a symbol, an emblem of something else; he is a living man in whom are met and resolved a diversity of problems. Hazel's fear vanishes when she comes to him to confess her pregnancy. He provides enough fragments of memory to make the young Grant's impression of his father more tangible and tolerable than the distorted image provided by his uncle, James Marshall, who has reared him. Richard gives solace to Alan who suffers from being the bastard of Hazel and Anse, raised as Grant's son and in love with Grant's daughter, Margaret, when Anse returns to disrupt the tenuous balance of their relations. He gives solace to Margaret and a measure of hope. And yet he is a quiet man, a loner, and given to outdated, outmoded ways. He keeps to himself and others come to him, as they do to Felix, but to him as a man and not as a symbol of some other more limited and, perhaps, more profound state of being.

There are similarities. But the differences are far more inescapable. The Channel Shore is a place of people, of memories and the patterns of lives. Like the community in *The Double Hook,* it is a world in miniature, but an actual world and not an abstraction. Passing within Grant's sphere of consciousness is a somewhat didactic explanation of the Shore's representative personality:

> . . .along the Shore you found all the differences that make up nationality: different ways of doing things; differences of upbringing and religion; differences between Findlay's Bridge with its touch of village superiority, and Currie Head; differences between Currie Head, full of Protestant Scots and English, and the Irish Catholics of Katen's Rocks and Mars Lake. Differences between all these and Forester's Pond, which kept the name though the last Forester was gone, and where, although the

> Catholic Church was there, you began to get a sprinkling again of the up-shore kind of people. The Channel Shore–a little nation.
>
> All getting along in a kind of working tolerance but divided by difference.. . .Differences that came down to people in the end. Differences between people.[30]

It is redundant to point out that the nation for which the Channel Shore is a metaphor is, or could easily be, Canada. My purpose, however, and I believe that of the novel, is not to dwell on such obvious intimations. It is enough to realize that the setting, ultimately, is people. Time and the landscape are the informing principles of their lives. But it is people with whom Bruce is concerned, on whom his vision is relentlessly focused. This, alone, sets him at the opposite extreme of aesthetic perception from Sheila Watson.

People, the characters, in *The Channel Shore* occupy interrelating patterns of reality. These are held in place by the landscape, even while they evolve through the passing of time. The past emerges for them all in the patterns of the continuous present, surging like the sea onto the shores of consciousness. And the present recedes into undercurrents of memory which turn back on themselves to gather and surge again forward in future experience. Bruce writes about patterns of convention, of "the usual," of habit, of chance, of change. He describes a reflexive response of Adam Falt's as "a pattern woven of memory and experience traced in the fabric of his brain by years of human contact on the Channel Shore road."[31] Alan's response to the return of Anse, his illegitimate father, picks up the metaphor, a generation later;

> Now the images began to lose their unreality, to become life, the beginning of a whole new story–a story that must fit itself by word and recollection, by glance and touch, into the pattern of the Channel Shore. What ravelling-out, what industrious reweaving. . .[32]

Bill Graham, the outsider, continues the image further, on hearing that Alan has moved away from home and in with Josie, his natural grandmother, as Grant had done from his own surrogate father years before: "Best way to begin the new design, woven of the old. Best way to begin the change in the pattern–in the memory and imagination and knowledge of the Shore."[33]

From the intricate context of an interwoven design emerge the primary stories of Grant and of Alan and Margaret, and the other stories that set theirs in motion and bring them through to resolution. Structurally, the whole is circumscribed by the consciousness of Bill Graham, the outsider who returns to his ancestral home on the Shore as a boy of thirteen and, twenty-seven years later, as a veteran of World War II. Enough is revealed about his family life in Toronto, the anxieties and frustrations, and about his personality, engaging and relaxed, to make it clear that Currie Head is peripheral to the facts of his life, yet the cornerstone of his existence. He, more than any other, represents the author. He is not present through much of the action and, when he is, it is as a sympathetic bystander rather than as one of the principals. He is not a narrator in whose awareness the patterns are arranged; nor would it be possible, given the controlled omniscience of the author, for him to be so. His function, it seems to me, is to provide a vital framework outside the narrative flow in which to contain the Shore, to give it definition within a single conscious, receptive, and sympathetic mind.

Early in the novel's chronology, Bill is one of the boys swimming at Kilfyle's Hole when Anse passes by on his way to a tryst with Hazel McKee. A few weeks later, he witnesses the shared intimacy of Grant and Anna Gordon as they part from an evening's walk. These pairings established, Bruce then allows him to recede into the background and the narrative progresses. Hazel and Anse, free-spirit and malevolent spectre, conceive a child, Alan. But before her pregnancy is known, Hazel has turned away from Anse, and he has fled, privately humiliated, to the outside world. Grant and Anna, Anse's sister and a Roman Catholic, are kept separate despite the quiet urgency of their love, by Grant's ambivalent submission to the imperious will of his stern Methodist uncle, James Marshall. Their love founders and Anna leaves the Shore for respite in Halifax. She is killed by a streetcar. In moral indignation, Grant leaves the house of his surrogate father and moves in with Anna's family, Josie and Stewart Gordon who, with Anse gone as well and Stewart rather confused by reality, cannot cope with their farm. As further contrition and to restore a moral balance, Grant brings Hazel back to the Shore from her refuge in Toronto, marries her, and accepts Alan as his own son. Hazel dies.

In the middle section of the novel, some thirteen years later, Grant is married again. He and Renie have a child of their own, Margaret, who is passionately attached to young Alan. The community has absorbed Alan's past and guards him from the knowledge of it. But when its revelation appears as an imminent threat, Grant determines to send Alan away. Alan does not submit, as Grant had done to James, to his father's will. He learns of his past from Josie, loves Grant the more for being a father by choice and compassion and moral necessity, and asks to remain. Grant relents, with covert satisfaction.

The final section, immediately following World War II, sees Bill Graham once again on the Channel Shore. Like Alan, he is a returned veteran, but Alan has returned to stay and Bill Graham is a visitor, a witness. Relations between Grant and Alan are strained by Grant's refusal to acknowledge Alan's maturity. Alan and Margaret admit their love for each other which, by now, in the eyes of the Shore and of their family is tantamount to incest. Yet it is closely akin to the doomed relations between Grant and Anna. As Alan prepares, in desperation, to leave Currie Head, his natural father, Anse, reappears on the scene after a generation's absence. Pride, the desire to protect Grant, and his love for Margaret demand of Alan some resolution to the complexity of his situation. Ironically, through Anse's misanthropy, one occurs. Anse attempts to disrupt thoroughly the close self-preserving structure of the community by revealing at a public gathering his complicity in the patterns it has attempted to subsume over the years. However, Alan rises to the occasion, acknowledges Anse as his parent and proudly asserts his independence by striking him down. Anse flees the public humiliation. Grant, meanwhile, has recognized Anna, who would have been Alan's natural aunt, in Alan and accepts him as a man who is not also his son but who is beloved, nonetheless. And Alan and Margaret are freed by the open knowledge of their separate family origins to love openly. Bill Graham's visit ends. He leaves the Shore, musing that "In a hundred years the tale would be part of that long hearsay, a thread in a dim forgotten fabric. . .linked through tenuous blood-lines to the moving Now."[34]

These are the stories central to the novel, which spin off in a gyrating fashion from one to the other in a sequence of repetition and change. The separate patterns into which the narrative structure may be broken down are ultimately parts of a single design. As Renie, another outsider but one who has married into the Shore, perceives, with ellipsis intact:

> If a person could be given the eye to see. . .One day out of each

> year would be enough, back to the beginning.. . .The Holiday or a Sunday service or a church supper around Christmas time. Given that sort of clairvoyance you could see the story of the Shore. And yet, what differed, across a hundred and fifty years? Horses and saddles, once; buggies later; and now flivvers, jalopies. Hand-made leather boots and homespun, then. Tweed now, from the mail-order houses. And always faces. Faces that didn't change, really, though worn by different people in different generations. . .[35]

Somewhat reminiscent of *Brigadoon,* this concept provides the informing principle of Bruce's other novel, *The Township of Time.* In *The Channel Shore,* however, it is not the structural basis but, rather, its effect. All that has happened and been on the Shore is arranged in the memories of its inhabitants at points equidistant from the present. And the present is continually, inexorably, absorbed into the interwoven design of the past.

When Alan, as an adolescent, surveys the remnants of other times in the loft over his grandfather's shop, he is saddened by the mutability of human things. But he is also elated. "For the first time, he was conscious of glimpsing yesterday, today and tomorrow as part of a continuing whole. It put things in balance, and in a kind of abstract way was comforting when you thought about it."[36] As James Marshall observes in pondering the existence of God, it would be difficult to know "where space ended and time began."[37] Margaret associates time with people, and "the sense of home,"[38] in her musings about the irretrievable past. Grant, working on his property after having heard the tragic story of its earlier owners, is taken by a more definitive relationship of time and place.

> This was land that had been his great-aunt Fanny's, land a red-headed man had planned to clear in the times between his voyages. He felt a little of it himself. Last week this had been merely a big wood-lot which people called Grant's Place. Now it was land with history, land with life. Aunt Fanny's and Grant's Place, merged in a marriage of time. Land with a past and a future.[39]

Ironically, the locus of his great-aunt's ill-starred love becomes the predominant setting in his own tragic affair with Anna, and a reproach to him for his moral reticence until he restores moral order, in his own mind at least, by marrying Hazel on the premise that "Not a damn thing matters but what people can do for each other, when they're up against it."[40] In this instance, as clearly as anywhere in the novel, a pattern from the past emerges, somewhat modified, in the present. It is repeated once again, with variations, in the potentially disastrous affair between Alan and Margaret, both of whom have grown up on the Place.

Few novels have such a powerful sense of the landscape, the land and its seasons, as this sleeper of Canadian fiction. Inevitably, the moral implications of Bruce's vision are derived from the setting which, in turn, is fused with its people and the passage of time. The righteousness of Grant's moving in with the Gordon's after Anna's death, for example, is implicit in Stewart's perception of the "curious illusion of time drawn out. . .as if Grant had been around the house and the woods and the fields for years."[41] The ninety acres of land, the Place, that Anna suspects are Grant's chosen alternative to their love become, as I have suggested above, a tangible and haunting reproach to Grant for failing her, for failing them both. Other places, Kilfyle's Hole, the hauling-road to Katen's Store, to McKee's for mail, each of these places shapes the moral patterns sustained by the Shore. Yet it is the Shore, collectively, that reveals the design of the author's moral vision. It is a design that is clear and yet, like the Channel Shore, indefinable because it reaches past an immediate context to other and all times and places. Ultimately, it is no less a universal vision than Sheila Watson's in *The Double Hook.* But the medium of its transposition into aesthetic reality is actual experience rather than art experience, the conditions of real geography and real people rather than their surrealist abstractions.

Bruce is a regionalist writer in the finest tradition of romantic realism that extends through Trollope's Barsetshire, Hardy's Wessex, and perhaps, reaches an apex in Faulkner's Yoknapatawpha. Capitalizing on the precedents of the genre, the moral dynamics of his novel are developed in the concatenations of geneology, sustained by the insistent presence of the landscape, and resolved in communal experience that extends infinitely beyond regional perimeters. The natural world is both the context of personal isolation, of the uniqueness of individual lives, and the medium that gives it community with the isolation of others. The Channel Shore is a region, a place, and a means of perceiving; or, as Bruce writes in the epigraph, "a country of the mind, the remembering blood," for those who have lived there or lived his vision of it.

Sheila Watson is determinedly anti-regionalist, yet regional nonetheless. The physical world in *The Double Hook* does not extend laterally beyond the sharp edges of her novel's reality. It exists in a separate dimension, defined with implosive descriptions of detail that place the isolation of individual beings in parentheses between primal substance and universal essence. The allusions adhering to the factors of landscape and weather are more structurally and thematically significant in a vertical pattern extending through the several planes of being, than for their inherent characteristics and relationships on the level of ordinary experience. By exploiting the ambiguities of reality she ultimately defines its limits. Unlike that of Charles Bruce, her conception of the geophysical world is determined by its simultaneous embodiment of the particular and the universal. Time, in *The Double Hook,* is irrelevant except as a necessary context. Yet both she and Bruce build the patterns of moral and physical isolation, the conditions of human existence, from those of the natural world. Both redeem their characters from the ultimate oblivion of isolation through a sense of community imposed by the conditions of their natural surroundings. Surrealist and magic-realist meet on the common ground of geophysical experience.

Notes

1. Sheila Watson, *The Double Hook* (Toronto: New Canadian Library, 1969), p.92. (Toronto: McClelland & Stewart, 1959.)
2. *Ibid.*, p.107.
3. *Ibid.*, p.134.
4. *Ibid.*, p.133.
5. *Ibid.*, p.113.
6. *Ibid.*, p.24.
7. *Ibid.*, p.129.
8. *Ibid.*, p.72.
9. *Ibid.*, p.132.
10. *Ibid.*, p.121.

11. *Ibid.*, p.126.
12. *Ibid.*, p.59.
13. *Ibid.*, p.59.
14. *Ibid.*, p.81.
15. *Ibid.*, p.23.
16. *Ibid.*, p.21.
17. *Ibid.*, p.44.
18. *Ibid.*, p.35.
19. *Ibid.*, p.36.
20. *Ibid.*, p.42.
21. *Ibid.*, p.127.
22. *Ibid.*, p.127.
23. *Ibid.*, p.29.
24. *Ibid.*, p.98.
25. *Ibid.*, pp.22-23.
26. *Ibid.*, p.126.
27. Charles Bruce, *The Channel Shore* (Toronto: Macmillan,1957), p.398. (1954.)
28. *Ibid.*, p.46.
29. *Ibid.*, p.273.
30. *Ibid.*, p.291.
31. *Ibid.*, p.48.
32. *Ibid.*, p.312.
33. *Ibid.*, p.394.
34. *Ibid.*, p.394.
35. *Ibid.*, p.375.
36. *Ibid.*, p.243.
37. *Ibid.*, p.249.
38. *Ibid.*, p.353.
39. *Ibid.*, p.88.
40. *Ibid.*, p.208.
41. *Ibid.*, p.153.

4.
The Ubiquitous Bastard

Conditions of human isolation and geophysical setting seem inevitably to converge on a moral plane in Canadian fiction. This is the case in other literatures as well, although it might be argued that it is more prevalent in Canadian than elsewhere. The patterns of convergence are as various as the land and the imagination of its people. Some emerge into characteristic prominence by the frequency of their occurrence. The focal image of one such pattern is that of frozen carcasses, stiff in the snow. Others derive from marital detente or disintegration such as exists amidst the natural and emotional wilderness of *As For Me and My House, Swamp Angel,* and, with ironic variations, *The Nymph and the Lamp.* Not unrelated are the patterns of sexual tension which are an integral part of these novels and *The Double Hook* and *The Channel Shore* as well. One concept in particular, however, stands above the rest as a correlative of geophysical and human isolation in moral conjunction–that evoked by the implications of bastard offspring and illegitimate origins.

In some novels, such as *The Channel Shore* and *Wild Geese,* illegitimacy provides the basic plot-structure, the moral conditions to be resolved. In both these novels, the apparently anti-social implications of illegitimate birth conform to the insularity of their settings. Bruce and Ostenso exploit hidden knowledge about such an event, but its isolating effect is quite differently conceived in their separate visions. Nevertheless, it is the source of malevolent power for both Caleb Gare and Anse Gordon, by which the former tyrannizes his family and the latter insidiously subverts communal stability. Other novels, like *The Double Hook* and Mazo de la Roche's *Possession,* conclude with illegitimate birth as a moral triumph, although in both these cases, the imminence of the natural setting tempers the triumph with a measure of resignation. In Watson's novel, young Lenchen's child is made clearly the inheritor of the mortal condition that afflicts the others, while in *Possession* the reconciliation of Derek Vale with mortality and solitude, and with Fawnie, is as much through his son's death as through his birth. More often, illegitimacy is absorbed into the narrative texture as a determing condition of characters' lives which fully conforms to the narrative conflict without being directly the cause of it. This is the case of Matt Carney, in *The Nymph and the Lamp,* born to a wayward girl in a remote Newfoundland outport and destined to live the isolation his origins imply. More directly, Alan Bentley's character is the product of illegitimacy. He is the son of a small-town waitress and an itinerant student minister. *As For Me and My House* is not overtly about the consequences of his unfortunate beginnings but their effect is implicit in the events surrounding his life with Mrs. Bentley in Horizon. Occasionally, the knowledge of illegitimacy emerges in the seemingly incidental revelation of detail. In *Swamp Angel,* Nell Severance admits to Maggie that she had never been married, that her devotion to Severance was a matter of will rather than conventional necessity. Ironically, her indifference to social decorum drives her bastard child into the role of an incorruptibly middle-class housewife. More important, it reinforces the moral righteousness of Maggie's desertion of Vardoe for the British Columbian wilderness. Similarly, the casual revelations of illegitimate birth amongst the Tonnerres in Margaret Laurence's Manawaka stories inevitably have moral implications far beyond their immediate contextual impact. This is the formative source, for example, of Piquette in "The Loons," who later burns to death with her own children, and of Valentine, in *The Fire-Dwellers,* who is consumed by the dissipation rampant in the core of Vancouver. Both the Tonnerre girls are apparently predestined by the social and moral deprivation of their origins, to extinction. Their isolation and the abuse they endure begins at their beginning, on the edge of the world beyond the community, which disowns them, and the land, which they, half-breed and dissolute, have disowned.

Variations on the concept in Canadian fiction of bastard offspring and bastard origins occur in the familiar situation of orphaned or abandoned children brought up by surrogate parents. This is a favourite device in Hugh MacLennan's novels. In *The Watch That Ends the Night,* Jerome has emerged from the wilderness of the Miramichi, his mother the victim of murder, and begins the course of an unconventional life of heroic proportions. Resulting in a somewhat more ignominious demise than MacLennan allows for Jerome Martell, Neil Fraser in Edward McCourt's *Music at the Close* dies as much alone on a Normandy beach as he had been when he was an orphan coming to live with elderly, indulgent relatives on their remote prairie farm. In *Barometer Rising,* the only one of MacLennan's novels in which the illegitimacy is actual and not a figurative device, MacLennan allows the retrieval of an abandoned child to provide moral sanction for the renewed conjugality of the unwed parents–and, unfortunately, an implied sanction to the disaster of the Halifax explosion. As in the Whiteoak saga of Mazo de la Roche, in which Maurice lives in open acknowledgement of his illegitimate daughter, Pheasant, or when the family takes the dead Eden's son back into their mainstream, or as Wakefield is brought up by Renny and Meg at Jalna, ultimate responsibility for the child of one's blood usually suggests more of social rectitude than of moral beneficence.

The farther the recurrent pattern of the isolated child is removed from the geophysical context, the less it seems to imply of the moral conditions of the characters involved. For Penny and Neil, as for the Whiteoaks, the misfortune of youngsters set alone by circumstance suggests familial unity, life independent of the natural world, rather than a divisiveness and spiritual estrangement concomitant with social and geophysical isolation. In *Music at the Close,* where the prairie is a relatively passive setting, Neil's adoption is the prelude to a lonely life of self-indulgent compromise which never achieves the profound dimensions of solitude that a more dominant landscape might have imposed. However, in the events surrounding the mature Jerome Martell, the discontinuity of childhood that was the result of wilderness experience is the source in his character of moral complexity and of his propensity to remain outside the conventional modes of behaviour. In *The Channel Shore,* where Alan is brought up by Grant and Renie, who are not blood-kin, the setting as perceived by Alan, as characterized by the author, is a correlative of his problematical isolation and also the substance, to a considerable extent, of its resolution. Less directly, the prairie setting of *As for Me and My House* offers a tangible equivalent to the relationship between Steve and his surrogate parents, in its relentless assertion of the separate conditions of all men. It also continues the impositions on Alan's solitary personality that his own discontinuous origins had begun years earlier. Inevitably, the more immediate the sense of geophysical place in Canadian fiction, the greater the moral burden it must carry. Where the context of birth is a significant factor of human isolation, this is more so than ever.

Bastard origin provides a disturbingly appropriate metaphor for the discontinuous conditions of individual life. With disarming clarity it embodies the moral conflict in human experience between natural and social principles. A threat to familial and communal unity, it demands a turning inwards upon individual resources, for better or worse, with an effect parallel to that of an imminent landscape.

At the convergence of geophysical reality and the conditions of individual being, the bastard child evokes patterns of isolation in Canadian fiction which embody an essentially moral vision at, perhaps, its most penetrating centre of focus. Other patterns offer other perspectives, but always the landscape and those who live with it close at hand sustain a reciprocal function which is the revelation of moral experience.

PART III
Irony and the Individual Consciousness

And suddenly Duddy did smile. He laughed. He grabbed Max, hugged him, and spun him around. 'You see,' he said, his voice filled with marvel. 'You see.'[1]

–The Apprenticeship of Duddy Kravitz

Nowhere is the dualism inherent in the experience of human isolation more evident than in the ironies sustained by individual consciousness in relation to the surrounding world. Irony is perhaps the concomitant of objective awareness in a country as anomalous and enigmatic as Canada–a country historically, geographically, and culturally rich, shapeless and contradictory. Certainly, in our fiction the ironic vision predominates. In our literature of exile, the pervasive irony is occasionally amusing, often bitter or tragic. Much of our regional writing effectively exploits the ironic dichotomy and convergence of moral and natural conditions. And in that vast body of fiction given to explication of individual consciouness in response to the self or the world around it, irony, too, is the distinguishing characteristic.

Other national literatures are as concerned with individuality. In the fiction of the United States, where the sanctity of the individual is enshrined in a Constitution, the concept of separate consciouness has largely been a matter of definition, of portraying the realization of innate potential: Hester Prynne and Captain Ahab pursue their separate selves with astonishing convictions of righteousness; Huck Finn journeys down the Mississippi on a voyage of self-discovery; Jamesian protagonists travel far to confront, ultimately, themselves; Hemingway's men and women enact their implicit strengths and weaknesses in public displays; Faulkner's Quentin Compson murders himself because he is who he is. The individual in American fiction tends to be a romantic figure, caught in the struggle of an emerging consciousness. It is seldom an ironic struggle, for the premise of personal identity and the objective of self-fulfilment are seldom ambiguous, however unclear the struggle itself may be.

The individual in British fiction is usually portrayed in confrontation with the conditions of his social environment. From Tom Jones and Tristram Shandy, through Becky Sharp, Dorothea Brooke, Pip, and Jude Fawley, to Gully Jimson and Joe Lampton, the individual character is seen in relation to a relatively rigid society, a conventional system of values and social custom. Often he is reduced to submission or annihilated, and occasionally he exuberantly prevails. Either way, individual and collective personalities converge. In England, it is society that is privileged, sanctified, and its members are obliged to conform or be rejected to an eccentric oblivion. There is little irony in such a movement of consciouness towards communal awareness, although there is a great deal of pathos, of comedy, and of socio-moral instruction.

The fulfilment of implicit potential in American fiction, and the expiation of eccentricity in British, converge in Canadian fiction. The result is irony. In works of those novelists who might by now be considered principal members of the Canadian literary establishment–Grove, Garner, Callaghan, and MacLennan–individual consciousness is conceived primarily as behavioural response to externals. In those of more recent members–Laurence, Richler, and Buckler–it emerges to a greater degree in conundrums of psychological awareness. All of these writers seem bent on representing the isolation endured by their separate characters on what is essentially an ironic plane. Their protagonists are different from others in their context, but the isolation so engendered does not make of them moral or social leaders, nor visionaries, nor righteous recluses, nor tragic nor comic celebrities. It merely makes them individuals whose difference from the norm is inevitably shaped by the dichotomy between their self-perceptions and the conditions imposed upon them by the world in which they live. This disparity, their measure as outsiders, contains the dimensions of irony that characterize their experience.

Perhaps a pair of brief sketches will more succinctly demonstrate what I mean, and escape the aridity of theoretic abstraction. Morley Callaghan's 1934 novel, *Such Is My Beloved,* and Mordecai Richler's

The Apprenticeship of Duddy Kravitz, first published in 1959, are both superb works of fiction, written in entirely different styles about different structures of experience, projecting different visions of reality. Yet thematically they are both operative primarily on an ironic level and their main protagonists endure a loneliness that is neither tragic nor comic but the ironic diminution of tragedy and comedy in the context of mundane reality.

Father Dowling is a young, robust, compassionate idealist. He seems unaware of his own suffocation within the absolutism of a Church sustained by dispassionate compromise but founded on principles of humility, love, and charity. Dowling befriends and attempts the salvation of two streetwalkers, Midge and Ronnie, who operate from a hotel across from his Toronto cathedral. His love for them is pure altruism, but it is misanthropically expressed. Like an impotent lecher, he buys them things, borrows for them, and enjoys the hurt of their using him, of their deceptions. His love is redeemed, however, by its purity of intent and its compassion. What he regards as a religious relationship is, rather, a spiritual relationship. But there is no room for genuine charity in Father Dowling's moral environment. The Bishop, a financier and administrator, is without sympathy. Charlie Stewart, the Marxist idealist, sees the girls as economic factors, Dowling as a victim. To Lou, the pimp, they are livelihood and Dowling is a threat. Robison, the fund-raising lawyer, and his vicious, vacuous wife have no sympathy. The only indication Callaghan allows of the spirit prevailing is in the peripheral character of Mrs. Schwartz, who fusses terribly about dying, but who, when she does, does so in peace, with grace and beauty. Somewhere beneath the hypocrisy of the Church and the self-conscious proselytes of charity, is the true church of God, the spirit of man. But Dowling is foreordained by the world in which he lives to failure in his redemptive quest. Only in his example are the prostitutes absolved: he ends in a mental hospital, in moments of ironic clarity writing a commentary on the spiritual love in *The Song of Songs.*

In Duddy Kravitz, Richler has created a Canadian Sammy Glick. Duddy's obsession to own land is as much a Canadian phenomenon as the dream of Schulberg's equally obnoxious, obstreperous, hustling, acquisitive, scheming, achieving protagonist in *What Makes Sammy Run?* to succeed as a Hollywood mogul, is American. Even as a student, Duddy tyrannizes friends, teachers, relatives. He alienates his father and yet aspires to emulate his father's hero, the Boy Wonder. He alienates his uncle Benjy, who puts Lennie through McGill medical school, and his grandfather, Simcha, and Lennie, his brother. Yet Duddy is a catalyst in his family. Through an overriding sense of loyalty, he retrieves Lennie from Toronto after his unpleasant complicity in an abortion; he brings Ida back from New York to be with Benjy when he dies. His feelings are something he controls, rationalizes, manipulates–all to achieve his own self-defined ambitions. He abuses his friends as he does himself. Yvette, with whom he sleeps and builds his dream of land, and the doggedly devoted, physically afflicted Virgil are both sacrificed ruthlessly to the cruel whim of aspiration. He is loyal without honour, determined and without integrity. Duddy is alone–he leads, hurts, and confounds those close to him but he is not one of them. His understanding of being a Jew is limited by his stereotyped concept of the brash, crass Jewish success in a Gentile world. In trying to beat both Jew and Gentile according to the rules by which he perceives them to play, he becomes a parody of the stereotype. He works so obsessively to belong, to be accepted, that he is excluded from either world and he has not the capacity to realize it, to understand that in gaining his coveted land he himself is lost.

Whether a character is conceived like Father Dowling as a simplistic creature incapable of comprehending the perverse nature of the simplistic world he occupies, or like Duddy Kravitz, as a complex contradictory person unable to comprehend himself, to bring himself into conscious focus against an equally complex, contradictory field of reference, the tendency in Canadian fiction is to exploit his ironic potential. Duddy is in many ways a comic character, and in some ways heroic. Father Dowling sustains an aspect of the tragic hero through to the end. Yet Richler's comic view serves only to make Duddy more human, to jape at the values of a system that would encourage such a man. Through a blend of hilarious exuberance and brutal cynicism, Duddy's success is made futile, his life an ironic encounter with himself. Callaghan, in comparison, imbues Father Dowling with a naiveté and graceless compassion that make his efforts at sharing salvation ironically empty, his life a grim parody of spiritual devotion–sad, but not tragic.

Irony is obviously not the exclusive property of Canadian novelists. In the critical cosmology of Northrop Frye it is the prevailing mode of our age. But as the distinguishing characteristic of authorial concepts of individual consciousness it would seem more prevalent in Canadian fiction than elsewhere. The patterns of individual isolation defined by the writers mentioned previously–Grove, Garner, Callaghan, MacLennan and Laurence, Richler and Buckler–do not necessarily emanate from within their characters' psyches. Grove and Richler, in particular, stay well on the outside of personality, observing behaviour with a clinical detachment that allows for the ironic manipulation of external conditions and events. Much to the same end, MacLennan usually delves only into the surface realities of his characters, as does Garner. Laurence and Buckler both allow external reality to take form according to the internal progress of their protagonists towards the integration of their own personalities. External and internal realities in Callaghan's novels equally tend to conform to predetermined thematic patterns. Whether events shape personality or are behavioural consequences or, as in Callaghan, event and character are both subservient to an ulterior purpose, these writers all explore the ironic potential of individual consciousness in patterns of isolation that are indigenous to the Canadian experience.

By consciousness, I am not referring to the vantage point of the author, the voice he speaks in, or his psychological objectives. I mean, quite simply, the self-conception of the protagonist, the characteristic quality of his awareness of being himself in relation to the world around him. Individual consciousness, in this sense, is the knowledge, ultimately, that he is different from others. This awareness, as in *The Mountain and the Valley,* may be the crux of the entire novel. Or it may be an intuitive condition of response to experience, as in *Cabbagetown.* It may be misunderstood, or a perverse motivating factor of a character's progress, as in Richler's Montreal novels and in Grove's entire canon. Awareness of personal difference may precipitate conflict, as it does in MacLennan's novels, or it may in itself be the conflict, as in the works of Margaret Laurence and Morley Callaghan.

The consciousness of himself as a unique creation that is given to a character is the common point of departure for these novelists in their variegated visions of human experience. It generates as wide a variety of patterns of isolation as the imagination can conceive. But as these patterns originate in Canadian experience it might be expected that they will display characteristics consistent with that experience, if not with each other.

The irony which I believe is particularly the response of individual consciousness to Canadian experience is generated by the divergence between two realities in our fiction: that of the protagonist's perception and that of the author's, of the protagonist and his environment. The patterns of isolation which emerge from this ironic encounter do not conform to any particular nationalist schema. They do, however, reveal a psychological set of mind that is distinctively Canadian, if not uniquely so. Literary analyses according to the dictates of rigid systems tend to omit much and to distort what they do reveal. The victim-survival concept imposed on our literature by Margaret Atwood, in *Survival,* is an exciting vehicle for authorial insights, for example, but excludes a great deal of material to which it does not apply. I believe that it is important to realize, always, that Canadian literature, or any other, contains systems and is not contained by them. There are various patterns of isolation within Canadian fiction, including those emanating from concepts of individual consciousness, and a knowledge of these patterns can contribute to our understanding of separate works as well as the collective tradition. But they must be perceived, not imposed.

Note

1. Mordecai Richler, *The Apprenticeship of Duddy Kravitz* (Toronto: New Canadian Library, 1969), p.319. (Don Mills: André Deutsch, 1959.)

1. Grove

Frederick Philip Grove's protagonists invariably suffer within the confines of a profound personal isolation that is the result of their particular responses to the fundamental realities of their lives. Each protagonist is in some way a unique and self-determining creation, fully conscious of the effects of being different, if not aware, quite, of the difference itself. The conditions impinging on their lives are those common to the rest of humanity: the inexorability of time's passage; the immutable laws of cause and effect; the intractability of the natural world and the impermanence of the human; the naiveté of pride; the emptiness of power; the futility and the grace of devotion. Each is enthralled with the mortal struggle to endure and conscious, at least, of that struggle.

Two of his protagonists are immigrants. Niels Lindstedt in *Settlers of the Marsh* and Phil Branden in *A Search for America* both embody the naiveté inherent in cultural transposition. Phil, however, is a highly sophisticated and somewhat insufferable *étranger,* who seemingly prevails over the North American experience that in fact moulds and manipulates him and spews him out, re-educated and unhumbled, to be a teacher, to explain life to others in the Canadian West. Niels Lindstedt, in comparison, is encumbered by a profound humility, rather than arrogance, that likewise keeps his ignorance and his idealism intact. He is the pathetic, the tragic, *alter ego* of Phil Branden.

Settlers of the Marsh operates primarily in a sexual dimension, like Grove's less successful novel set in the same terrain, *The Yoke of Life.* It draws the experience of immigrants in the rugged landscape of northern Manitoba into a dynamic pattern of sexual confrontation and conflict. Niels has grown to manhood ignorant of sexual relations. He is, nevertheless, powerfully drawn to Ellen Amundsen as the complement to his immigrant dream of home and family. Her sexuality, however, has atrophied as a consequence of her parents' murderous intimacies. Niels turns to the district tramp, Clara Vogel, and, with a misguided sense of responsibility, marries her. Eventually, he murders her, does penal restitution, and returns to Ellen. His determined pursuit of fulfilment carries him through to the sad completion of his original dream.

Contrary to those critics who reject the apparently happy ending as an inconsistent contrivance, I would suggest that it is not happy but positive and, in context, the inevitable consequence of a cathartic encounter of innocence with ignobility, of ignorance with the brutality of experience. Niels and Ellen meld their separate solitudes because they have no alternative:

> These two have been parted; and parting has opened their eyes. They have suffered; suffering has made them sweet, not made them bitter. Life has involved them in guilt; regret and repentance have led them together; they know that never again must they part. It is not passion that will unite them; what will unite them is love. . .
>
> They are older. Both feel it. Older than they were then when threaded those thickets before. They are quieter, less apt to rush to conclusions, too close in a struggle with life.. . .[1]

They have endured thus far, alone, and suffered. Their mutual complicity in Clara's death imposes the ultimate necessity of enduring together, if they are to endure at all. And there is no indication in Grove's vision that they should do otherwise.

Phil Branden is not innocent. He is the product of a cosmopolitan European education. His naiveté is of the privileged class immersed in the acquisitive, morally chaotic New World. As an omnibus-waiter in Toronto, he is confronted by graft. Selling travelogue books out of New York, he is enmired in hustling and then, selling hyper-expensive history books, in fraud. Never does he lose his self-satisfied righteousness. He tramps westward; eventually works in a factory; becomes a hobo; a farm labourer proselytizing for socialist reform; and thence to Canada. to teach–maintaining to the end an independence sustained by his conviction of superior knowledge. The irony, of course, is that he is not a Horatio Alger hero, or even a Kafkesque foundling in an alien world, but the buffeted victim of his own inability to adjust, to perceive the similarities between New World and Old disguised by their obvious differences. Unfortunately, he is a rather repulsive, patronizing prig in spite of Grove's autobiographical attachment to him. This creates a disturbingly paradoxical tone which might have been readily avoided, perhaps, by making him a third-person creation. As it is, the reader is too much inside his consciousness for his response to isolation to be tolerable, even where it is most meant to be. Phil Branden is, in my opinion, the least convincing of Grove's suffering *isolatoes.*

Grove maintains an effective distance between his own and the protagonist's consciousness in his other novels. This is particularly so in *Two Generations* and *Our Daily Bread.* The subject matter of both demands objectivity–where isolation is conceived primarily in terms of family structures; pathos and tragedy in terms of familial disintegration. John Elliott, in *Our Daily Bread,* is a man tortuously alone because time passes; because children become adults; because death comes not by convenience but on a whim of indifference; because generations are simultaneously antithetical although, through time, identical; because an old man has already been young whereas the young have not yet been old. In presenting the tragedy of John Elliott, Grove is not so reactionary as might be superficially apparent. He does not venerate the tried and true, the old and established; John Elliott does. Rather, Grove shows that the real world of the old man is not the real world of his children. All ten of his offspring branch out into their own lives; to Winnipeg, to being an impossible wife, to compliance with a crooked husband, to poverty, to farming. But none of them is more than a fragment of his progenitor–from Elliott's perspective, at least. John Elliott discovers himself adrift, alone, without continuity. The horror of his isolation culminates in his desperate flight back into the irretrievable past, to the deserted farmhouse and death.

In the first chapter of *Second Image,* Ronald Sutherland dwells on the similarities amongst *Maria Chapdelaine, Thirty Acres,* and *Our Daily Bread* in regard to the land and divine order. While not wanting here to dispute either his premise of bilateral coincidence or his conclusion of bi-national identity, I believe the suggested comparison is worth pursuing for what it might reveal in regard to the nature of John Elliott's tragic deterioration and demise and of the determining moral vision of Grove. My rejection of the Sutherland hypothesis is implicit but, in itself, peripheral.

For Hémon, the violence of François Paradis' freezing to death in the wilderness and the consuming challenge to Samuel Chapdelaine of a frontier farm are equally expressions of a God of whom Maria's world is certain. The conditions of her life are ultimately determined by her environment, which is God made manifest. This determinism and the transcendent authority of divine order are quite in keeping with Québécois *romans du terroir.*

Ringuet's *Thirty Acres* is, in this respect, the antithesis of *Maria Chapdelaine.* The life of Euchariste Moisan is a cycle. He is left a farm by his uncle, whose own life cycle has run its course, who has become in Euchariste's eyes, although not in the author's, redundant. Moisan in turn leaves the farm when he becomes, according to his family who have been reared upon it and sustained by it, similarly redundant. Significantly, he is sent to the United States for the completion of his death, in contrast to Maria Chapdelaine who resists the impulse southward in favour of continued participation in the processes of the past. In fact, Maria cannot leave Quebec, for the world beyond is chaos, whereas Moisan must leave, for rural Quebec has become chaos and America is an enclosing vacuum, offering the surcease of oblivion.

Any doubt of the cyclic nature of *Thirty Acres* is dispelled by the arrangement of its four sections according to the seasons, which are the seasons of Euchariste's life, ending in Winter. The cycle conforms to a tragic determinism, from Moisan's point of view. But that is not the vision of the author. Ringuet's overview of Moisan's story provides an almost classic display of free will distorted by *hubris* and renewal confronted by stasis. Moisan's tragedy is that as he grows he does not adjust to change. Change, like Hémon's God, is indifferent and inexorable but, in itself, is neither constructive nor destructive except as it is perceived. In Ringuet's scheme of things, the divine order is the order of nature and not the arbitrary inclinations of a disinterested supreme being. The processes of life, of man and the land by which he lives are, in *Thirty Acres,* not objectively deterministic, as they are in *Maria Chapdelaine,* but subjectively so. Life is not a matter of learning to accept, but of learning to adjust. The ironic counterpointing of Ringuet's vision as author and Moisan's point of view within the context of the novel is its sustaining force.

The common aspirations of Euchariste Moisan and John Elliott–growing out of their relations with the land–for farm and family and themselves, and the disintegration of their dreams and their eventual dispossession by both land and kin provide a notable coincidence. But John Elliott neither accepts the divine order, like the characters in *Maria Chapdelaine,* nor does he resist adjusting to the natural order, as does Euchariste Moisan. Grove's purpose is much more sinister, in terms of deterministic schemes.

John Elliott believes in a relationship of mutual respect between himself and the land. He is not hell-bent to be its master, which, in *Fruits of the Earth,* is the characteristic of Abe Spalding that eventually brings about his collapse into humility. Nor is he imprisoned by his own response to its demands, as is Ralph Patterson in *Two Generations.* John Elliott is the victim of time. Its cyclic movement is totally dissimilar to Ringuet's continuing gyre, however. It is a consuming wheel. Elliott is Ixion on the other side of the hill, perpetually feeling the wheel at his back and with perpetual futility attempting to resist its pressure. The changes which time brings about are as important to *Our Daily Bread* as the processes of change are to *Thirty Acres.* But in John Elliott's world, they are not the cycles of life to which one must adapt or be lost. They are, as elsewhere in Grove's writing, revolutions on a linear plane, a sequence of endings. When Elliott crawls back to his farm, he arrives at his own conclusion–which is both pathetic and fitting.

In Grove's world, there is neither retreat nor retrieval. The only external order is the order of a sequence. How his characters fight back, resist the pressure of the wheel, is in spite of the inevitability of their defeat, the source of both their compelling strength and their private agonies. For John Elliott, defeat is particularly bitter. He is not given the same chance as Abe Spalding or Ralph Patterson to modify his aspirations to changing circumstances. Ultimately, he is the victim of his own inability to understand that he cannot win. Unlike the land, with which he is so closely identified, there is not for him the option of renewal. Unlike his scattered family, there is not for him indifferent resignation to the inevitable. He is crushed by his own awareness of himself and an awareness of his ultimate separation from either the land or his family, and by the conflicting presence of this knowledge in the mechanistic order of being.

Two Generations is the only one of Grove's novels, with the arguable exception of *The Master of the Mill,* in which this mechanistic order is not operative upon a single lone protagonist. Even though he is isolated within the midst of his family, John Elliott meets crisis and adversity on his own and those around him are relatively unaffected by his misery and ignorant of its origins. Ralph Patterson is similarly isolated from his children and his dreams by time and the force of his personality. He is a powerful, quiet, domineering man, successful at farming in Southern Ontario and, like so many of Grove's protagonists, destructively self-righteous. But in this novel, the members of the family are not limited by Grove to being submissively functional. Patterson's wife, Di, matches the force of his character with her own. It is she who ultimately welds together the intangible family ties in her winterbound house at Sleepy Hollow. Grove maintains an omniscient poise above events–more here than elsewhere–and the younger generation is allowed a realistic presence. In *Fruits of the Earth,* the children are cut-out emblems in Abe Spalding's lonesome and heroic quest for achievement. In *Our Daily Bread,* they are the graphic details of Elliott's personal torment. In *The Master of the Mill,* the generations meld together into a single composite identity; but, in *Two Generations,* they are as substantial and individualized as the main protagonist, making the generation gap, itself, the tragedy.

Henry, with Catherine and their greenhouses, and George, with Nancy, the New York showgirl, and their eventual child, are fully realized characters. Even Mary and Tom, young enough to be considered the Patterson's second family, are known despite their distance from the centre of the action. But it is Phil and Alice, the middle children, who most come alive and with whom the confrontation between generations is most dynamically apparent. They are the nearly incestuous, brilliant, sensitive, ambitious and utterly cynical heroes of the novel who, through the machinations of Di, force Ralph into tragi-pathetic reconciliation with the unalterability of change. Individual isolation, in *Two Generations,* is seen from the perspectives of both youth and maturity. It is seen as being the inexorable consequence of a continuous process which can only be overcome through its acceptance.

In two of Grove's novels, *The Master of the Mill* and *Fruits of the Earth,* the consuming determination of the main protagonists isolates them within the domineering proportions of their own ambitions. Sam Clark and Abe Spalding are both towering figures in their separate worlds, both too isolated by power and achievement from humanity and from reality to perceive or understand their own frailties and the relentless processes of time and change. It is a testament to Grove's genius that two such characters could be so differently conceived, defined in fictional contexts so vastly dissimilar, and in novels so strikingly unalike in time sequence, structure and subject matter.

The Master of the Mill is built around a corporate industrial monolith and the intricate relations of those who bring it into being and are ironically its servants, its victims. It is related in a temporally chaotic, fragmented consortium of flashbacks, documentary sketches, ruminative conjecturing, and forward progress. It is a highly thoughtful novel, sometimes–as always, in Grove–a bit naive. It explores the Orwellian implications of the industrial-technological age on society as a composite whole and on the incredibly powerful, wealthy, and suffering individuals who are at its centre, giving it shape. In comparison, *Fruits of the Earth* is an epic chronicle of a rural district of Manitoba and of a single man. Through single-minded perseverance and a profound ambition to prevail over the obstacles of natural process and his own humanity, Abe moulds history and accrues wealth and respect and then, inevitably, sees his achievement fall victim to pride and progress. His story is told as a straightforward sequential narrative. Grove begins with Abe's arrival from Ontario in the summer of 1900, and maintains a relentless focus on him throughout the ironic course of his rise to tragedy, his fall to secular grace. *Fruits of the Earth* is metaphysically, philosophically, prototypic of the whole Grove canon–often cranky and rigid; occasionally cynical, perverse; but always with a profound sympathy for man's mortal condition in an indifferent, capricious continuum.

Just as narrative simplicity is appropriate to the subject matter of *Fruits of the Earth,* the intricate complexity of *The Master of the Mill* is contextually justified. Sam Clark is preparing himself for death, quite consciously struggling to impose a retrospective order on the events of his life. Sam's ultimate purpose is to know who he is, and what he is, before he ceases to exist. Grove's purpose, which includes his protagonist's, is apparently to know who and what all of us are before we, modern man, inevitably cease to exist.

Sam Clark is a troubled man, lonely and misunderstood; a protomythic titan with a human conscience. He perceives the conflicts and contradictions of his experience as an inexplicable chaos which is resolved into tenuous clarity only by the imminence of his death. But in ironic contrast to Sam's perception of reality, Grove has created for him an environment, a context, which is arbitrarily ordered to an improbably extreme degree–improbable were it not deciphered through the sphere of consciousness around the dying mortally-perplexed septuagenarian senator, Sam Clark.

Sam is the focal centre of a multi-personal, composite structure, his conscience the response to his father's ambition, the antithesis of his son's bloodless quest for power. The three generations are melded into one, literally, for Sam outlives both progenitor and progeny, and figuratively, for Sam ingenuously goes far to achieve the aspirations of the other two in spite of himself. As Maud Dolittle explains about Sam's apparently compassionate bequest to the indigent of Canada–

> Do you know what, to me, today, appears as the greatest of all ironies? It is this: that the senator, throughout his life, fought consciously against the logic of the mill while unconsciously he promoted it. Even in his will. He created that fund from charity, as a protest against the action of his son. But that fund is precisely what the son would have advised his father to create had he been asked. It is this contradiction between the senator's desires and the consequences of his actions which led to the very things he abhorred; so that he fought his father as well as his son while promoting their designs.[2]

The son, Sir Edmund, is described variously as both the resurrection of his father and of his grandfather.[3] They are, all three, parts of the same conglomerate being whose consciousness as well as conscience is Sam.

The Clark women are similarly aspects of a composite personality, whose relations with Rudyard, Sam, and Edmund bind the lot of them inextricably together. Maud Carter is Sam's wife and the beloved beneficiary of his father. Maud Dolittle is Sam's secretary, Vice-President of the mill, and beloved elder mistress of young Edmund. Maud Fanshawe becomes Lady Clark, Sir Edmund's wife, and beloved companion of the old senator. A delicate balance, a foil for each of them, is Miss Charlebois–companion, competitor, friend, devoted to all. As the three Clark men form a trinity of ambition, conscience, and power, the three Mauds embody mind, heart, and soul.

In this highly ordered universe, Sam is at the focal centre but the whole is contained by the presence of the mill itself. The mill is a pyramid, a dynasty, a mechanistic monstrosity, a determining god of the new age. Grove's vision of man's impotence in the face of external order is here consistent with his rural novels. Like the others, *The Master of the Mill* offers a somewhat sardonic, naturalistic conception of reality. But the arcane world of corporate technology and the aesthetic imposition of bewildering disorder on lives that are ultimately as rigidly structured and interrelated as the imagination permits, have enabled Grove to formulate a vision that is ominously prophetic. Sam Clark's personal isolation, ironically the concomitant of Grove's insistence that he is not a separable and separate individual, and the uniquely overwhelming dimensions of the monolithic mill, join in the most cosmopolitan of Grove's novels to project what is perhaps the least universal of his fictional conceptions of reality's inexorable process. Such, I would suggest, is the nature of the best utopian fiction. The impact of the visionary is due, at least in part, to the convincing idiosyncrasy of his vision.

In an entirely different context, Abe Spalding perceives the essential conundrum of Sam's world, although not its implicit tragedy:

> If, at one time, he had thought that machines were going to bring the millenium, he came to see now that the machine itself is nothing: what is needed is the mechanical mentality; and that he did not have. The use of machines might "pay" in a money sense; it did not pay in terms of human life. The thing done is nothing; the doing everything.[4]

What Abe, a pioneer of the land, cannot comprehend, of course, is that the machine is the creator of mechanical mentalities and that the doing of something becomes no more relevant to human life than the thing done. But Abe's world is fundamentally different from Sam Clark's. His ambitions for the land and for Spalding District are more humane, perhaps, than those which generate and are sustained by the mill, but they are also more profane.

Abe Spalding conceives of progress only in terms of his own achievement. He had been "dimly aware of changes going on about him. The years were piling up. He had given it no thought; it could not be helped."[5] Blind to the reciprocal needs of his wife Ruth and of his children, he forges a vast farm complex out of the recalcitrant land, and isolates himself from human and natural orders through the pride and determination of his achievement. Then his son, Charlie, is killed beneath the wheels of a farm wagon. The unremitting process of destruction is begun. As the years pass, Abe is increasingly aware of his shortcomings, yet increasingly withdrawn from family and the community which he has shaped in his image. His children grow and leave–Marion weds a lawyer, Jim becomes a mechanic, and Frances violates his trust and, pregnant, falls into disrepute. Following World War I, Abe opposes consolidation of the district and is humiliated at the polls. The dynastic dreams crumble around him and when there is nothing left, the myth becomes man. There is a measure of triumph in Abe's learning to accept and to renew the struggle of his life from the premise of his own frailty:

> The decay of the human faculties impressed him as part of the human tragedy inherent in the fundamental conditions of man's life on earth. That was a thing ever present now. What, as compared with this fact–that, having lived, we must die–did such inessentials matter as economic success or the fleeting happiness of the moment?[6]

It is a sobering realization for Abe that he is intrinsically alone and as vulnerable as others, that he is human. It is a sad triumph; a vision of hope, tinged with despair, or of tragedy, redeemed by the consolation of self-consciousness.

At best, all of Grove's protagonists suffer an ignominious conclusion to their stories. To a large extent, they determine their own demise and, where applicable, their own limited salvation. They have no control over the mechanistic processes of the universe: but they do have control over their own responses. Ironically, it is seldom judiciously exercised. Their inability to see themselves as they are prevents them from adjusting to the unalterable. Inevitably, they are subsumed by the world in which their confrontation has taken place with the realities of self and surroundings.

Notes

1. Frederick Philip Grove, *Settlers of the Marsh* (Toronto: New Canadian Library, 1965), p.216. (New York: Doran, 1925.)
2. Frederick Philip Grove, *The Master of the Mill* (Toronto: New Canadian Library, 1967), p.331. (Toronto: Macmillan, 1944.)

3. *Ibid.,* pp.74, 180.
4. Frederick Philip Grove, *Fruits of the Earth* (Toronto: New Canadian Library, 1969), p.132. (Toronto: Dent, 1933.)
5. *Ibid.,* p.110.
6. *Ibid.,* p.199.

2.
Garner's *Cabbagetown*

Hugh Garner's *Cabbagetown,* like Grove's *Fruits of the Earth,* is a chronicle. Unlike Grove's account of a fictional, representative district that is continuous with historical time and place quite arbitrarily, according only to narrative necessity–the price of wheat, the War, the origins of the settlers are externally derived–Garner's novel is an authentic representation of historical actuality. *Cabbagetown* is a chronicle of a particular time, the Depression, with primary focus on a particular place, the Cabbagetown district of Toronto which Garner describes in the Author's Preface to the Pocket Book Edition, 1971, as "a sociological phenonemon, the largest Anglo-Saxon slum in North America."

In keeping with the documentary requirements of his approach, Garner's protagonist, Ken Tilling, is necessarily a representative character rather than being, like Abe Spalding, larger-than-life and removed from the mainstream. Tilling is very much a life-sized creation and he is wholly immersed in the mainstream of his time and his place. That is not to say that he is ordinary or average. He is not. He both suffers and triumphs as a result of an inborn pride, a consciousness of being the same as others, yet different. In many ways he is the emerging writer in a *bildungsroman.* Although Tilling is not Garner, Garner, perhaps, is Tilling. Ken sustains a determination to fulfil his potential and that, rather than the potential itself, is what sets him apart. He is the embodiment of an archetype rather than a prototype. His isolation is self-imposed, yet subject to the conditions of his external environment in a way that would have reduced Abe Spalding to the eccentric, but elevates Tilling to the heroic. Spalding is an epic protagonist in mortal combat with himself; Ken Tilling is a prosaic hero struggling to be only himself in an imposing world.

The opening and closing paragraphs of *Cabbagetown* provide suitable parentheses for Garner's story of a young man and an era. The novel begins with a sixteen-year-old Ken quitting a central Toronto technical school, early in 1929:

> "Goodbye, Tilling, and good luck," said the principal, Mr. J.K. Cornish, proffering his hand. "Today is the big day in your life. Your are going out into society–into business–into the business world, and from now on it is up to you. I hope you will retain pleasant memories of your association with us here, and that you will–er–curb your, shall we say spirits?" He smiled wanly. Then concluded hurriedly, "Goodbye, my boy!"[1]

At the corner down the block, Ken turns and thumbs his nose at the school. Opportunity awaits him–and the Crash, the Depression, the incredible poverty, despair, and ideological fantasies, the destruction or degradation and compromise that overtake his world and reduce it to miserable submission. The novel concludes with Ken, a self-styled Communist sympathizer, a member of the International Brigades in Spain, in 1937:

> The dawn can be seen to the east, but it really comes from the west. It comes across the watcher's shoulders and envelops him in its light as he watches for it. It starts as a narrow ribbon of lighter darkness, then squeezes together before it fans high into the sky. As the watcher looks for its birth it begins at his feet and lights him, so that he becomes a part of it. The dawn is in the crease of his trousers and in the new-appeared eyelets of his shoes. The dawn is in the new shapes around him, and in the lighted fields. The dawn is a widening earth–a populated earth. The dawn is not only the beginning of the day, but the ending of the night.[2]

The movement from sardonic naiveté through to contemplative sanguinity is what *Cabbagetown* is all about. Garner, in my opinion, is a consummate intuitive craftsman who has effectively adjusted his prose style, the tonality, the syntactical and expositional patterns of his narrative, in accordance with this movement from high-spirited youth to the wary optimism of maturity. It is a change in keeping with the sentiments of the era, at least as he perceives them.

Between 1929 and 1937 the world, of which Cabbagetown in this novel is the perceptual centre, convulses in the throes of destitution and futility. Garner portrays the Depression era with the clinical objectivity of a social realist. He explores the implications of capitalism, fascism, communism, the tyranny of populism and of elitist socio-political structures. His approach to political and economic philosophies is intelligently temperate. Set against this solidly realistic background, vividly and rationally treated, is the highly melodramatic, emotionally persuasive, plausibly stereotyped cast of characters associated with Ken Tilling's Cabbagetown. Taken separately, these two visions account for the opposing responses to this novel: some regard it as the definitive document of Depression Canada, and ignore its immense power as a work of fiction, while others deplore its cliché-ridden characters and the proto-conventional ends to which they fall, and discount, once again, its immense power and the profound quality of authenticity it projects.

Perhaps my syntax has already indicated my lack of sympathy for either response. It seems to me that Garner has successfully wedded document and melodramatic sentiment into a steadfastly singular and ironic vision of reality. He has done so through the character and personality of Ken Tilling, who occupies the middle ground between the two extremes and who is aware of both as perimeters of his experience. He is committed to his friends, but he reamins quite separate from them. He is immersed in the Depression, but he does not participate in the socio-political movements it engenders, although he is their acute observer. Not until the last do the people he knows and the causes he follows merge in his committed participation in a foreign war.

The characteristic that sets Ken apart is pride. It is pride that makes him ashamed of his squalid background, that turns him self-righteously away from Myrla when he discovers she is pregnant, that drives him to bum around, to read and to think and finally to commit himself to a cause, to gain self-respect. It is pride which loses him his first job at McDonald's Wholesale Grocers because he will not be corrupted except by himself, and pride, later, that keeps him from active participation at the political action meetings he frequents. Pride prevents him, as well, from sacrificing his integrity, his free-willed control of the effects the events of his life have on him. Insouciant with employers, capricious with friends, embittered by poverty, unemployment, and loneliness, Ken nevertheless remains essentially his own man.

On the one side of his experience are the examples of Myrla's father, a frustrated painter lapsed into insanity; Mr. Gurney, the establishmentarian who tries to sell Ken on the virtues of the Y.M.C.A. and pornography at the same time, with a pudgy trembling hand on Ken's knee; and Noah Masterson, a wise old cynic and Ken's political mentor. Characters such as these, and the preponderance of factual detail, and the events of his own life, articulate Ken's sociological context. But his emotional context is characterized by his mother, who dies a drunk, by his friends–Billy Aldington, who drowns with horrific plausibility in a vat of chocolate; Bob McIsaacs, shot after escaping Kingston Penitentiary and terrorizing Toronto; and Theodore East, who becomes a civil servant and a snob–and, most of all, by Myrla Patson, who travels the inevitable course from idealized girlfriend to streetwalking whore, turning five tricks a night.

The relationship between Ken and Myrla perhaps best typifies Garner's over-all vision of social and personal transition. They meet at a party at the Patson's. Two years later they meet again: Ken is on probation for stealing a toilet from a construction site; Myrla's employment as a maid has resulted in her pregnancy. They live in a private world of innocent love–until Ken discovers her condition. He leaves to work across the continent at casual labour; Myrla waitresses, mistresses, and then whores. They meet briefly, twice, after their break-up. The first time, in a restaurant, he scorns her advances:

> He walked out of earshot. He paid the blonde waitress for the soft drinks, and ignored the look she gave him. When he reached the sidewalk it struck him that this was the second time he and Myrla had parted in just about the same way. But this time it was an anticlimax, as everything had been an anticlimax since the Sunday afternoon when she told him she was having another man's baby.
>
> He felt free once more. Myrla still had the power to hurt him, but she no longer had the power to draw him back.[3]

The second time, encountering her walking the streets according to her profession, he takes her to a beverage room. This time it is Myrla who resists Ken, Myrla who leaves him sitting. He is not crushed, however. He has grown up and accepts their separate lots, as she has done. She will continue whoring and Ken will enlist in the International Brigades. It is a cruel outcome to their original devotion; but the world around them is cruel and they have both managed to endure.

It is ironic that Ken's quest for self-realization promises to be achieved through martial conflict–as ironic as Hitler's military termination of the Depression. The irony of Ken Tilling's life, between 1929 and 1937, however, is not limited to the culmination of his experience during that time in a war-torn foreign land. It is exhibited in the continuous tension between Depression conditions, as documented by Garner, and their effects on those close to his protagonist, as perceived by Ken himself, albeit under the control of Garner's authorial hand. Ken's consciousness of himself as an individual, different from the rest of humanity if for no other reason than that he is self-conscious, where the others in his context are not, is the source of his pride. And with irony appropriate to his awareness of himself and his socio-historical context, his pride generates the tenacious integrity through which he endures his own self-righteousness as well as the tragic indignities imposed by Cabbagetown and the Depression.

Garner, as I have suggested, is an intuitive writer. He seems, as well, to be an intuitive thinker, if the oxymoron will be permitted for the sake of accuracy. He has a profound ability to perceive universal conditions in the pedestrian as well as the bizarre. His prose style, while occasionally haphazard in critical close-up, is from a less demanding distance well modulated to convey human behaviour and response, through which an acute social conscience is indirectly revealed. The depth of insight in his novels, those such as *Cabbagetown* and *Silence on the Shore* which are not obvious pot-boilers, is the depth of experience, of actuality, rather than of philosophy or moral vision.

Inevitably, as in the two novels just mentioned, it is human community as much as individual isolation that is the object of Garner's aesthetic pursuit. But, almost invariably, the sense of community is achieved through evolving patterns of isolation. That, at least, is the structural basis of *Silence on the Shore* and the informing principle of Ken Tilling's ironic confrontation with the realities of the Depression.

Notes

1. Hugh Garner, *Cabbagetown* (Richmond Hill: Pocket Book, 1971), p.12. (Toronto: Collins, 1950.)
2. *Ibid.,* p.368.
3. *Ibid.,* p.244.

3.
Callaghan and MacLennan

Morley Callaghan and Hugh MacLennan have been discussed extensively elsewhere, by other critics. They are two of Canada's best known and most accomplished novelists. To say, as it has been said, that there is little that is intrinsically Canadian in either is a misapplication of the national modifier, a chauvinist delimitation. The fact that both are primarily urban writers, that Callaghan explores a moral topography in what is incidentally a Canadian milieu while MacLennan seems doggedly determined to map out the peculiarities of the Canadian experience, that both are urbane, self-conscious, and intellectual writers, these facts make them neither failed aesthetes nor failed nationalists.

It seems to me that it should not be incumbent upon a novelist to conform to the needs of his time and place, whether those needs are derived from insecurity or from a new-found national confidence. I just heard on the radio, while writing this, someone say that only a French Canadian can really understand Jack Kerouac–that is the kind of delimiting nationalism to which I am referring. Kerouac may have a special meaning to the Québécois sensibility, born of his ancestral heritage, but to suggest that his personal confrontation with America as it is universalized in his careless, intense, profound prose vision, is somehow the peculiar property of his genetic kin, is nothing short of silly. Similarly, to condemn Callaghan for his exploration of the moral patterns encompassed by individual isolation, or MacLennan for defining the nature of collective experience through patterns of individual solitude, is largely indefensible, except as they are flaws within their aesthetic creations.

My concern here, then, is not with the responsiveness of Callaghan or MacLennan to contemporary historical needs. As social documentarians, they are both questionably inadequate: Callaghan is apparently unconcerned and MacLennan tries, perhaps, too hard. My assumptions are based on the concept that Canadians define Canada; not Canada, Canadians. Clearly, I would not agree, either, with those who insist that MacLennan is the prototypic Canadian novelist, that Callaghan is a displaced American or the definitive Canadian internationalist. Where novels fit into a Canadian tradition–that is, in my opinion, significant. Where their authors' visions fit into contemporary socio-historical trends is irrelevant to literary *qua* literary criticism. With these assumptions in mind, I shall briefly approach one aspect of several of the novels of Morley Callaghan and Hugh MacLennan.

A word that keeps cropping up in MacLennan's novels is "solitude." The implications are clearly political in the novel which incorporates that word into its title. But in *Two Solitudes,* as elsewhere, it suggests the condition of individual as well as collective self-consciousness, the effect of the isolating forces of previous events. Solitude is a state of isolation but, more, it is a condition of mind within that state. MacLennan describes the Canadian ethno-political dichotomy in his Foreword:

> No single word exists, within Canada itself, to designate with satisfaction to both races a native of the country. When those of the French language use the word *Canadien,* they nearly always refer to themselves. They know their English-speaking compatriots as *Les Anglais.* English-speaking citizens act on the same principle. They call themselves Canadians; those of the French language French Canadians.[1]

In this brief exposition are the premises upon which the epic dimensions of his novel are sustained. But, within the fictional framework, the separateness, the frustration, and the loneliness of individuals for whom the larger solitudes are merely a dramatic context occupy the central patterns of his vision. Paul, in particular, is at the centre. Each of those around him inhabits a separate solitude, each pulling him apart: "Marius on one arm and his mother on the other, Athanase at the head, and the priest with his powerful hands on both feet."[2]

Read as a whole, this novel is the story of Paul Tallard, of the struggle around and within him, and of his gradual emergence into a consciousness that is determinedly his own. His father's pathetic efforts to accommodate the capitalist *anglais* machine, the fierce reactionary caprice of Father Beaubien, the insurgent and rebellious nationalism of his brother Marius and the indulgent complacency of his mother–these are the forces wrenching Paul asunder, as it were, while recreating him as a unique individual, a writer, who can one day attempt to resolve them as complementary aspects of his own personality. His father destroyed, his mother an American bride, Marius, a radical anomaly, and the village behind him, Paul determines to transcend enmity and ignorance by acknowledging its existence, by writing of it, transmuting it into a personal tradition which can stand for them all:

> Must he write out of his own background, even if that background were Canada? Canada was imitative in everything. Yes, but perhaps only on the surface. What about underneath? No one had dug underneath so far, that was the trouble. Proust wrote only of France, Dickens laid nearly all his scenes in London, Tolstoi was pure Russian. Hemingway let his heroes roam the world, but everything he wrote smelled of the United States. Hemingway could put an American into the Italian Army and get away with it because by now everyone in the English-speaking world knew what an American was. But Canada was a country that no one knew. It was a large red splash on the map. It produced Mounted Policemen, Quintuplets and raw materials. But because it used the English and French languages, a Canadian book would have to take its place in the English and French traditions. Both traditions were so mature they had become almost decadent, while Canada herself was still raw. Besides there was the question of background. As Paul considered the matter, he realized that his reader's ignorance of the essential Canadian clashes and values presented him with a unique problem. The background would have to be created from scratch if his story was to become intelligible. He could afford to take nothing for granted. He would have to build the stage and props for his play, and then write the play itself.[3]

Presumably, Paul was the ghost-writer of *Barometer Rising,* and ghosted *Two Solitudes, The Precipice* and *Return of the Sphinx* as well, for in all of these MacLennan follows Paul's advice to himself.

Paul's thoughts were formulated by MacLennan, or at least published, in 1944. From the present historical perspective, MacLennan's clarion declamation seems as curiously outmoded as many of his political judgments. But as the triumphant call to exploit his own solitude, the two, the many solitudes that are within one man, Paul's declaration is at once as individuated and as universal as the vow of Joyce's hero, at the close of *A Portrait of the Artist as a Young Man,* "to forge on the smithy of my soul the uncreated conscience of my race."[4] Paul will speak for the races and the histories that are mingled in his blood. But he will speak as a man, an individual conscious of his heritage and, more, of its residual presence. Like Stephen Daedelus, awareness of himself has made him different from those around him, and the difference gives him the authority to speak for the others. The complexities of solitude are not resolved; they are unified, redeemed.

Morley Callaghan, never to be accused of being too much a Canadian spokesman, is as concerned with individual being, with specificity of experience. But in Callaghan's fiction, the focus is on the common patterns of life, the psycho-moral dimensions of personality, and not on the behavioural texture of those living it. Behaviour and event to Callaghan are elements in a moral drama rather than the converse, as in MacLennan's novels. Callaghan's characters live out the implications of their separateness from the mainstream of life around them. They are seldom memorable, in the way MacLennan's are, because they are tentative, groping, largely unshaped creatures isolated from but continuous with universal reality.

Hugh MacLennan's fictional worlds are meticulously defined–they are clear finite spheres of being, superimposed on the historical continuum. His grasp over events and personalities controls their impact, their meaning–they are complete, structured, finite, known. In contrast, Callaghan occupies what is perhaps a narrower region of consciousness, and of more amorphous perimeters. There is no definition overtly imposed on the characters in Callaghan's fiction. They are internalized, indistinct, given to conflicting propensities towards survival on their own terms and self-annihilation, because those terms are unclear or ambiguous. Father Dowling, for example, ultimately commits himself to the oblivion of insanity in his pursuit of redemptive charity for Midge and Ronnie. Jim McAlpine, in *The Loved and the Lost,* finds himself ensnarled in Peggy Sanderson's pathological quest for self-realization, and he is ruined. Peggy, in comparison, is the enticingly tragic victim of wanting only to be wholly herself, without knowing who she is. Kip Caley, based on the real-life rise and fall of arch-criminal Red Ryan, perhaps more than any other of Callaghan's major protagonists, is the tragically ambiguous embodiment of clear moral principles in conflict. The irony of his novel is conveyed by the title, in retrospect. *More Joy in Heaven* names the celestial consequence of the redemption of a single sinner over the maintenance of ninety-nine just men in their innocence.

The irony of this concept is itself implicit in a number of Callaghan's novels. Michael Aikenhead in *They Shall Inherit the Earth,* for example, and Father Dowling both representatively exhibit the precedence of redemption over innocence or virtue–Michael by atonement through remorse, Dowling by figurative ascension through humility. But the irony of Kip Caley's story is twofold. That he should be lionized for his reformation is unsettling. That he should then fall victim to the joyous self-righteousness that his change engenders in himself and those around him brings his tragedy to ironic completion. After he is prematurely paroled from Kingston Penitentiary because of the influence of Senator Maclean and Father Butler, he returns to Toronto. There he is fêted as the prodigal son. But others use him to their own separate ends: Maclean and the Mayor to display their good worth to the public; Jenkins, opportunistically, hires him as a greeter at the Coronet Hotel; Ellen Maclean, for thrills; the self-righteous Judge Ford, for self-satisfaction; Whispering Joe, the insidious voice of his own violent corrupt core, to pull him down, make him one again with his past. Whispering Joe is the reflection of Kip's *hubris* or, perhaps, original sin. At the opposite extreme of Kip's experience is Julie Evans, whose love for him is too pure, too spiritual and compassionate to survive reality. Kip accepts the impositions of all as adoration. With humility dissipated, he perverts and has perverted for him his salvation and gains not Heaven but a violent death. Julie dies across his expiring body–a cross, together. Over them, Father Butler prays and they are, at least in death, redeemed. Kip is a giant, exciting, child-like man. His isolation is imposed upon him by a corrupt world, invited by his corrupted values. As a personality, he does not engage the imagination. As a reproach, an example, he is a deeply disturbing creation.

Callaghan's characters are psychologically predictable, given the conditions imposed on their lives by the author. Each of his protagonists enacts a carefully contrived drama and embodies the spiritual and emotional complexity of that drama. They are personae, characters through whom the author can explore the implications of particular fragments of the cosmos–that is not to say that they are failed creations. Quite the contrary; according to the dictates of their implicit functions they are well-conceived and powerfully presented. But Callaghan is not writing realistic fiction. His novels are morality tales embroidered with authenticating details from external experience. His characters participate in the external world, but they are not parts of it. They are voices, not beings. Their words, their visions, are uttered from the inner reaches of separate possible conditions of human consciousness.

Consider what many would call his most successful novel–perhaps only, however, because it is the least self-consciously religious–*The Loved and the Lost.* The characters are intrinsically bland. Even Peggy Sanderson remains largely an unprepossessing mystery. Others react strongly to her, usually with hostility and suspicion, but there is little in the character, herself, apart from mildly engaging coyness and a certain self-willed determination to be herself, that would excite interest. We are told she does; we seldom see evidence to corroborate the response of others to her in her context. And certainly McAlpine is a cliché-ridden creation–bright young columnist professor with the promise of his wealthy publisher's beautiful daughter at hand. The individual characters are fey clichés. But their relationships are dramatically powerful. They are so because they are thematically inevitable and Callaghan is a master at plumbing the depths, the moral and psychological implications, of the obvious.

The effect of people within his fiction on one another is all-important in Callaghan's fiction. Jim McAlpine is hopelessly infatuated with Peggy Sanderson. She, in turn, is helplessly capricious. Her neurotic predilection for the company of Negroes, not as individual black people, but as an expiating milieu, allowing her an exotic context for her determined pursuit to be her own self, has given her a reputation as a loose woman. She makes the blacks uneasy. She disturbs everyone who comes in contact with her:

> "There's the root of the matter," McAlpine said. "Why is everybody so damned eager to prove she's a tramp? So everybody can feel more comfortable and forget their own stinking trampishness? And aren't you overlooking something? Don't you no-

> tice that Wagstaffe admits he didn't sleep with her? He thinks he could do it. Well, I know what he means. He thinks she wouldn't resist, and yet he had to leave her as she was. He's black and I'm white, but we were brothers in wanting to let her stay as she is. But we all suspect each other. And Wagstaffe is suspecting the trumpet player."[5]

There is little in Peggy's uncompromising innocence to account for the responses she generates in others. Yet to be with her becomes an obsession with McAlpine. Another man is driven to murder her. And like the hockey player at the Ranger-Canadian [*sic*] game, she is "an indifferent innocent."[6]

Ironically, the incident at the Forum convinces McAlpine that she is being wronged by them all. He has become that much the victim of Peggy's own obsessive behaviour that he sees fault only in the frenzied fans jeering at the referee, sees her vindication in their hostility. He does not recognize her similarity to the Ranger forward who skates lazily around the ice after the *mêlée* while others bear the burden of his guilt in the penalty box.

She thrives on the corruption of others. Her innocence, beneath the facade of a fallen woman, is as contrived as her guilt:

> She would move around the room, and sometimes he would reach out and circle her hips with his arms and put his head under her breast, listening to the beating of her heart, and she would stand still, unprotesting, but uninterested, till her stiff stillness gradually took the heart out of him. Then she would smile to herself.[7]

As the heart continues to go out of him, McAlpine flounders–professionally, emotionally, and spiritually. His life becomes a commitment to the quest of her innocence; not to possess it but to prove its existence. She dies, a raped virgin–apparently. Jim is racked with guilt; as lost as the little church of their early intimacy that he cannot find after her death.

Whether beneath the indifferent and uncompromising innocence which has such a destructive impact, there is a pure, an uncorrupt innocence, is unlikely. She is fallen because she is a human, a woman, and in a fallen world her refusal to acknowledge guilt or innocence leaves her open to harsh judgment and hostility. It also makes her immensely attractive to as Presbyterian a disposition as McAlpine's. Their relationship is explosive because of her negation of innocence, his negation of guilt. Individually, they are mere humans. Together, they are a vision, a vision that is as complex as it is ambiguous–innocence corrupted in a world sustained by guilt.

Callaghan's individuals are emotionally dynamic. MacLennan's are occasionally volatile, yet somehow static in comparison. The characters in Callaghan's novels are intensely conscious of interior realities, although their inability to understand and cope provides the primary movement in their contexts. MacLennan's characters are more conscious of their conditions in the external world, responding directly to people and events rather than to their own selves in relation to their experience. Both writers perceive individual consciousness primarily in terms of irony. In Callaghan's fiction, the irony is in the resolution of moral complexity: Dowling ends in an asylum; Kip and Ellen form a corporeal cross in their death postures; Michael Aikenhead atones for his step-brother's death through suffering, and is redeemed through love, despite the misery he has inflicted on those who love him. MacLennan's irony is less metaphysical, more pervasive throughout his novels.

The relationships between generations, sexual and kinship, and between the past and the present, in *Return of the Sphinx,* create a resounding irony that is the novel's didactic strength as well as its narrative weakness. The affairs between Chantal and Gabriel Fleury, an old friend of her father's; between Daniel and Marielle Jeannette, a girlfriend's mother; the rhetorical declamations of Aimé Latendresse and of Moses Bulstorde; the heroism and statesmanship of Alan Ainslie's past and his present political and familial impotence; the many ironic balances deployed throughout *Return of the Sphinx* give dimension to the polemical themes of divisiveness from a common base and regeneration through change. They are also, unfortunately, rather cumbersome and obvious, drawing attention to the author's contrivances of personality and event and away from his sophisticated insights into political and moral behavior.

In other of his novels, MacLennan's ironic impulse is more carefully controlled. In the best, in my opinion, *The Watch that Ends the Night,* it provides a brilliantly effective device, exploited primarily through the author's consummate manipulation of time. The reader is given a vantage-point equidistant from the chronological sequence of events. Thus, their impact conforms to an emotional logic rather than to a temporal progression. This novel is a carefully wrought complex of temporally discontinuous experience, in which events from disparate times are drawn together into a moving vision of human sadness, of spiritual reconciliation with mortality, of acceptance. Although there are a number of dramatic changes in circumstance for the characters, they remain essentially unchanged. Through their essential constancy, the irony of human life is made tragically apparent. George Stewart finally allows his wife, Catherine, to "live her own death" following the embolism she suffers when her first husband, Jerome Martell, returns from presumed death. There is a profound affirmation in Stewart's acceptance of Catherine's imminent death:

> So the final judgement of the human plight–the final vindication of God Himself, for that matter–is revealed in a mystery of the feelings which understand, in an instant of revelation, that it is of no importance that God appears indifferent to justice as men understand it. He gave life. Life for a year, a month, a day or an hour is still a gift. The warmth of the sun or the caress of the air, the sight of a flower or a cloud on the wind, the possibility even for one day more to see things grow–the human bondage is also the human liberty.[8]

George Stewart has not changed. But he has seen far more of what he is and has been.

The source of the bond between George and Catherine is described by Catherine, when she disavows the existence of a similar bond between herself and Jerome, in "that line of Rilke, 'Love consists in this, that two solitudes protect and touch and greet each other.'"[9] The union of separate beings, the acceptance of separate solitudes, did not exist in her first marriage. It is the quiet strength of her second. In *The Precipice,* the concept of solitude is equally pervasive, and with many of the same marital implications. The feelings between Bruce and Lucy, which are never consummated, are described as follows: "The vessel which had neared her solitude was already sailing past."[10] Bruce comes close to comprehending her great loneliness, but does not. Later, Steve is described as having "invaded her solisude,"[11] after she learns of his impending divorce. She becomes a passionate, vulnerable woman, who had before been a sexless, small-town Presbyterian spinster. Awake late on the first night of her honeymoon with Steve in New York, however, she ponders the fact that "No solitude she had ever known had been like this." Her virginity is gone; the isolation remains: "Her mind was bursting with strange new images, but she could think of nothing." Her ecstasy is foredoomed: "even God seemed irrelevant in this region of random lights."[12] Yet, like George Stewart, she ultimately prevails, solitude intact, reconciled to the conditions of individual isolation which are, ironically, both the reward and the suffering of her consciousness of self in the universe.

Hugh MacLennan and Morley Callaghan are mature, accomplished novelists. Their separate conceptions of individual isolation reflect vastly different visions of reality. Yet they have in common the accomplishment of their contributions to the continuing traditions of Canadian fiction. Whether their novels are definitively Canadian is unimportant. They participate in and contribute to the Canadian imagination and their achievement is continuous with the larger traditions of world literature. The individual confronted by the conditions of his environment, moral or socio-political, is universal.

Notes

1. Hugh MacLennan, *Two Solitudes* (Toronto: Popular Library, 1945), Foreword.
2. *Ibid.,* p. 71.
3. *Ibid.,* p.341.
4. James Joyce, *A Portrait of the Artist as a Young Man* (New York: Random, 1928), p.299.
5. Morley Callaghan, *The Loved and the Lost* (New York: Signet, 1959), p.82.
6. *Ibid.,* p.136.
7. *Ibid.,* p.120.
8. Hugh MacLennan, *The Watch that Ends the Night* (Toronto: Signet, 1969), p.322. (Toronto: Macmillan, 1959.)
9. *Ibid.,* p.290.
10. Hugh MacLennan, *The Precipice* (Toronto: Collins, 1948), p.43.
11. *Ibid.,* p.154.
12. *Ibid.,* p.181.

4.
Three Canadian Originals

Three novels stand out in contemporary Canadian fiction for their sensitive portrayals of individual protagonists engaged in the mortal struggle to know themselves, to accept the conflicting conditions of inner and external realities within their separate consciousnesses. Ernest Buckler's *bildungsroman, The Mountain and the Valley,* published in 1952, was one of the first and most successful attempts in Canada to explore the special problems of the creative person born into an inarticulate world. Mordecai Richler's second novel, *Son of a Smaller Hero,* appeared first in 1955. In it, Richler dramatizes Noah Adler's commitment to an indefinable self-realization through rejection of the forces that created him. *The Stone Angel* by Margaret Laurence, published in 1964, explores the convergence of Hagar Shipley's past experience with her present condition as she approaches death. All three define individuality in terms of the conflict between behaviour and consciousness.

David Canaan, Noah Adler, and Hagar Shipley, do not share in some unique experience, common to themselves alone. They are three of the most successful of a new breed of protagonists in Canadian fiction, a breed that has its origins in the mainstream of the mid-twentieth century behavioural sciences. From the psychology of "I" in the earlier years of this century, under the dispensation of Freud, Jung, and their various followers, the psychoanalytic protagonist evolved–the vastly dissimilar heroes of Lawrence and Woolf, of Faulkner, and in Canada, of Knister, McCourt and Ross. But the psychology of "me," the individual as interacting object rather than responding or expiating subject, came into the fore in mid-century. Under the indirect influence of B.F. Skinner, C.L. Hull, and others, the focus shifted from inner depths to the interaction of inner and outer realities of individual experience. Novelists like John Braine in

England, John Barth and John Updike in the United States, and Laurence, Richler, and Buckler in Canada tacitly give their approval to the behaviourists. Similarly, the movements in sociology and anthropology in this century, away from the exotic or the documentary into our own back and front yards, has coincided with shifting perspectives in fiction. The social realism blended with awakening consciousness that characterizes the works of Grove, Garner, Callaghan, and MacLennan gave way to a considerable extent to the participatory familiarity of Laurence, Richler, and Buckler with their surrounding environment.

Other writers have more recently explored the ironies of individual consciousness in a contemporary Canadian context with great technical skill and depth of insight. Clark Blaise's *A North American Education,* 1973, is a book of "short fiction" in which the main characters are merged in an autobiographical identity. As immigrants to their ancestral homeland, they struggle desperately to participate in Canadian experience as they observe it and expect that it should be felt. But their American backgrounds impose restraints: just as the consciousness of their Canadian heritage prevented them from growing up as participants in the American experience, so, with the United States determinedly behind them, they respond to Montreal with an alien sense of commitment. The retrieval of lost identity is in large part a voyeuristic illusion which Blaise defines with unerring precision. It is subtle and brutal fiction, revealing much of the Canadian propensity to take for granted our history and belabour the need for self-definition. Margaret Atwood's *Surfacing,* 1972, details a young woman's quest into the dark heart of her origins which ultimately prove to be the universal source of human experience, the dream night world of prehistory. In *Lives of Girls and Women,* 1971, Alice Munro traces Del Jordan's growth to womanhood as she learns to accept the isolating effect of her acute awareness of reality, to accept her own consciousness of experience. She is a soul-sister of David Canaan, just as the protagonist of Atwood's novel is related to Hagar Shipley, and Blaise's personae share with Noah Adler the suffering of their own drives to assimilate in an alien world. And all of them share the need to integrate internal and external realities in a Canadian context.

These writers are Canadian without trying. They are concerned with the growth of individual consciousness. Canadian materials provide the details of context, the contributing and ironically conflicting external structures for their fictional quests into the source of identity. It is interesting that in Richler's *Son of a Smaller Hero* there is an implicit command of Canadian experience, but blatant self-consciousness in regard to exclusively Jewish phenomena. The back streets of the ghetto, the main arteries and the habits of Montreal, Canadian weather, the political climate, the relationships between Jew and goyim, Jew and the New World are all subsumed with confidence into the narrative flow of the novel. Unfortunately, Richler displays no such confidence in his treatment of esoteric Jewish materials. Here and there throughout the novel are capsule explanations of Jewish terminology, Jewish custom. Although the context of Wolf's funeral makes it clear to the uninitiated what it means to say *kaddish,* Richler notes that "*Kaddish* is the prayer for the dead."[1] Again, despite its implicit clarity, he gratuitously explains: "During *Shivah,* a Hebrew term that means seven days of mourning. . . ."[2] In an otherwise mature work of fiction, this consciousness of his readers' lack of prior knowledge is curiously demeaning, almost a betrayal of trust. Richler writes to a goyim audience instead of a universal readership. The irony is that such a patronizing attitude is implicitly unnecessary. Narrative clarity makes such extra-contextual definitions redundant.

When fiction will not support its materials, the writer prevails on the indulgence of his readers by expecting them to integrate explanatory insertions into the totality of their response. Documentary detail can be effectively incorporated into narrative patterns. Melville and Frances Brooke and Hugh MacLennan do so with varying degrees of success. Richler does so exceedingly well with his descriptions of Montreal in *Son of a Smaller Hero.* Part 3, "Spring 1953," for example, opens with an evocative medley of images suggesting the resurgence of life that accompanies the changing weather. They are terse, ironic, expositional images, culminating in the single pronouncement that in Montreal in April, "Everybody is full."[3] This section of the novel ends with the recovery of Wolf's body from the burnt-out office of his father's coal-yard and the beginning of the fallacious myth that he died heroically trying to rescue the Torah. Spring's promise of renewal proves to have been hopelessly false. In this pivotal section of the novel, conditions do change dramatically, as its opening indicates, but towards disintegration of familial and amorous relations and the coalescence of deceit and not towards renewal or truth. Richler's rhetorical devices are here an integral part of his narrative.

Elsewhere, the cynical as well as the clinical observations of the Montreal milieu are equally incorporated into the structure and the movement of his novel. Only when he writes intimately of Jewish experience itself does the apologist subvert the novelist's achievement.

By addressing their fiction to what I have described as the universal reader, Margaret Laurence and Ernest Buckler and Richler, with the notable exception discussed above, display a maturity seldom found previously in Canadian novels. *The Stone Angel* and *The Mountain and the Valley,* like *Son of a Smaller Hero,* treat Canadian experience as the valid continuation of a larger world. In all three, Canada is taken for granted, as a matter of course, a viable realm of existence. They each direct their focus to implicitly circumscribed segments of external reality and then concern themselves with the dynamics of individual consciousness within these perimeters. They portray the ironic dichotomy between self-concept and how others perceive the individual. Canada, as it were, is left to look after itself.

The Stone Angel is not regional fiction. It exploits few of the thematic possibilities inherent in the landscape, in the peculiarities of Hagar's setting in Manawaka or Vancouver. Hagar lives within her own mind more than in a particular time and place. Her milieu is incorporated graphically with the rest of her experience and not arranged as its complement or determinant. Richler describes Noah's Montreal as an experienced reality, often misapprehended by his characters but, nevertheless, their world. Buckler defines the Annapolis Valley of David Canaan as if it were a complete reality within the fictional context, albeit a part of a larger world beyond. Location, in all three novels, is contiguous with the rest of their characters' experience of themselves.

The quests of Hagar and David for self-realization culminate in death, and for Noah, in departure to another world across the Atlantic. Each is locked within his or her own restricted consciousness, restrained by the differences in his or her personality from others, and unable even through the universal communion of sexuality to participate fully in the experience of their social environment. Each is largely defined by family relationships and they all strain under their imposed personae. Hagar tempestuously refuses to play the roles demanded of her and the outcome is alienation, bitterness and an inner rage that even imminent death cannot quell. David endures the deferential and conciliatory gestures by which his family shape his growing up in their midst. As the family disintegrates into the separate solitudes of despondency or death his need to define their shared experience becomes clear, but the struggle has already been lost and he dies in an epiphany of quiet despair. Noah finds the demands of old Melech, his grandfather, both to honour tradition and be the spirit of revolt, as intolerable a burden as the requisites of his parents, his uncles, or his gentile mistress. With grim determination to be himself, whatever that may be, he turns away from them all.

Richler, Laurence, and Buckler exploit the ironic potential between demands upon the self of their protagonists and demands made by others. Noah, for example, does not simply reject his family as irrelevant to his quest:

> He wanted, all at once, to squeeze Melech, Wolf and Leah, Panofsky, Max, to his breast and consume them with his love. . . .But he saw little hope of a reconciliation. Before him always, wringing his heart, was a picture of Melech–an old man crumpled up in a chair: Leah–safe only with the dead: Wolf–wiggling his ears and raising his eyebrows. *Oh, God, I love them all.*[4]

But if he gives in to them, they will consume him. He is sure of that. Particularly Melech will consume him, for Melech is an enigma which Noah's rational determinism could not long resist without crumbling. Yet the love between grandfather and grandson is a powerful bond. It is forged from a mixture of admiration and guilt. Each is a separate reproach to the other. Noah's determination to go his separate way forces the old man to acknowledge his own weakness in leaving, years ago in Lodz, the young girl he loved. Melech struggles for self-justification: "My father was a scribe, he thought. He wouldn't let. *I am a strong man.* I didn't go against my family the way he does. I had respect. *Helga has blonde hair and walks straight. She claps her hands together when she dances.*"[5] He lapses into sorrow; Noah's strength, his scourge. But Noah, too, suffers from the example of his *zeyda.* The old patriarch was the strength of the family, the embodiment for Noah of the Jewish traditions of compromise with the goyim, but none with their own. Looking at the yellowed photographs of a young Melech with his lost Helga, Noah laments, and promptly rejects his weakness:

> It was difficult to see the relationship between the righteous and God-fearing Jew and the young lover embracing a giggling girl

> at a village fair. Oh, Melech, Noah thought. My poor, suffering *Zeyda.* Still, he thought, you did wrong to punish us.[6]

Noah cannot afford too much sympathy for the old man without losing his resolve to be free of him. Yet it is to Melech he goes for absolution, as it were, before setting out for Europe. Melech is ultimately his source and Noah must necessarily depart with his love.

Hagar Shipley's retrospective of her life in *The Stone Angel* involves a whole series of role demands, none of which she is able to meet. She is an obdurate woman. Obduracy is the crux of her personality, of the unbreachable edifice of pride that separates inclination and response. When her brother Dan is dying and Matt asks her to put on their dead mother's shawl and comfort him in her arms, she refuses: "however much a part of me wanted to sympathize. To play at being her–it was beyond me."[7] Later, she sees Matt draped in the shawl, holding their dying brother. Displaying a similar restraint, Hagar refuses to show emotion when she leaves her father for finishing school in the East: "Later, in the train, I cried, thinking of him, but, of course, he never knew that, and I'd have been the last to tell him."[8] Suffering the role of her father's chatelaine, on her return, she rebels and marries Bram Shipley. Her relations with Bram are characterized by ossifying restraint:

> It was not so very long after we wed, when first I felt my blood and vitals rise to meet his. He never knew. I never let him know. I never spoke aloud, and I made certain that the trembling was all inner. He had innocence about him, I guess, or he'd have known. How could he not have known?Didn't I betray myself in rising sap, like a heedless and compelled maple after a winter? But no. He never expected any such thing, and so he never perceived it. I prided myself upon keeping my pride intact, like some maidenhead.[9]

Hagar's pride repeatedly imprisoned her within the confines of thwarted affections and misdirected emotion. She could not play the roles, in the past, required by her sons, John and Marvin, even when John was on his deathbed, Marvin departing for war. And in the continuing present from which her retrospective is perceived, she will not succumb to the demands of Marvin and Doris that she behave like the old and cumbersome woman she has become.

Ironically, the restraints that isolated her in the episodes of the cumulative past are her greatest strength in the stages of the present that move her inexorably towards death. She will not submit to frailty and deferential concern. She rages "against the dying of the light" with the same wrongheaded spleen that she had always displayed. In the counterpointed present, as Laurence portrays it, her splenetic pride is heroic.

It seems to me that the ambiguous source of power in *The Stone Angel* lies in this anomaly. The book is structured in such a manner that the chronological sequence of the past is entwined with the movement of the present action. Memory and event achieve coincidence at the point of her death. There is the truth of actual experience in this binary movement. But what gives Mrs. Laurence's vision the resonant dimensions of universal truth is the anomalous interlacing of the destructive and constructive effects of her protagonist's recalcitrant pride. The same indomitable will that prevents Hagar from playing the roles her life demands of her, prevents her from submitting to the inevitable consequences of old age. Pride is a double-edged sword.

The continuing present is structured in a series of stages which, contrary to the episodes of the past, signify movement towards reconciliation for Hagar of her self with her soul, her public demeanour with her interior condition. She rejects the imprecations of Mr. Troy, "God's little man,"[10] who like Marvin and Doris would have her consigned to meet eternity in the Silver Threads Nursing Home. The minister and Dr. Corby, to whom she also responds with disgust, are scorned by Hagar for their apparent complicity in her approaching demise. Inside, at least, she will not bend to God nor to modern medicine. She will rage against the death for which they would have her prepared. Yet, externally, she submits to both. She is an old woman and has no choice. And through the whole process, Marvin and Doris are like ministering angels, menacing at the periphery of her consciousness. In the symbolically laden sequence at the deserted fish cannery, she meets Murray F. Lees, a life insurance salesman. Ironically, it is he, more than minister or doctor, who forces the communion of interior and exterior realities on Hagar. A man whose living depends on the acceptance of death, the acknowledgment of its eventual coming, brings Hagar to accept her own. The next and final stage is her commitment to the hospital where she dies, rebellious to the last. The pride that destroyed her relations with others has given her the strength to be herself to the end–and let death do what it may.

The ironic tension between past and present is effectively exploited in a number of ways. Hagar's repeated confrontation with her mirror image is possibly the most significant, in the present context. While talking with Mr. Troy, she surmises:

> If I were to walk up to my room, approach the mirror softly, take it by surprise, I would see there again that Hagar with the shining hair, the dark-maned colt off to the training ring, the young ladies' academy in Toronto.[11]

Yet the mirror holds no such image. She is old and fat and awkward:

> I give a sideways glance at the mirror, and see a puffed face purpled with veins as though someone had scribbled over the skin with an indelible pencil. The skin itself is the silverish white of the creatures one fancies must live under the sea where the sun never reaches. Below the eyes the shadows bloom as though two soft black petals had been stuck there. The hair which should by rights be black is yellowed white, like damask stored too long in a damp basement.[12]

Thinking back to a humiliating incident in the past, she recalls satisfying a desperate need to see her reflected appearance: "I stood for a long time, looking, wondering how a person could change so much and never see it. So gradually it happens."[13] What Hagar is, inside, and what Hagar appears to be, on the outside, never coincide. The divergence between appearance and reality is the source of both Hagar's embittered isolation and her triumphant contumacy. It is a divergence founded on indomitable pride, resolved through the coming together of two sequences of time, the sequence of memory and the sequence of event. She dies, a whole, reintegrated, recalcitrant being. In her tragedy is triumph; in her death, great dignity.

Time has a quite different function in the ironic resolution of David Canaan's personal dichotomy. Time in David's consciousness is more than a continuous context; it is a tangible, dynamic milieu containing the major events of his life like a series of bursting cocoons. He feels time as shape, as spatial dimension. In marked contrast, past events for his grandmother, Ellen, are equidistant from the present: time is the texture of present memories. Her incipient senility makes causality irrelevent, distorts reality, discards lives, and renews them according to emotional necessity. She accepts. David, however, is slowly suffocated by the passing of time: one cocoon bursts into another and another and only in the end, with death, is there a bursting forth beyond time.

Time is the concomitant condition of David's self-consciousness, for he is the most self-conscious of protagonists and he scrutinizes his life as it moves raggedly towards completion. Words are his only recourse to the isolation that is imposed upon him by external events. Yet, ironically, it is his sensitivity and his ability to articulate that separates him from the others. The ultimate epiphany on the mountain is that for him life must be translated from event to experience through words. Only then will the separate solitudes of them all be redeemed. But as words are his shield against time, death is time's ultimate weapon. In David's realization of himself on the mountain, the two clash directly. Inevitably, death penetrates his defence. The artist is cruelly, perhaps fittingly, refined out of existence despite his obsession to participate in the life he has observed as an outsider.

David is articulate on all matters except death. At the cemetery with his family he struggles to comprehend its meaning:

> Sometimes David stood beside a grave and willed himself to know just what it was to be standing at the spot where someone lay no longer alive. But the thing had no language for him. The inaccessible mystery itself, coming physically from the ground, kept brushing away the thought that was seeking to touch it.[14]

He is a child, here, and he does not understand that some things are not understood but are lived with, nonetheless. In the same sequence, his grandmother shows a beauty of acceptance that remains unattainable to David to the end:

> Ellen knelt where someday she would lie, smoothing out the white lake sand on the surface of her husband's grave. She felt no sadness. Not even the watered sadness of memory. No pictures sprang into her mind, as they did when she tore rags for a rug. This was the one sure spot, the spot where her husband lay. All of him with her was gathered here, unchangeably ended, nothing to be added now or taken away. It was like a focus of light she stood in so that all the separate images disappeared. The

> quiet warnings on the tombstones about her–Aged 23 years, Aged 51 years–had no message of urgency or fear. Those were places she had passed. Now years were no longer footholds in the treacherous cliff going up. She had reached the plain. She knelt by her husband's grave in this focus of peace. She felt nothing but the peace of her hands moving in the warm white sand.[15]

David, however, does not attain the plain until events and his own weakness have exhausted him. He clings to the treacherous cliff, pursued by death, fending it off with words, so that when he is driven, at last, to the summit, death overtakes him.

After Effie died, "David tried to hide from the unremittent now. He tried to pretend that, by sheer will, he could reach back through the transparent (but so maddeningly impenetrable) partition of time,"[16] and manipulate the past. His attempt is pathetically inept. He had humiliated Effie to show his city friend, Toby, his accomplishment with girls; to gain Toby's envy. Instead, Toby is merely amused, and Effie is uncomprehendingly hurt. Reconstructing the incident in his mind, he shows Effie affectionate consideration and, of course, he discreetly avoids telling Toby about their intimacy. "Then a gust of fact would bare the pretence, without warning."[17] He is impaled by the truth, suffocated by the irrevocable and irretrievable past.

David's knowledge of himself makes him different from the others who, he believes, simply live what they are. David lives for what he should be and should have been. As the family disperses, disintegrates, he becomes more and more haunted by his ineptitude for living, until on the mountain he breaks down and the voices and faces of those lost to him accuse him of their loss. They have been his creation, in a sense, known to him only as they exist within his own consciousness. Yet some other reality has determined their lives: Anna is now Toby's widow; Chris is separated from his wife and lives awkwardly next door; Joseph, his father, dies crushed under the keel-tree and Martha, his mother, dies of a withered heart. Ellen endures in a world of dream-memory and senility. David has created them in his mind, through the years. But their lives do not conform to his needs. They have existed apart from the illusion in which he has perceived them. Desperately, he envisions the possibility of re-creating them with words. But that is what he has always done. He could never truly conceive of their separate realities, no more than he could comprehend Effie's hurt or Toby's apparent indifference on the train, passing by David in the field, on the way to war.

The implicit irony is intensified as David hopes to reconstruct his vision of their common past, a vision which has always excluded their independent identity.

> As he thought of telling these things exactly, all the voices came close about him. They weren't swarming now. He went out into them until there was no inside left. He saw at last how you could *become* the thing you told.[18]

But it cannot *become* him. Such creation is annihilation.

> It wouldn't be necessary to take them one by one. That's where he's been wrong. All he'd have to do. . .oh, it was so gloriously simple. . .was to find their single core of meaning. It was manifest not differently but only in different aspects, in them all. That would be enough. A single beam of light is enough to light all the shadows, by turning it from one to another.[19]

True, but it is a light that neither love nor art can generate nor endure.

Richler's Noah Adler suffers no such restriction of consciousness. Nor is his consciousness confined by restraints such as Hagar knows. Noah's family and his past are external adversaries. He is little encumbered by their interior presence from overcoming their impositions on his life. This makes him appear ruthless, particularly to Miriam and to his mother. Yet he is not ruthless. He is determined, but he is not without conscience; he does not avoid suffering. In fact, that is why Noah Adler is, perhaps, the greatest and most convincing of Richler's protagonists–because he has the capacity to suffer, and he does so, and he proceeds in spite of it to fulfil what he conceives to be his destiny or, at least, the conditions of its prelude.

Miriam interprets Noah's uncompromising determination to be with her, to take her away from her husband, as lack of feeling. "Noah's ruthless manner alarmed her and yet she felt more disgust than compassion for Theo."[20] His manner, however, is only that of a man who places priority on one set of circumstances over another and struggles to meet the requirements of his choice. Later, when the young lovers break up, Noah is anything but ruthless. He is bumbling, stupid, and concerned. But when Miriam turns him out to preserve her dignity, he regains his own: "Outside, there was a mess of cigarette butts on the porch steps. Sun glistened on the empty whiskey bottle that had been flung into the grass." He walks by these remnants of their mutual sorrow: "It was going to be a fine day."[21] He needed, then, to be free of Miriam as much as he earlier needed to have her. Neither event takes place without suffering, without humiliation in the first instance and anxious confusion in the last. But Noah does not exist in a vacuum. His needs have paralleled Miriam's–to have him; to be free of him; to travel the distance from indifferent companion for a dull husband to promiscuous neurotic. Noah was not the cause of her transformation but the catalyst, just as she was the catalyst in his change from intuitively rejecting the past to consciously accepting responsibility for his future.

Noah's mother practises an insidious form of blackmail to keep him near her after his father's death. She has always prevailed upon him to be grateful for her love and for the respectability of her origins. But after Wolf becomes the "smaller hero" of the title, consumed in the fire while trying to save Melech's money-box, she threatens Noah with her sickness. If he does not stay by, if he does not please, she will die. She tries to consume her son, to possess his identity. There can be no fault in his desire to break free, despite the possible truth of her morbid prediction. Noah refuses to play the role of a husband such as she had never had. Wolf was stupid and oafish and bitchily pliant, pathetic even in the journal he kept that recorded his innermost secrets–such trivia as the time of his life spent on the toilet and the number of steps taken each day around the coal-yard. He was a smaller hero in every way. Noah will not submit to being an alternative surrogate of his father, neither for Leah nor for Melech. He displays great moral courage in leaving his mother to her own demise. Her closing words to him provide ample explanation of the necessity for doing so: "Write, don't write. To put a knife into my back would have been kinder. Now go. Go. Be happy."[22] Noah loves her but to survive on his own he must escape her grasp that threatens to strangle him.

The forces with which Noah must contend are externalized, clear adversaries in an ambiguous world. They are his family, friends, class, Jewish heritage, immigrant background. Yet there is little triumph in his overcoming them. That which would destroy what he is, has made him what he is. His adversaries are his origins and in going to Melech for a token of the old man's love before he departs, he shows their continued importance to him. They are clearly defined but his responses to them are ironically ambivalent, painful, and confused.

For Noah, Miriam provides a transition from the past into the future. Sexuality is a medium in which to discover himself. He loves Miriam exuberantly because she lets him live. For David Canaan, sexual relations are quite the opposite, embodying no commitment at all. Effie gives him a thrill and he humiliates her. Effie's mother makes love to him and he cries. Just as Noah Adler's love-making is an expression of his irrepressible will to endure, David's expresses his inability to participate, to share in the experience of others. Hagar's sexual relations with Bram are similarly consistent with her general condition. She recalls: "His banner over me was only his own skin, and now I no longer know why it should have shamed me. People thought of things differently in those days. Perhaps some people didn't. I wouldn't know. I never spoke of it to anyone."[23] Between desire and function, desire and the demands it imposes on her, there is always her unyielding pride.

Hagar and David and Noah all live the struggle between reality and illusion. Their lives embody the implicit ironies in such a struggle, where both reality and illusion depend on the perspective from which their experience is perceived. Each of them is conscious of being different from others. Each lives more within his own consciousness than in the surrounding world. Yet in each case, the environment is meticulously detailed, the impositions it makes, as well as its virtues, are clearly defined.

Laurence, Buckler, and Richler share in common a vision of individual isolation that is both universal and contemporary. Their protagonists endure the ironies of their separate consciousnesses confronted by their own formative contexts. The fact that these contexts are characteristically Canadian, although quite different from one another, insures that the three novels I have been discussing participate in the traditions of Canadian fiction. That they are also continuous with the cosmopolitan tradition of contemporary literature written in English is not irrelevant. It suggests that with writers such as Buckler, Richler, and Laurence, the Canadian imagination has achieved a maturity that provides sanction for the serious consideration of novelists who preceded them–sanction that the separate qualities of the earlier works should have made unnecessary.

Notes

1. Mordecai Richler, *Son of a Smaller Hero* (Toronto: New Canadian Library, 1969), p.134. (London: André Deutsch, 1955.)
2. *Ibid.,* p.156.
3. *Ibid.,* p.107.
4. *Ibid.,* p.97.
5. *Ibid.,* p.38.
6. *Ibid.,* p.160.
7. Margaret Laurence, *The Stone Angel* (Toronto: New Canadian Library, 1968), p.25. (Toronto: McClelland & Stewart, 1964.)
8. *Ibid.,* p.42.
9. *Ibid.,* p.81.
10. *Ibid.,* p.40.
11. *Ibid.,* p.42.
12. *Ibid.,* p.79.
13. *Ibid.,* p.133.
14. Ernest Buckler, *The Mountain and the Valley* (Toronto: New Canadian Library, 1969), p.91. (New York: Holt, 1952.)
15. *Ibid.,* p.90.
16. *Ibid.,* p.148.
17. *Ibid.,* p.149.
18. *Ibid.,* p.298.
19. *Ibid.,* pp.298-99.
20. Richler, *op.cit.,* p.106.
21. *Ibid.,* p.171.
22. *Ibid.,* p.200.
23. Laurence, *op.cit.,* p.81.

5.
Fool-Saints

Isolation of the individual in Canadian fiction has not by any means been limited to perspectives of consciousness. The isolated protagonist appears in many shapes and guises. Some display no awareness at all of the conflict between inner and external realities, despite the discontinuity of their experience. Robert Moray, in Parker's *The Seats of the Mighty,* for example, is the hero of an historical romance, a prisoner of the French régime in old Quebec. He responds to captivity according to the dictates of the genre, with honour, valour and good sense. He is individuated without being an individual. Adam More amongst the fantastical Kosygin in James DeMille's *A Strange Manuscript Found in a Copper Cylinder* is an engaging archetype of everyman, as befits his representative role in the utopian vision of an alternative reality. In contrast to these two, Wes Wakeham, the anti-hero of Richard Wright's contemporary novel, *The Weekend Man,* exists almost solely within his own mind. His isolation, however, is not a condition of consciousness but of his conscientious determination to be different through being extraordinarily ordinary, through being committed to disengagement. His consciousness is a sustaining condition of his own contrivance in response to the meaningless milieu around him. Wakeham, like More and Moray, is an ironic creation. Yet the irony they embody is not implicit in their own experience but imposed by authorial conceptions of their isolating environments.

Canadian fiction is rich with individual characters in isolation from conventional reality. Usually they occupy an ironic dimension by the very nature of their presence as an alternative to the collective experience of the norm. Nowhere is this more apparent than in the numerous variations on the concept of the fool-saint. I would not wish to speculate on whether the paradoxical presence of the fool-saint is more indigenous to the Canadian experience than to any other. It is enough to realize that Canadian writers have exploited permutations of the concept repeatedly with narrative effectiveness.

Fool-saints are elusive beings; intentionally so, for ambiguous oxymoron is the source of their function in literature. They are the demented, the idiot-savants, touched by an informing grace. They are the wise fools, recluses from the world, with consciousness restricted accordingly. Billy Budd is a fool-saint of sorts, a simple-minded paragon. So is Prince Myshkin and so is Faulkner's Benjy in *The Sound and the Fury.* David Canaan's senile grandmother, Ellen, is a variation of the fool-saint. Old age has released her from the bondage of time to see past events equidistant from the present, to sort out the sum of her experience according to meaning and not chronological necessity. The fool-saint is an outsider who one way or another has the vision to see or the capacity to convey a vision beyond the limitations of ordinary experience. Variations on the concept may be subtle indeed. They include visionary hermits, false heroes, indifferent proselytes, sanctified fools, foolish martyrs, corrupting as well as incorruptible innocents. Ultimately, I mean the term to include all outsiders who embody paradox out of which their worlds are informed with transcendent meaning.

Two recent novels which deal most directly with the implications of sainthood are Robertson Davies' *Fifth Business* and Leonard Cohen's *Beautiful Losers.* Dunstable Ramsay, in Davies' novel, pursues a quest through life for the meaning of sanctity. He becomes an authority on the lives and trivia of the dead saints and he attempts to beatify one of his own, Mrs. Dempster, who was reduced to dementia by a snowball meant for him. Her three attested miracles are the redemption of a tramp in the town dump through sexual intercourse, the apparent raising of Ramsay's brother from the dead, and her hallucinatory presence to Ramsay when he is wounded at Passchendaele. She is his saint, but that of no other–and, what is most important, not to herself. Ramsay is a Protestant searching for meaning in Roman Catholic structures and he finds only Protestant salvation in his own integrity. Davies' quest is self-evidently Jungian, but his protagonist's, while mythopeic perhaps, is on a more consciously religious plane. Cohen's Catherine Tekakwitha is an authorized saint in the Church calendar. By reducing her to a suffering, stupid, repulsive persona in the erotic phantasmagoria of his narrator's perceptions, she is re-beatified as one of life's losers, who wins because she is lost, who is beautiful because she endures not only the distorted history in the narrator's reconstruction of her life, but because she endures him. She is elevated from the ignominy of sainthood to the sanctity of being a fool-saint in a world where only fools prevail.

Just as Mrs. Dempster and F., the narrator's mentor in *Beautiful Losers,* end up in asylums, their perverse grace too much for them or the world to endure, Father Dowling in *Such Is My Beloved* and Abraham in *The Sacrifice* are consigned to institutions for their transcendent visions–albeit, the priest had become mentally incompetent, the old Jew, a murderer. Often, in Canadian fiction, visionary experience is the prelude to incarceration, insanity, or death. David Canaan's mountain-top epiphany is followed by death; A.M. Klein's Melech Davidson, in *The Second Scroll,* ascends from the horrors of Nazi mass-murder to exaltation an an Israeli prophet, and dies a martyr of Zion; Peggy Sanderson, ambiguously imbued with a tragic innocence which corrupts what it cannot contain, is murdered in bed. While none of these may be dubbed a visionary in fact, Martin, the scourge of the mosquitoes in Cohen's *The Favorite Game,* inescapably is, and is doomed by occupying a separate reality to be crushed by a bulldozer while pursuing his vocation.

Callaghan's Peggy Sanderson and Grove's Niels Lindstedt represent a type of corrupting innocence that sets them as individuals apart from ordinary experience, yet makes them its victims. In contrast, the incidental similarity of Wolf Adler in *Son of a Smaller Hero* and Isaac in *The Sacrifice* both apparently giving their lives to rescue the Torah from fire, suggests the imposition of innocence on the undeserving. Isaac's motives are misunderstood, for he was serving not God but his father's distortion of God. Wolf was killed trying, in fact, to save his father's money that he mistakenly thought was in the box where the scrolls were kept. Both die, pathetic, false heroes.

A case might be made, as well, that Gander Stake, in Robert Stead's *Grain,* is a corrupting innocent for the effect that his refusal to join the Army in World War I has on his beloved Jo Burge and on their relationship. Yet Gander's story is much larger than his inept love affairs. He is an incorruptible innocent, attached passionately to the land. He cannot envision the threat of a foreign war and will not demean himself to participate in it. However, he is not a coward; his conscientious objections tear him to the limited depths of his soul. His innocence is born of his inability to understand the profound attachment he has to the farming life. It is this inability that causes him to suffer and, as well, to endure. Lilka Frahm in *The Atonement of Ashley Morden* is a far more triumphant innocent. But none can match Earle Birney's incomparable Turvey. *Turvey* is somewhat of a precursor to *Catch-22,* founding its sardonic humour on order in the midst of chaos. The title character is a picaresque hero in reverse, a wise fool, an insouciant rogue. Turvey passes through all possible phases of the enlisted man's war and emerges, miraculously, unscathed. His simplistic innocence, by the deft manipulations of his creator, makes a mockery of global conflagration. Turvey wins; humanity loses. He is a fool-saint at the centre of an absurdist vision of moral anarchy.

Variations on the concept of the fool-saint can be subtle, undefined, integrated fully within their narrative contexts. Occasionally, as in W.O. Mitchell's *Who Has Seen the Wind,* the fool-saint is an entirely distinct presence. Saint Sammy, the mad hermit-sage in his piano-box hovel, with his collection of underwear labels, talks directly to his Lord. Brian's quest for God reaches a temporary impasse with Sammy, whose God is a perverse caricature of the vengeful Lord of the Old Testament, a Lord who maintains a pact with his chosen prophet, Saint Sammy. Brian's quest continues, but he has been impressed by the old man's vindictive grace. It is a grace, of course, that only a demented old man could possibly achieve.

The hermit-sage is a common enough character in Canadian fiction. Felix, in *The Double Hook,* is described as a saint, yet his beatification is as much in being disengaged from the reality of others, and seeing himself subservient to it, as in any positive function he performs. Richard McKee, in *The Channel Shore,* is a more secular, less ambiguous saint, a man of profound insight, alone by choice; hardly a fool. Ken Tilling's mentor, Noah Masterson, in Garner's *Cabbagetown,* is another example of the wise man disengaged from the reality around him, yet able to penetrate it with a depth of understanding that belies his benign demeanour.

Apart from Saint Sammy and Mrs. Dempster, the examples of the fool-saint I have suggested are departures from the seminal concept. Yet each in some way suggests the moral, intellectual, and emotional paradox implicit to this most individual of individuals. The fool-saint does not occupy a centre of consciousness, so much as he generates consciousness in others. In Canadian fiction, his function is widely exploited as one of the most effective means of defining the experience of the individual in a Canadian context.

This and other patterns of isolation in Canadian fiction provide one of a number of its distinguishing characteristics. Whether they display concepts of exile or express what I have called the geophysical imagination or, as in the present discussion, arise from the ironic conflicts of individual consciousness, they equally reflect the progress of the Canadian imagination towards a positive identity. An examination of other patterns might reveal as much about the processes of our emergence into national being. It seems to me that none, however, better defines the indigenous character of our Canadian community.

Bibliography

Atwood, Margaret. *Surfacing*. Toronto: McClelland and Stewart, 1972.

______. *Survival*. Toronto: Anansi, 1972.

Bach, Richard. *Jonathan Livingston Seagull*. New York: Avon, 1973.

Barrie, J.M. *The Admirable Crichton*. New York: Scribner's, 1925. London: Hodder and Stoughton, 1914.

Bellow, Saul. *Henderson the Rain King*. New York: Fawcett, 1969. New York: Viking Press, 1958.

Birney, Earle. *David, and Other Poems*. Toronto: Ryerson, 1942.

______. *Turvey*. Toronto: *New Canadian Library*, 1969. Toronto: McClelland and Stewart, 1949.

Blais, Marie-Claire. *Mad Shadows*. Tr. Merloyd Lawrence. Toronto: *New Canadian Library*, 1971. *La belle bête*. Québec: Institut Littéraire du Québec, 1959.

Blaise, Clark. *A North American Education*. Toronto: Doubleday, 1973.

Bodsworth, Fred. *The Atonement of Ashley Morden*. New York: Dodd, Mead, 1964.

______. *Last of the Curlews*. Toronto: *New Canadian Library*, 1967. London: Museum Press, 1956.

______. *The Strange One*. New York: Dodd, Mead, 1960. 1959.

Brooke, Frances. *The History of Emily Montague*. Toronto: *New Canadian Library*, 1969. London: Dodsley, 1769. 4v.

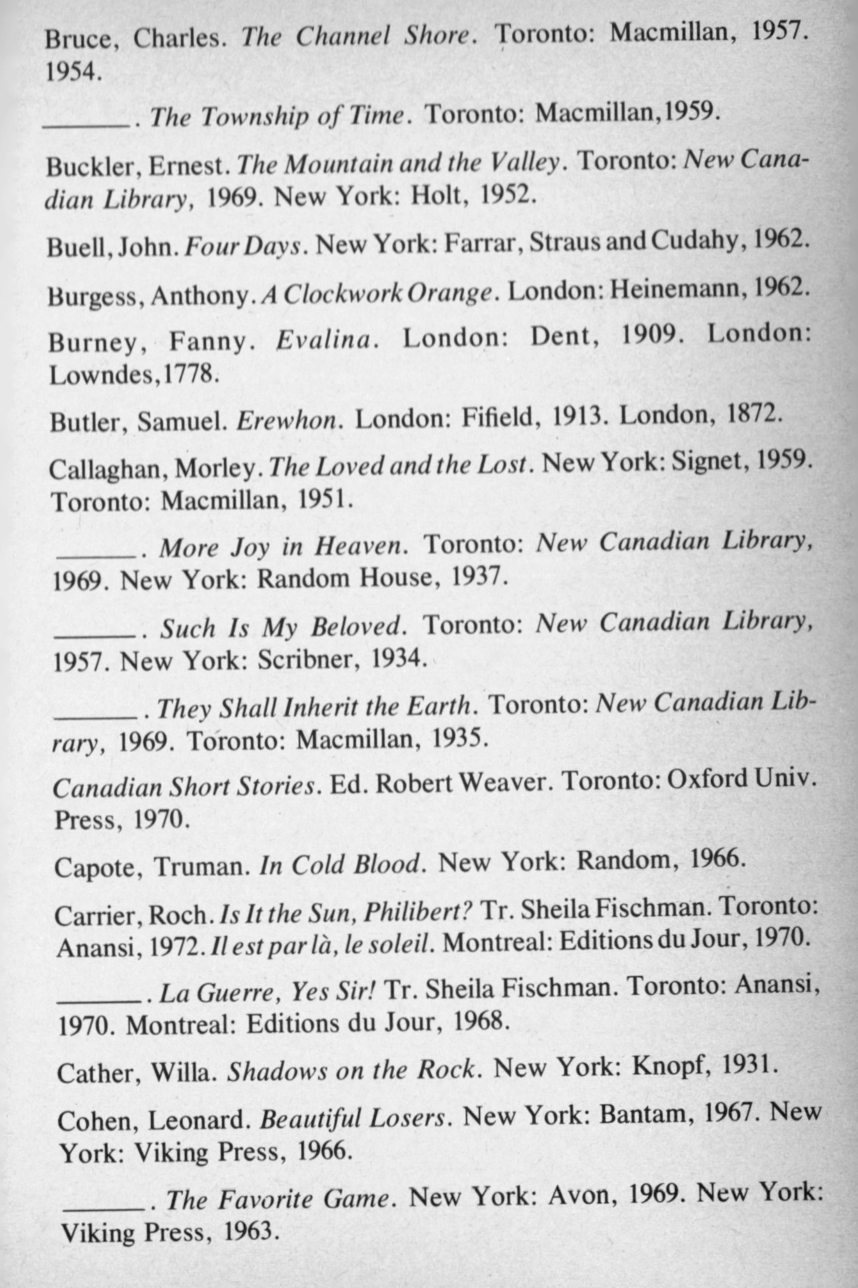

Bruce, Charles. *The Channel Shore*. Toronto: Macmillan, 1957. 1954.

______. *The Township of Time*. Toronto: Macmillan,1959.

Buckler, Ernest. *The Mountain and the Valley*. Toronto: *New Canadian Library,* 1969. New York: Holt, 1952.

Buell, John. *Four Days*. New York: Farrar, Straus and Cudahy, 1962.

Burgess, Anthony. *A Clockwork Orange*. London: Heinemann, 1962.

Burney, Fanny. *Evalina*. London: Dent, 1909. London: Lowndes,1778.

Butler, Samuel. *Erewhon*. London: Fifield, 1913. London, 1872.

Callaghan, Morley. *The Loved and the Lost*. New York: Signet, 1959. Toronto: Macmillan, 1951.

______. *More Joy in Heaven*. Toronto: *New Canadian Library,* 1969. New York: Random House, 1937.

______. *Such Is My Beloved*. Toronto: *New Canadian Library,* 1957. New York: Scribner, 1934.

______. *They Shall Inherit the Earth*. Toronto: *New Canadian Library,* 1969. Toronto: Macmillan, 1935.

Canadian Short Stories. Ed. Robert Weaver. Toronto: Oxford Univ. Press, 1970.

Capote, Truman. *In Cold Blood*. New York: Random, 1966.

Carrier, Roch. *Is It the Sun, Philibert?* Tr. Sheila Fischman. Toronto: Anansi, 1972. *Il est par là, le soleil*. Montreal: Editions du Jour, 1970.

______. *La Guerre, Yes Sir!* Tr. Sheila Fischman. Toronto: Anansi, 1970. Montreal: Editions du Jour, 1968.

Cather, Willa. *Shadows on the Rock*. New York: Knopf, 1931.

Cohen, Leonard. *Beautiful Losers*. New York: Bantam, 1967. New York: Viking Press, 1966.

______. *The Favorite Game*. New York: Avon, 1969. New York: Viking Press, 1963.

Connor, Ralph. *The Man from Glengarry*. Toronto: McClelland and Stewart, 1965. Toronto: Westminster, 1901.

Davies, Robertson. *Fifth Business*. New York: Signet, 1971. New York: Viking Press, 1970.

———. *A Mixture of Frailties*. New York: Scribner's, 1958

de la Roche, Mazo. *Jalna*. Toronto: Macmillan, 1927.

———. *Possession*. Toronto: Macmillan, 1923.

De Mille, James. *A Strange Manuscript Found in a Copper Cylinder*. Toronto: *New Canadian Library*, 1969. Anonymous; New York: Harper, 1888.

Dostoevsky, Fedor. *The Idiot*. Tr. David Magarshack. London: Everyman's, 1929. 1882.

Duncan, Sara Jeannette. *The Imperialist*. Toronto: *New Canadian Library*, 1961. Toronto: Copp Clark, 1904.

Eggleston, Wilfred. *The Frontier and Canadian Letters*. Toronto: Ryerson, 1957.

Faulkner, William. *The Sound and the Fury and As I Lay Dying*. New York: Modern Library, 1946. New York: Cape and Smith, 1929; and New York: Cape and Smith, 1930.

Fiedler, Leslie A. *Love and Death in the American Novel*. New York: Dell, 1969. New York: Stein and Day, 1960.

Franklin, Stephen. *Knowledge Park*. Toronto: McClelland and Stewart, 1972.

Frye, Northrop. *The Anatomy of Criticism*. Princeton: Princeton Univ. Press, 1965. 1957.

———. *The Bush Garden*. Toronto: Anansi, 1971.

Galbraith, John Kenneth. *The Scotch*. Boston: Houghton Mifflin, 1964.

Garner, Hugh. *Cabbagetown*. Richmond Hill: Pocket Books, 1971. Toronto: Collins, 1950.

———. *Silence on the Shore*. Richmond Hill: Pocket Books, 1971. Toronto: McClelland and Stewart, 1962.

Gibson, Graeme. *Communion*. Toronto: Anansi, 1971.

Gide, André. *Symphonie pastorale*. Paris: Lettres Modernes, 1970. Paris: Editions de la Nouvelle revue française, 1919.

Godfrey, Dave. *Death Goes Better with Coca-Cola*. Toronto: Anansi, 1967.

Gogol, Nikolay. *Dead Souls*. Tr. Bernard Guilbert Guerney. New York: Modern Library, 1965. 1842.

Greene, Graham. *The Quiet American*. London: Heinemann, 1955.

Grove, Frederick Philip. *Consider Her Ways*. Toronto: Macmillan, 1947.

______. *Fruits of the Earth*. Toronto: *New Canadian Library*. 1969. Toronto: Dent, 1933.

______. *The Master of the Mill*. Toronto: *New Canadian Library*, 1967. Toronto: Macmillan, 1944.

______. *Our Daily Bread*. Toronto: Macmillan, 1928.

______. *Over Prairie Trails*. Toronto: *New Canadian Library*, 1969. Toronto: McClelland and Stewart, 1922.

______. *A Search for America*. Toronto: *New Canadian Library*, 1974. Ottawa: Graphic, 1927.

______. *Settlers of the Marsh*. Toronto: *New Canadian Library*, 1965. New York: Doran, 1925.

______. *Two Generations*. Toronto: Ryerson, 1939.

______. *The Yoke of Life*. New York: Smith, 1930.

Haggard, Sir H. Rider. *She*. London: Hodder and Stoughton, 1920. London: Longmans, 1887.

Hardy, Thomas. *Jude the Obscure*. London: Macmillan, 1951. London: Osgood, McIlvaine, 1896.

______. *Tess of the D'Urbervilles*. New York: Harper, 1950. London: Osgood, McIlvaine, 1891.

Harlow, Robert. *Scann*. Port Clements: Sono Nis Press, 1972.

Hart, Julia Beckwith. *St. Ursula's Convent*. Kingston: Thomson, 1824. 2v.

Heller, Joseph. *Catch-22*. New York: Dell, 1964. New York: Simon and Schuster, 1961.

Hémon, Louis. *Maria Chapdelaine*. Tr. W.H. Blake. Toronto: Macmillan, 1922. Montreal: Le Febvre, 1916.

Huxley, Aldous. *Brave New World*. London: Penguin, 1968. London: Chatto and Windus, 1932.

Jameson, Anna. *Winter Studies and Summer Rambles*. Toronto: *New Canadian Library*, 1969. London: Saunders and Ottley, 1838.

Jarvis, W.H.P. *A Remittance Man's Letters to His Mother*. Toronto: Musson, 1907.

Jones, D.G. *Butterfly on Rock*. Toronto: Univ. of Toronto Press, 1970.

Joyce, James. *Finnigan's Wake*. New York: Viking Press, 1944. 1939.

______. *A Portrait of the Artist as a Young Man*. New York: Random, 1928. London: Egoist, 1916.

Kirby, William. *The Golden Dog*. Toronto: *New Canadian Library*, 1969. Montreal: Lovell, 1877.

Klein, A.M. *The Second Scroll*. Toronto: *New Canadian Library*, 1969. New York: Knopf, 1951.

Knister, Raymond. *White Narcissus*. Toronto: *New Canadian Library*, 1962. New York: Harcourt, 1929.

Kreisel, Henry. *The Rich Man*. Toronto: *New Canadian Library*, 1961. Toronto: McClelland and Stewart, 1948.

Kroetsch, Robert. *But We Are Exiles*. Toronto: Macmillan, 1965.

Laurence, Margaret. *The Fire-Dwellers*. Toronto: *New Canadian Library*, 1973. Toronto: McClelland and Stewart, 1969.

______. *The Stone Angel*. Toronto: *New Canadian Library*, 1968. Toronto: McClelland and Stewart, 1964.

Lawrence, D.H. *Sons and Lovers*. London: Penguin, 1959. London: Duckworth, 1913.

______. *Studies in Classic American Literature*. London: Martin Secker, 1964. New York: Seltzer, 1923.

Lewis, Wyndham. *Self Condemned*. Toronto: *New Canadian Library*, 1974. London: Methuen, 1954.

Literary History of Canada. Gen'l. Ed. Carl F. Klinck. Toronto: Univ. of Toronto Press, 1967.

Lowry, Malcolm. *Dark Is the Grave Wherein My Friend Is Laid*. Toronto: General, 1968.

______. *Hear Us O Lord From Heaven Thy Dwelling Place*. New York: Lippincott, 1961.

______. *October Ferry to Gabriola*. New York: World, 1970.

______. *Ultramarine*. Toronto: Clarke, Irwin, 1963. London: Cape, 1933.

______. *Under the Volcano*. London: Penguin, 1963. New York: Reynal, 1947.

MacLennan, Hugh. *Barometer Rising*. Toronto: *New Canadian Library*, 1965. New York: Duell Sloan, 1941.

______. *Each Man's Son*. Toronto: Macmillan, 1951.

______. *The Precipice*. Toronto: Collins, 1948.

______. *Return of the Sphinx*. Toronto: Macmillan, 1967.

______. *Two Solitudes*. Toronto: Popular Library, 1945.

______. *The Watch That Ends the Night*. Toronto: Signet, 1969. Toronto: Macmillan, 1959.

McClung, Nellie. *Clearing in the West*. Toronto: Thomas Allen, 1935.

______. *Sowing Seeds in Danny*. Toronto: Ryerson, 1939. New York: Doubleday, 1908.

McCourt, Edward. *Home Is the Stranger*. Toronto: Macmillan, 1950.

______. *Music at the Close*. Toronto: *New Canadian Library*, 1966. Toronto: Ryerson, 1947.

Melville, Herman. *Moby Dick*. New York: Modern Library, 1926. New York: Harper & Brothers, 1851.

Mitchell, W.O. *Who Has Seen the Wind*. Toronto: Macmillan, 1967. 1947.

Montgomery, Lucy Maud. *Anne of Green Gables*. Boston: Claus, 1908.

Moodie, Susanna. *Roughing it in the Bush*. Toronto: *New Canadian Library*, 1969. London: Bentley, 1852.

Moore, Brian. *I Am Mary Dunne*. New York, Viking Press, 1968.

———. *Judith Hearne*. Toronto: *New Canadian Library*, 1968. London: André Deutsch, 1955.

———. *The Luck of Ginger Coffey*. Toronto: *New Canadian Library*, 1972. Boston: Little Brown, 1960.

———. *The Revolution Script*. Toronto: McClelland and Stewart, 1971.

More, Sir Thomas. *Utopia*. New York: Da Capo Press, 1969. 1516.

Munro, Alice. *Lives of Girls and Women*. Toronto: McGraw-Hill Ryerson, 1971.

Orwell, George. *1984*. London: Secker and Warburg, 1949.

Ostenso, Martha. *Wild Geese*. Toronto: *New Canadian Library*, 1971. Toronto: McClelland and Stewart, 1925.

Our Sense of Identity. Ed. Malcolm Ross. Toronto: Ryerson, 1954.

Pacey, Desmond. *Essays in Canadian Criticism: 1938-1968*. Toronto: Ryerson, 1969.

Parker, Sir Gilbert. *The Seats of the Mighty*. Toronto: *New Canadian Library*, 1971. London: Methuen, 1896.

Paton, Alan. *Cry, the Beloved Country*. New York: Scribner's, 1948.

Poe, Edgar Allan. *The Complete Tales and Poems*. New York: Modern Library, 1938.

Pratt, E.J. *Collected Poems*. Toronto: Macmillan, 1970.

Raddall, Thomas H. *The Nymph and the Lamp*. Toronto: *New Canadian Library*, 1965. Boston: Little Brown, 1950.

Richardson, Major John. *Wacousta or The Prophecy*. Toronto: *New Canadian Library*, 1967. London: Cadell, 1832. 3v.

Richler, Mordecai. *The Apprenticeship of Duddy Kravitz*. Toronto: *New Canadian Library*, 1969. Don Mills: André Deutsch, 1959.

______. *A Choice of Enemies*. London: André Deutsch, 1957.

______. *Son of a Smaller Hero*. Toronto: *New Canadian Library*, 1969. London: André Deutsch, 1955.

Ringuet. *Thirty Acres*. Toronto: *New Canadian Library*, 1968. Tr. Felix and Dorothea Walter. *Trente Arpents*. Paris: Flammarion, 1938.

Roberts, Theodore Goodridge. *The Harbour Master*. Toronto: *New Canadian Library*, 1968. Boston: Page, 1913.

Ross, Sinclair. *As For Me and My House*. Toronto: *New Canadian Library*, 1969. New York: Reynal, 1941.

______. *The Lamp at Noon and Other Stories*. Toronto: *New Canadian Library*, 1968.

______. *The Well*. Toronto: Macmillan, 1958.

______. *Whir of Gold*. Toronto: McClelland and Stewart, 1970.

Roy, Gabrielle. *The Cashier*. Tr. Harry Binsse. Toronto: *New Canadian Library*, 1970. *Alexandre Chenevert, Caissier*. Montreal: Beauchemin, 1955.

______. *Windflower*. Tr. Joyce Marshall. Toronto: McClelland and Stewart, 1970. *La rivière sans repos*. Montreal: Beauchemin, 1970.

Salverson, Laura Goodman. *The Viking Heart*. Toronto: McClelland and Stewart, 1925. New York: 1923.

Schulberg, Budd. *What Makes Sammy Run?* New York: Modern Library, 1952. New York: Random House, 1941.

Stead, Robert J. *Grain*. Toronto: *New Canadian Library*, 1969. Toronto: McClelland and Stewart, 1926.

Story, Norah. *The Oxford Companion to Canadian History and Literature*. Toronto: Oxford Univ. Press, 1967.

Sutherland, Ronald. *Second Image*. Toronto: New Press, 1971.

Swift, Jonathan, *Gulliver's Travels*. New York: Modern Library, 1958. London: Motte, 1726.

Theriault, Yves. *Agaguk*. Tr. Miriam Chapin. Toronto: Ryerson, 1967. Québec; B. Grasset, 1958.

Traill, Catharine Parr. *The Backwoods of Canada*. Toronto: *New Canadian Library*, 1971. London: Knight, 1836.

Watson, Sheila. *The Double Hook*. Toronto: *New Canadian Library*, 1969. Toronto: McClelland and Stewart, 1959.

Wiebe, Rudy. *The Blue Mountains of China*. Toronto: McClelland and Stewart, 1970.

______. *First and Vital Candle*. Toronto: McClelland and Stewart, 1966.

______. *Peace Shall Destroy Many*. Toronto: *New Canadian Library*, 1972. Toronto: McClelland and Stewart, 1962.

Wilson, Ethel. *Hetty Dorval*. Toronto: Macmillan, 1947.

______. *Swamp Angel*. Toronto: *New Canadian Library*, 1962. Toronto: Macmillan, 1954.

Wiseman, Adele. *The Sacrifice*. Toronto: Macmillan, 1968. 1956.

Wright, Richard B. *The Weekend Man*. Scarborough: Signet, 1972. Toronto: Macmillan, 1970.

Author-Title Index